CASSELL GUIDE TO LITE

Also available from Continuum:

Christopher Robinson, *Scandal in the Ink:*
Male and Female Homosexuality
in Twentieth-Century French Literature

Valerie Worth-Stylianou, *Cassell Language Guides: French*

Cassell Guide to
Literature in French

GENERAL EDITOR:
VALERIE WORTH-STYLIANOU

CONTINUUM
London and New York

Continuum
The Tower Building
11 York Road, London SE1 7NX

370 Lexington Avenue, New York, NY 10017-6550

First published 1996
Reprinted 2000

British Library Cataloguing-in-Publication Data
A catalogue record for this book is available from the British Library.

ISBN 0-304-33194-5 (hardback)
       0-8264-5393-7 (paperback)

Library of Congress Cataloging-in-Publication Data
Cassell guide to literature in French / edited by Valerie Worth-Stylianou
                    p. cm.
            Includes bibliographical reference and index.
            ISBN 0-304-33194-5.— ISBN 0-8264-5393-7 (pbk.)
            I. French literature—History and criticism. 2. French literature—
Foreign countries—History and criticism. I. Worth-Stylianou, Valerie.   II.
Continuum Ltd.
PQ103.C27 1996
840.9—dc20
                                                                    95-25347
                                                                        CIP

Typeset by Ben Cracknell
Printed and bound in Great Britain by Redwood Books, Trowbridge, Wiltshire

Contents

The Contributors

Valerie Worth-Stylianou is Lecturer in French at King's College London.

Colin Davis is Fellow and Tutor in French at Lady Margaret Hall, Oxford.

Toby Garfitt is Fellow and Tutor in French at Magdalen College, Oxford.

Angelica Goodden is Fellow and Tutor in French at St Hilda's College, Oxford.

Anne Green is Lecturer in French at King's College London.

Christina Howells is Fellow and Tutor in French at Wadham College, Oxford.

Belinda Jack is Lecturer in French at Birkbeck College, London.

Karen Pratt is Lecturer in French at King's College London.

Acknowledgements

We are grateful to colleagues, friends, families and students for their encouragement and comments. We would particularly like to thank the following, who read the draft of one or more chapters: Nicholas Cronk, Michael Heath, John Taylor, Wolfgang van Emden. We also thank our editors at Cassell, Steve Cook, Janet Joyce and Sandra Margolies, for their enthusiasm and very practical support. All errors of fact or interpretation are our own.

Introduction

The *Cassell Guide to Literature in French* is a guide in the sense of both a work to lead the reader through familiar and less familiar territories and a compendium of itineraries to sample at leisure. It provides a continuous narrative and analytic account of French literature from its origins (in the early Middle Ages) to the 1990s, but each chapter can equally be read as an independent critical essay. As experienced university lecturers, engaged in research in their specialist fields, the contributors have been mindful of the need to combine an introduction to their subject with a discussion of areas of recent study and of continuing debate. If this volume encourages you to go away and read a new author or work, or return to a familiar one with new insights, it will have achieved its fundamental goal.

There are ultimately as many ways of reading literature as there are readers. The late twentieth century has witnessed a particular flourishing of theoretical debates (see Chapter 10), and before looking in more detail at some of the recurrent preoccupations of this book, it is appropriate to say a word about the challenges implicit in producing a historical account of literature. Sartre's essay 'Qu'est-ce que la littérature?' (1948) provides but one of the most famous question marks hanging over a term we frequently take for granted. Can we, for example, limit literature to the outstanding works of each generation preserved in written form (and outstanding by what criteria?) or, conversely, can literature include every example of the written form from Flaubert's finely crafted prose to an illustrated children's book? Does literature exist for its own aesthetic sake, or does it necessarily both shape and reflect values? Where does literature stop and where do such categories as history, philosophy and even theology start? In this single volume, we have taken the pragmatic approach of acknowledging the literary interest of works which might be argued to belong at least equally to other disciplines (Calvin's theological treatises, Rousseau's social writings, Derrida's philosophical discussions are among the many examples). Although in general we concentrate on works with obvious literary merit, we suggest the need to compare these with contemporaneous 'popular' writing, be it medieval theatre or the rapidly growing daily press of the nineteenth century.

However broadly we define literature, we are still left with the question of how far we can or should view it from a historical perspective. Briefly, is a given work to be seen as a product of its cultural/social/political environment? On the one hand, such an approach may mean that we are tempted to give undue emphasis to those groups in society who have succeeded in making their voices heard. And on the other hand, are we thereby undervaluing the relationship between a work and the unique mind and sensibility of its author? It is a truism that real masterpieces defy attempts at rigid generic or historical classification. So can the modern reader not fully enjoy a work of an earlier period on its own terms, unencumbered by background information? Ahistorical readings sometimes achieve new insights – witness Barthes's uneven but striking study *Sur Racine* (1963). But to refuse the importance of historical context in any circumstances is to deprive some texts of their fullest resonances. Interestingly, this is no less true of a contemporary writer such as Elie Wiesel, preoccupied with the Holocaust, than of Voltaire, concerned throughout his life with the denunciation of all forms of intolerance and tyranny. Again, our response in this volume has been a practical compromise. Each of the first eight chapters opens with a brief summary of major historical events within France or affecting the French, and the accounts which follow underline the complex interplay of historical, social and literary pressures, ranging from the relationship between poetry and patronage in the Renaissance to the ideological debates arising from the Dreyfus affair. Yet we also stress that some writers are far from typical of their age, and not all wrote expecting public recognition. Ultimately, it is often a judicious combination of modern critical approaches and informed historical scholarship which provides the most stimulating readings (see for example the exploration of feminist approaches to medieval epic and romance).

We chose to devote separate chapters to two aspects of later twentieth-century French writing: francophone literature (Chapter 9) and recent French thought (Chapter 10). In both cases, the texts covered and the issues raised could have been treated within a study of literature from 1940 to the present (Chapter 8). However, the explosion of interest in both these areas has been such that we felt they required separate treatment in order to do justice to the complexity and wealth of writings available. As both the discussions and cross-references make clear, though, much francophone and theoretical writing is concerned precisely to challenge the artificial boundaries within which any attempts at a large-scale synthesis are obliged to operate.

At an early stage of writing this book, the question arose of the extent to which we saw our task as a revision of established canons. Now that our work is completed, it seems appropriate to use the more neutral term of a review. First, the 'canon' has been challenged by both French- and English-speaking critics for some decades, so that once-revisionary statements may now pass as common observations: for example, if some of Corneille's plays do not conform to strict neo-classical rules, this makes him not a 'failed' author but an interestingly independent playwright able to exploit the (baroque) elements of suspense and surprise. Equally, new names have gradually been added to the canon. Thus our readers can expect such authors as Béroalde de Verville, Isabelle de Charrière, Marguerite Duras, Tahar Ben Jelloun to be conspicuous by their presence. Secondly, though, in a book for undergraduates and non-specialist readers, it would have been perverse to refuse to confront traditional labels or to discuss the pre-eminence still generally accorded to the 'great names'. So our index testifies to the fact that we examine the usefulness (and limitations) of such terms as *amour courtois* or Romanticism and Realism, and we try to give a balanced evaluation of the achievement of Chrétien de Troyes, Molière, Balzac, Proust, etc. But we have also drawn attention to issues, works and writers we believe to merit closer attention than they have sometimes received. Since several of these approaches inform a number of chapters, it is useful to draw the threads together here.

The study of literature necessarily involves an awareness of the nature and evolution of language itself. While this *Guide* cannot offer a history of the French language, in some form the concern spans all the periods examined. Interestingly, it is particularly prominent in both the opening and closing chapters. The account of the Middle Ages looks at the problem of when French can be distinguished from Vulgar Latin, and highlights the co-existence of various dialects (as well as the language of Occitan or Old Provençal). The chapter on francophone writing draws attention to a similar phenomenon: the creation of texts united by an apparently shared tongue, but with marked variations which here call into question the hierarchical assumption that there is a standard, normative form. French has, to a greater degree than English, been associated with intense debates over the relationship between thought and linguistic systems. Chapter 4 shows that in the seventeenth century, an age character-ized by a wish to codify and purify the language after the energetic but almost unfettered expansions of the Renaissance, many writers strove after absolute goals – clarity, simplicity, elegance. Yet they and their readers were intensely aware that language is only an approximate vehicle for the expression of reality. It is a very similar apprehension which lies at the heart of the fiction of the New Novelists (see Chapter 8) in their self-reflexive fascination with the limits and nature of narrative. And the relationship between language and the categories in which we represent our view of the world is again a key subject of modern critical theory (see, for example, the analysis of Foucault and Derrida in Chapter 10).

In contrast to the more abstract debates over the nature of language and thought, our work also reflects contributors' interests in issues of literacy, and in the status of the book (or manuscript) as a physical and commercial object. Recently there has been a substantial body of scientific research into these topics, which is significant for any assessment of the way writings may be influenced by the reception which they are expected to enjoy. Writers of all periods have often had at least one eye on the impact their work might make on the public or distinguished patrons, and many depended precisely on what we would now term the commercial success of their work. We recognize today the significance of a novelist winning the Prix Goncourt, but earlier ages had their own measures of success (which noble or monarch accepted the dedication of a collection of poetry in the Renaissance, which theatre performed a play in the seventeenth century, which journal serialized a work in the nineteenth). Whereas in the later twentieth century we have precise information on sales of books, and even categories of readers, for earlier periods the evidence is far less complete, and requires interpretation. Similarly, literacy levels today are closely documented (albeit that their interpretation is still open to debate), but for earlier periods our information is at best indicative. Thus we can assert that by 1789 about half the male population of France could read, but this masks the enormous gap between Paris (*c*. 90 per cent male literacy) and the south-west (*c*. 11 per cent). Furthermore, many who were notionally literate were very unlikely to read the kinds of book we are discussing.

However, this does not mean that a history of earlier literature must be confined to a study of the reading habits of the upper social classes, for any account of the reception of literature before the Revolution must take into account the importance of the oral transmission of texts. In the Middle Ages, this is paramount. Even after the spread of the printing press in the Renaissance, many works (such as those of Rabelais) retain marked oral characteristics, and poetry is frequently set to music or recited at court. In the seventeenth and eighteenth centuries, salons perpetuate the shared reading and discussion of literature for the upper classes, while for a wider public the theatre becomes a focus of both popular celebration and political discontent. The emergence of something like the modern newspaper in the nineteenth century is an essential factor in the burgeoning of the novel. Yet even as the institution of universal, free, compulsory primary education in 1882 (under the *lois* Ferry) set the seal upon public literacy, and as a handful of novelists and authors of school texts reached huge audiences, reading was about to be challenged by the rival attraction of the moving image. Such information helps us to appreciate writers of distinction within the context of their period, surveying their likely readership or audience. It also allows us to go some way towards answering the questions 'Was Madame de Lafayette/Prévost/Zola . . . widely read in her/his period?' and 'How does she or he compare with other writers of the time?' Readers of this *Guide* may be surprised to find how little 'popular' taste has changed over the ages – it is not only the late twentieth century which favours fast plots, love, adultery and murder, and larger-than-life characters!

In considering the question of reviewing canons, we were aware both of the challenges posed by recent feminist theory and of the increasing attention many women writers have enjoyed. The latter point means that in some chapters, notably those dealing with both French and francophone literature since 1940, the position of women is central. In some earlier periods, it has been easy to identify particular flowerings of writing by women, such as sixteenth-century poetry or the eighteenth-century novel. In other cases we have approached the question differently. Anonymous medieval works might conceal female authorship; some literary partnerships have obscured women's roles (Colette initially published under her husband's name). It is, in any case, useful to address the question of why women published relatively little in certain periods. Another fruitful approach has been to focus on women as readers, either individual women encouraging specific writers (as patrons and critics) or women collectively as a section of the public with distinct tastes for certain genres. For much of the seventeenth century, for example, the influence of literary salons hosted by women is crucial. Some modern feminist theory, however, invites us to be more radical in our reappraisal, and from this perspective the section on feminism in Chapter 10 might serve as a preface rather than a conclusion to the whole book.

We hope that you will enjoy reading and reflecting on this volume. If you find statements with which you disagree or emphases you would like to change, they may demonstrate that literary criticism is essentially an act of dialogue, both with the text we are reading and with other readings of it. Montaigne remarked rather ironically of the late Renaissance that 'Tout fourmille de commentaires',* and four hundred years on, that, at least, has changed little.

Valerie Worth-Stylianou
General Editor

---

* 'Everything is swarming with commentaries.'

CHAPTER I

The Middle Ages: Beginnings

KAREN PRATT

During the so-called Dark Ages, from the fall of the Roman Empire (AD 476) to the ninth-century 'Carolingian renaissance', literature in Western Europe was mainly produced by the Church, in its official language, Latin. Gradually, however, as the language spoken in Gaul diverged from its Vulgar Latin source, the Church was obliged to communicate to the masses in the vernacular, giving rise to the first monuments of Old French literature. The earliest surviving literary texts are saints' lives, but it is likely that secular genres such as epic poetry, adventure stories of Celtic inspiration and popular plays were being recited and performed by professional *jongleurs* or entertainers for decades or even centuries before works began to be composed and preserved in written form from the early twelfth century onwards. This chapter will concentrate on extant *written* texts from the early Middle Ages; however, if we are to appreciate the true nature of Old French literature we must remember that these works originated in a strongly oral culture.

The term 'Middle Ages' was coined by Giovanni Andrea in 1469, and probably reflects his contemporaries' view that their immediate forebears were merely paving the way for a more significant cultural flowering during the Renaissance. Yet in the medieval period France in fact witnessed two 'renaissances': that under Charlemagne, when important Latin texts were preserved for posterity by scribes working in the monasteries and schools of the Empire, and the 'twelfth-century renaissance'. Between these two periods of relative political stability, conducive to learning, came the feudal age, dominated by barbarian invasions and the breakdown of the centralized government set up by Charlemagne. Feudalism, based on a personal bond of mutual dependence between a lord and vassal, and ritualized by the ceremony of homage, provided the vassal with protection and land (a fief) and the lord with military service and counsel (*auxilium et consilium*). Even after the decline of feudal society, as national monarchies became established and power was increasingly removed from local barons and concentrated in the hands of the king, the vassal swearing allegiance to his lord and the loyalty fundamental to this reciprocal relationship were still popular motifs in literature, especially as a metaphor for courtly relations between the sexes, and for relations between the Christian and God.

Twelfth-century France under the Capetians Louis VII and Philippe-Auguste witnessed a remarkable consolidation of royal power. However, the king's court was not the only source of artistic patronage. Great barons, their wives and secular bishops commissioned works as well, hence the flourishing of courtly literature in this period. The eight crusades to the Holy Land between 1096 and 1270 also left their mark on contemporary literature.

Until the arrival of the printing press in France in 1470 (see page 43), literary works were composed by hand onto parchment or paper, and copied and recopied by scribes. There was no fixed orthography or grammar and this led to polymorphism (marked variation in spelling). Frequently changes, both deliberate and accidental, were made to the exemplar; lines were omitted or copied twice by a hasty or inattentive scribe, others added or altered by one with ideas above his station. Extant manuscripts are rarely autograph copies (a notable exception being those of Christine de Pizan, who supervised the copying of her own works), but rather copies of copies, many intermediaries having been lost on the way. The modern editions we use contain either reconstructions of the author's original, arrived at by comparing variants in the surviving manuscripts and rejecting readings judged to be inauthentic, or the version found in the 'best' extant manuscript, with only the most obvious scribal errors corrected. It is editors who supply punctuation and diacritic marks (such as accents), expand abbreviations and clarify word division for the modern reader. Titles are also often supplied by editors, though many are based on the scribal incipits and explicits of the kind 'here begins/ends the tale about ... '.

The chronology of medieval works is often approximate and relative; while the order of composition and intertextual influence can usually be established, accurate dating is generally impossible. The dating of manuscripts is based on characteristics of the scribal hand and linguistic features; however, the date of a work's composition, which can be decades (if not centuries) earlier, rests on available internal evidence. Only rarely do we have a reference to a patron or a historical event to aid dating. Moreover, medieval literature is frequently anonymous, and even an author's name is of little help if no biographical details are available. A work's geo-graphical provenance or that of its target audience can be ascertained by studying the dialectal features of its language: the major dialects of Old French are *francien* (spoken in the Île de France and the forerunner of Modern French), *picard*, *normand* and *anglo-normand* (the dialect spoken in England after the Conquest). However, the original author's dialect may be different from that of the scribe who copied the work, and rhymes and metre in verse texts are sometimes the only tenuous way of identifying the poet's dialect. A further complication arises from the influence of *occitan*, the language spoken in southern France, as far north as Poitiers, and also known as Old Provençal. Although we shall concentrate on works in Old French, some show the linguistic effects of *occitan*, and the role played by the literature of the south in the development of northern culture will be taken into account (see pages 9 and 36).

Vernacular texts are therefore elusive artefacts requiring detective work and ingenuity from their editors. They were produced alongside both oral and Latin literature at a time when there was a far weaker sense of authorial property than there is today. In many cases they were the products of collaboration: of authors (mainly male, although some female writers have been identified, and others may be hidden behind the 'anon.' label), of scribes, of patrons and of performers; for most medieval works were intended to be read or recited aloud, to large court audiences or to more intimate family groups. On the whole they were designed to be received aurally at a time when lay literacy was in its infancy.

Piety and Politics: Christian Martyrs and Epic Heroes

The medieval public's thirst for elevating but gruesome stories of torture and martyrdom was satisfied by the earliest genre to be written down in the vernacular: hagiography or saints' lives. Both entertaining and didactic, these works provided models of Christian behaviour to be admired if not easily emulated. While some saints' lives had Latin sources, the eleventh century saw the composition directly into the vernacular of the lives of indigenous (French) saints, no doubt to encourage medieval pilgrims to visit local shrines, thus combining the financial and pastoral concerns of the Church.

The *Cantilène de Sainte Eulalie* (*c*.880) has the distinction of being the oldest hagiographic text in Old French and is a monastic adaptation of a Latin liturgical sequence sung in church. It tells (in only twenty-nine lines) of the martyrdom of an obscure Spanish saint who prefers to die rather than forsake her faith, and it seems to have been composed just after her relics were found in Barcelona. Other early saints' lives include the tenth-century *Vie de Saint Léger*, written in a mixture of authorial French and scribal *occitan*, and the eleventh-century *Chanson de Sainte Foy*, another story about the torture and decapitation of a young girl, yet described by its prologue as a song sweeter than honey.

These early experiments in hagiography were all short, and are mainly of interest now for linguistic and metrical reasons. The *Vie de Saint Alexis*, however, first translated from the Latin *c*.1050, narrates the saint's life in some detail, from his refusal to consummate his marriage to the miraculous cures which followed his death. This is an improving tale of asceticism and self-sacrifice, with the saint attempting to live in imitation of Christ. It is humanized, however, by the speeches given to Alexis's parents and his wife. In later French versions this dialogue is expanded to enable the saint to explain to his spouse why chastity within marriage is preferable to acquiescing to the aristocracy's needs for legitimate heirs. This is a prime example of the medieval predilection for *remaniement*, the constant rewriting of material, adapting it to the tastes of new audiences. Thus a twelfth-century public familiar with romance was entertained by this recently added bedchamber debate, and the Church's new teaching on consent within marriage was emphasized through the innovation of allowing the wife to agree to Alexis's holy plan prior to his departure.

Appearing with the *Alexis* in at least two manuscripts is the Anglo-Norman *Voyage de Saint Brendan* by Benedeit (early twelfth century). This mixture of hagiography and travelogue was dedicated to Henry I of England's first wife, Maud, and relates Brendan's miraculous adventures during his voyage west in search of heaven and hell. The 'scientific' information which this work contains on the strange beasts and phenomena the saint encounters is similar to that provided by lapidaries, bestiaries and herbals. These were being translated into the vernacular at the time and contained descriptions and symbolic, religious interpretations of the natural world, exploitable by fictional writers.

It is to the late eleventh century that we owe the first written version of the epic, a genre in many ways reminiscent of the saint's life both in form (appearing first in assonance, then in rhyme) and in content, for heroes like Roland and Vivien (*Chanson de Guillaume*), while less humble than Alexis, nevertheless sacrifice themselves in the service of God. Around one hundred *chansons de geste** have survived, the genre continuing to be popular long after the birth of romance. They probably originated in orally composed heroic songs from the Germanic past, yet the stages they passed through remain unclear, as is the nature of the *Roland*, supposedly sung before the Battle of Hastings to inspire the Normans. However, the extant examples appear to be written compositions despite their oral features (no doubt included to aid aural reception and recitation by *jongleurs* accompanying themselves on a stringed *viele*).

In classifying epics we tend to adopt the three groups mentioned

---

* songs of heroic exploits

by Bertrand de Bar-sur-Aube in his *Girart de Vienne* (*c*.1180): the *geste du roi*, the Guillaume cycle and the epic of revolt. The first cycle concentrates on Charlemagne and his wars against the infidel and contains the best-known song, the *Chanson de Roland*. The second tends to present the king (no longer Charlemagne, but his weak son Louis) unfavourably, and as dependent upon Guillaume d'Orange to preserve his authority and to protect the monarchy and Holy Church. Thus it is Guillaume who, in the *Couronnement de Louis*, forces the reluctant Louis to assume the duties of king, kills rival claimants to the throne, and goes to the aid of the pope. Despite their serious political messages, epics in this group are characterized by a vein of humorous realism rare in the other two cycles. Thus we find within the *Chanson de Guillaume* a hilarious, scatological description of fleeing cowards and the amusing heroic exploits of the giant Rainouart with his club juxtaposed with the tragic death of the Christ-like martyr Vivien.

The final group of epics depicts rebel barons, whose revolt often seems justified, yet whose pride can either bring about their downfall, as in *Raoul de Cambrai*, or has to be expiated, as in *Les Quatre Fils Aimon* and *Girart de Rousillon*. Moral messages concerning the punishment of the hero's *démesure** are accompanied by an examination of political issues, such as feudal justice, the inheritance and distribution of fiefs, internecine war and the obligations of lord and vassal.

Although many epics are based on historical events which occurred in the eighth and ninth centuries, they portray the tensions and concerns of the age in which they were composed. For example, the skirmish between Charlemagne's rearguard and the Basques in the Pyrenees in 778 has become in the *Roland* (*c*.1098) a full-scale war between Christians and pagans, reflecting the crusading fervour of its late-eleventh-century author. It portrays the betrayal of Roland by his stepfather Ganelon, and the tragic consequences of bringing private grievances into the public arena. Moreover, through conflictual dialogue between Roland and his companion-in-arms Oliver, the poet is able to explore issues such as honour, heroism and the appropriate behaviour of a military leader, lord's vassal and servant of God.

---

* lack of moderation

The epic is usually characterized as masculine, monologic (promoting one authoritative viewpoint) and concerned more with collective ideals than with the desires of the individual. Yet epic heroes can often be individualized through the effective use of dialogue, and there are many *chansons de geste* that offer better roles for women than the purely functional one given in the *Roland* to Aude, whose death on learning of her fiancé's demise merely enhances Roland's reputation. In the *Chanson de Guillaume*, for instance, Guillaume's resourceful wife Guibourc is presented as his ideal mate, for she encourages her husband to fight, serves up a meal to a soldier with a monstrous appetite, then assembles a huge army for her husband. In later epics such as *Doon de la Roche, Aye d'Avignon, Aiol* and the *Siege de Barbastre* the function of Saracen princesses or Christian wives is not only to question the assumptions underpinning patriarchal society, but also to represent conflicting viewpoints not completely neutralized by the plot. In some respects these heroines are less willing to toe the line than their romance counterparts.

The 'Twelfth-century Renaissance': Lyric and Romance

The prologue to the eleventh-century *Vie de Saint Alexis* begins with a *laudatio temporis acti*,* the notion that the world has been degenerating ever since God's perfect creation. A consequence of this commonly expressed world-view was a respect for ancient learning, appreciated for the moral truths it contained, despite the pagan beliefs of its authors. However, medieval humility towards the *auctores* was also tinged with pride, which is summed up in Bernard of Chartres's oft-quoted claim that medieval scholars were 'dwarves perched on the shoulders of giants', thus enabled to see further than their predecessors, whose works they were engaged in glossing. This was the spirit of the 'twelfth-century renaissance'.

The romance writer Chrétien de Troyes is emblematic of the twelfth century in which he flourished. In the prologue to his second

---

* Golden Age topos (literally, 'praise of time past')

extant romance, *Cliges*, Chrétien presents himself and his contemporaries as worthy successors to the Greeks and Romans; for just as political power had passed from Greece to Rome and now to France (by a process called *translatio imperii*) so learning had similarly been transferred, with Chrétien expressing the hope that it would remain in France for ever. This 'translation' of culture (*translatio studii*) was effected through the actual translation of classical texts, and in this respect too, Chrétien is representative of his age. For, as the *Cliges* prologue also reveals, he began his career by translating into French several works by Ovid, including the *Ars amatoria*, *Remedia amoris* and some of the *Metamorphoses*.

Indeed, romance, the forerunner of the modern novel, began life as a translated genre. Although we now associate romances with love because that was their main subject-matter, *romanz* (from the Latin *romanice*) originally meant 'in the Romance language/ vernacular' as opposed to Latin. The earliest romances, the *romans antiques* (*c.*1150–70), were all based on Latin or Latinized Greek sources, the *Roman de Thèbes*, *Roman d'Enéas* and *Roman de Troie* drawing on Statius, Virgil, and Dictys and Dares respectively, while also being influenced by Ovid. The *Troie* by Benoît de Sainte-Maure was dedicated to Eleanor of Aquitaine, wife of Henry II of England, and a great patroness of the arts, as was Marie de Champagne, her daughter by her first husband, Louis VII of France. Two shorter Ovidian *lais*, *Piramus et Tisbé* and *Narcisus*, were produced around the same time along with various versions of the *Roman d'Alexandre* (containing marvellous travel tales not unlike those found in the *Voyage de Saint Brendan*).

Although twelfth-century writers respected their classical sources, they showed no compunction in modernizing them. Thus Enéas is a medieval knight and lover; God partially replaces the pagan gods; battles reflect contemporary warfare; and amorous dialogue imitates the contemporary troubadour lyric. Moreover, the oriental subject-matter allowed for elaborate description of Eastern exotica (clothing, spices, luxury goods) made popular by the Crusades. The authors of romance were Latin-educated clerics, trained in the seven liberal arts – the *trivium* (grammar, rhetoric and dialectic, learned through imitating the classical *auctores*) and the *quadrivium* (arithmetic, music, geometry and astronomy) – in one of the cathedral schools, the forerunners of the thirteenth-century universities. That they were particularly proud of their learning is evident in the rhetorical embellishment of their sources and in their consciousness of the tradition they were perpetuating.

Another influence on Old French romance was the Occitan lyric produced by the troubadours in southern France. Male poets' expressions of (often unrequited) desire for an apparently unattainable, sometimes haughty, but always idealized lady played a vital role in the development of the concept of what modern critics call 'courtly love'. *Amour courtois* may have been introduced to northern writers via the court of Louis VII of France and subsequently into Henry II of England's court by Eleanor of Aquitaine, married first to Louis, then to Henry, and the granddaughter of the first known troubadour poet, William IX of Aquitaine. The love poetry of troubadours such as Cercamon, Jaufré Rudel, Bernard de Ventadour and Marcabru is generally characterized by a spring setting with bird song (giving rise to feelings of love and a desire to sing), descriptions of love symptoms (many Ovidian, with an emphasis on suffering), lamenting over separation, a fear of spies and gossips, promises of fidelity and discretion, the ennoblement of the male lover through the cultivation of refined behaviour and language, and the constant hope that his love service will result in the lady granting solace, healing love's wounds, and giving joy to the suitor in sexual union. The lover's emotions, his hopes and anxieties, are expressed in hyperbolic, highly stylized language and versification, rich in imagery and enhanced by the lyrical music composed by the poets themselves. Such features were adopted not only by the *trouvères* or lyric poets of northern France (see also page 36), but also by romance writers in their love monologues and dialogues. They are to be found codified in Andreas Capellanus's *De amore* (*On Love*). While this treatise was traditionally thought to have been commissioned by Marie de Champagne (who is mentioned along with her mother, Eleanor, as presiding over 'courts of love'), it is now viewed as a humorous, ironic, Ovidian treatment of literary passion by a cleric writing for the king of France, Philippe-Auguste. Andreas's advice to young Walter on how to woo women of different social classes, how to behave in the presence of his beloved and, in Book Three, how to rid himself of love is no longer read as serious teaching on 'courtly love'.

Love and relations between the sexes are the subjects of several romances produced in the second half of the twelfth century and based on classical or oriental material. They include the *Sept Sages de Rome*, in which seven wise men tell stories exemplifying female malice, and two versions of *Floire et Blancheflor*, an idyllic romance depicting young love triumphing over parental objections and religious differences. The anonymous *Partonopeus de Blois* and Renaut de Beaujeu's Arthurian *Bel Inconnu* show lyric influence in their inclusion of female addressees within pseudo-autobiographical frame narratives, which claim that the fictional adventures to be related mirror their authors' own amatory experiences. While love is usually the stuff of romance, faith in God is the theme uniting the disparate elements of hagiography, *fabliau*-style comedy (see page 30), courtly romance and epic in Gautier d'Arras's *Eracle*, which portrays the life of the historical emperor Heraclius. Gautier (a lesser-known near-contemporary of Chrétien, who counted amongst his patrons Marie de Champagne, Thibaut V of Blois, Baudouin V of Hainault and Beatrice, Empress of Rome) followed *Eracle* with a Breton chivalric romance *Ille et Galeron* on the theme of the man with two wives, treated also by Marie de France in her *lai Eliduc*.

Marie de France, associated with the court of Henry II of England around 1180, is thought to have composed three works: the *Espurgatoire Saint Patrice* telling of the knight Owein's descent into Purgatory; a collection of *Fables* based on Aesop; and a group of twelve *lais*. The latter draw on the *matière de Bretagne*, oral Celtic tales probably introduced into the French-speaking world by bilingual Breton story-tellers. This *matière* gave French literature the legendary King Arthur, his magician friend Merlin, his half-sister Morgan the Fay, and the famous couples Lancelot and Guinevere, and Tristan and Iseut. Marie's *lais* are miniature romances, too short to portray evolution of character or complex plotting, yet the collection as a whole covers a wide range of variations on the theme of love. Like the *romanciers*, Marie employs traditional Ovidian metaphors to depict the process of falling in love and its symptoms: lovers are the victims of arrows shot by the god of love; they join his army as faithful vassals; Cupid's torch sets them on fire; the wound caused by his dart can be healed only by the beloved's medicine (that is, reciprocal feelings which lead to consummation); in the meantime the lovers cannot eat or sleep and are found weeping, sighing and even yawning! Other Ovidian devices are the go-between (transformed by Marie into a bird messenger in the case of *Milun*) and internal dialogue, enabling the lover to examine and question his or her emotions. Marie's treatment of love is not, however, purely Ovidian, for she employs the specifically medieval feudal metaphor of the man becoming his lady's vassal and receiving in return for his loyal service her body as a fief. This 'courtly view' of love appears to give greater power to the lady, whose commands her lover is expected to obey. However, this is not necessarily an attitude Marie condones, for in the two of her *lais* which seem most to invoke courtly conventions, *Equitan* and *Chaitivel*, the lovers do not achieve a happy union.

What Marie approves of is 'natural' love. Rejecting the artificial conventions of *amour courtois* and the pressures of feudal society, which encourage loveless marriages for dynastic reasons, she portrays the *mal mariée* (a girl married to an older, jealous man) finding happiness in an adulterous affair. She does not condone the excesses of young love, yet still presents the fated pair in *Les Deus Amanz* sympathetically. Several *lais*, in portraying active heroines willing to declare themselves, seem to represent female wish-fulfilment, especially those in which the Celtic *merveilleux* aids the women in their quest for true love (*Yonec, Guigemar*). However, *Lanval*, whose hero is mistreated by King Arthur and falsely accused of attempted seduction by Guinevere, but is ultimately rewarded with riches and love by a fairy mistress, is clearly an example of male wish-fulfilment. While there are signs of female authorship in the *lais* (though this is disputed), Marie was not a feminist in the modern sense. Despite their often courageous behaviour, her heroines are normally rewarded for their 'feminine' patience and altruism, rather than for any more active virtues (*Fresne, Eliduc*).

Marie de France's *Chevrefeuille* depicts Tristan's attempt to arrange a rendezvous with Iseut by leaving her a message carved on a hazel stick; the hazel, along with the honeysuckle of the title, symbolizing the inseparability of the lovers. This *lai*, in its concentration on one episode from the Tristan legend, resembles two other short texts: the Anglo-Norman *Folie d'Oxford* and the *Folie de Berne* (both late-twelfth-century). In these Tristan, disguised as a fool, tries to make contact with Iseut right under the nose of her husband King Mark, thus elaborating a theme common in the Tristan material: the ambiguity of language and the deceptiveness of appearances. More substantial, though unfortunately both fragmentary, versions of the legend are to be found in Beroul's *Tristran* (*c.*1190, but perhaps much earlier) and the Anglo-Norman romance by Thomas (*c.*1176). Beroul gives us an exciting episodic narration of the lovers' attempts to preserve their adulterous relationship in a hostile world. In his romance the fateful love is *caused* by the love potion, intended for Iseut and her prospective husband, Tristan's uncle King Mark, but drunk by mistake by the lovers. The lovers, as victims of an uncontrollable, anti-social passion, win the sympathy of the intrusive narrator. The ethical implications of adultery are, however, introduced by the waning of the potion half-way through the fragment, thus allowing moral responsibility to play a role in this tragic narrative.

It seems that in Thomas's more clerkly version of the story the protagonists were in love prior to the taking of the potion, which therefore becomes symbolic of the intensity of their feelings. Here the emphasis is on the psychological investigation of the hero's emotions, and in particular his jealousy at having to share Iseut with her husband, which he tries to remedy by marrying a second Iseut, with tragic consequences.

The *matière de Bretagne* similarly provided the subject-matter for Chrétien's five Arthurian romances, the first of which was *Erec et Enide* (now dated by some *c.*1184, formerly *c.*1164). Chrétien's source, according to the prologue, was a *conte d'aventure* which he transformed into a 'molt bele conjointure' – a beautifully wrought, carefully structured, complex narrative. While episodes concerning Erec were probably supplied by an oral legend, King Arthur and the concepts associated with him, namely chivalry and courtesy, were known to Chrétien from Geoffrey of Monmouth's *History of the Kings of Britain* (*Historia regum Britanniae*, *c.*1138) via Wace's Anglo-Norman translation *Le Roman de Brut* (*c.*1155, written for Eleanor of Aquitaine). These works by Geoffrey and Wace could be classified as histories, for they present Arthur as a historical figure. However, Geoffrey's elaboration upon the sparse historical facts about the British warlord Arthur and his transformation of him into a Christian king symbolizing twelfth-century ideals of monarchy place the *Historia* and translations of it firmly in the genre of romance.

In Wace's *Brut* later poets found all the major Arthurian characters, as well as the first mention of the Round Table and a greater elaboration than in Geoffrey of the concepts of *courtoisie* and *chevalerie*. It is Wace's Gawain who, in defending peacetime activities such as tournaments against a war-hungry old warrior, describes a role for women which characterizes much later Arthurian romance: ladies inspire knights to great feats of arms, thus enhancing their own reputation and that of their lover. Here love and chivalry are mutually beneficial, and fighting is no longer the purely masculine affair it generally was in the epic.

At the point in the *Brut* where we are told that twelve years of peace ensued, during which Arthur's court became famous for chivalry and *courtoisie*, a thirteenth-century scribe has inserted into his copy Chrétien's five Arthurian romances. The copyist has thereby re-established the historicity of the king and his knights, treated as purely fictional by the French poet, whose Arthurian settings are temporally and spatially imprecise. Chrétien's romances focus less on Arthur and more on the adventures of young knights in their quest for maturity and identity. *Erec et Enide* charts the progress of the protagonists towards an ideal royal partnership, ratified by Arthur. Erec's early adventures enable him to avenge his chivalric honour and win a bride. Yet Chrétien's romance does not end with marriage, for Erec's inability to combine desire for his wife with his public obligations results in neglect of his chivalric duties, and a marital crisis when Enide repeats criticisms of her husband's uxoriousness. Although the effects of her speaking out are positive, for Erec is thus propelled into a series of adventures during which he proves his valour and rehabilitates himself, Enide's *parole* is often criticized, and her wifely obedience put to the test in the form of a prohibition on speech. Notwithstanding the couple's reconciliation once Erec has proof of his wife's love, the romance's ambiguous presentation of gender roles leaves the audience with much to ponder.

Chrétien's second romance, *Cliges*, is a neo-Tristan in comic mode. It portrays the love of Cliges's parents before relating their son's story, thus reflecting the theme of generational *translatio* introduced in the prologue. Cliges's adulterous love for his uncle's wife Fénice does not have fatal consequences, thanks to potions which enable Fénice to remain true to Cliges until her husband's convenient death (this *is* comedy). Yet despite her refusal to become a second Iseut, Fénice's ultimate fate is to be compared to the deceitful wife of Solomon, and to provide subsequent emperors with an excuse to lock up their wives. The ending is characteristically ironic and playful, making it very difficult to judge Chrétien's moral position in relation to his subject-matter.

This is true also of his third romance, *Lancelot* or *Le Chevalier de la charrete*, dedicated to Marie de Champagne, and the first work to link Guinevere romantically with Lancelot. Possibly Chrétien was unhappy treating the subject of adultery, apparently imposed on him by his patroness, for he appears to have handed the romance over to a certain Godefroi de Leigni to complete. However, many of the 'authorial' remarks which appear in the prologue and epilogue may again reflect Chrétien's habitual irony. The romance narrates Guinevere's abduction to the other world, where some of Arthur's subjects are imprisoned, and the attempts of Lancelot and Gawain to rescue her. The fact that Lancelot, inspired by an adulterous love (presented as courtly service and near-religious devotion), succeeds where Gawain fails lends the romance an ambiguous morality. Is Chrétien promoting an ideal of love, more perfect than anything possible within marriage with its conjugal rights, or is he, at moments when Lancelot's excesses are portrayed comically, critical of this love? The irony and ambiguity characteristic of Chrétien encourage modern (and doubtless contemporary) readers to debate these issues and arrive at their own conclusions.

Another *casus* or case study on love is provided by *Yvain*, or *Le Chevalier au lion*. It is similar to *Erec et Enide* in structure, with its bride-winning followed by a marital crisis and then apparent resolution of it through a series of adventures. However, in this case the hero's fault is to neglect his wife rather than chivalry, for Yvain, off with Gawain on a tournament-crawl (the morality and social usefulness of which were being debated at the time), forgets to return to his wife after a year's leave of absence. In the prologue to *Yvain*, Arthur's court is idealized, thereby setting up audience expectations that are soon to be thwarted by the narrative proper. For Yvain, although an Arthurian knight, not only proves to be flawed as a lover, he also lacks a proper understanding of chivalry. He therefore undergoes a series of adventures, through which he learns punctuality, responsibility and chivalric altruism, mostly in the company of a lion. This gives the new, improved Yvain the sobriquet 'le chevalier au lion'. Whilst Lancelot loses the shameful appellation 'the knight of the cart' when Guinevere addresses him by his real name, Yvain rejects his old persona in favour of a more positive *surnom*. Thus the evolution of the hero is reflected in Chrétien's choice of names, a feature found also in *Perceval*. *Yvain* apparently ends happily with the married couple's reconciliation. Yet, as in *Cliges*, the ending is tinged with irony, for Laudine is tricked into taking her husband back. Although it is clear that Yvain (and the reader too) has achieved a deeper understanding of *courtoisie*, love and chivalry, the audience is asked not only to re-examine critically its received ideas and those ideals represented by Arthur and his court in the prologue, but also to question the plausibility of the happy ending promoted by this romance's often unreliable narrator.

Chrétien's final romance, *Perceval* or *Le Conte del graal* (dedicated to Philippe d'Alsace, Count of Flanders, who died on crusade in 1191), introduces the Grail into European literature. Perceval is a young Welsh nobleman, whose naivety and lack of education produce much humour, but who gradually learns the meaning of chivalry. In *Perceval*, however, Chrétien has developed the concept further to include not only the socially useful functions of protecting the weak and oppressed, demonstrated in *Yvain*, but the more religious function of protecting Holy Church – knights now being presented as members of an 'order' reminiscent of monastic orders. The crisis in *Perceval* is not marital, but spiritual, brought about by the hero's inability to ask vital questions at the Grail castle. Eventually he learns that it was his state of sin (having unwittingly but selfishly caused his mother's death) that prevented him from enquiring whom the Grail served and why the lance was bleeding, questions which would have healed the impotent Fisher King and restored fertility to the wasteland. When the fragment breaks off Perceval has not yet found the Grail again, but his chivalric and spiritual progress suggests he would ultimately have been successful. Gawain, sent on a parallel quest for the bleeding lance, but with an accusation of murder to answer, seems secure in his reputation as a great worldly knight (and womanizer), but is apparently not destined for spiritual perfection.

Chrétien's Grail, shaped like a dish, has features reminiscent of Celtic cauldrons and horns of plenty, yet by virtue of its contents – a consecrated host – it has been semi-Christianized, a process completed by the late twelfth-century writer Robert de Boron in his *Roman de l'Estoire dou Graal* or *Joseph*. For Robert, the Grail is the chalice used by Joseph of Arimathea to collect Christ's blood at the crucifixion. Its Celtic origins effaced, it has become a holy relic, brought to Britain by Joseph's brother-in-law, and in later tradition given to Perceval. Thus Robert links sacred history with Arthurian history, providing fertile ground for thirteenth-century romancers to continue the tradition.

Tradition and Originality: Rewriting Romance

Writers of the thirteenth century onwards, while respectful of the traditions set up by their predecessors, were nevertheless keen to experiment, to challenge (perhaps under the influence of Aristotelian logic being taught in the recently established universities), and to rewrite inherited material in a new way. Characteristic of this period is also the tendency to continue unfinished texts (e.g. the several verse continuations of Chrétien's *Perceval*, which narrate further adventures of Perceval or Gawain), and to organize works into cycles. *Chanson de geste* cycles had already been produced in the twelfth century by adding poems about a hero's ancestors or descendants to the epic narrating his finest hours. In thirteenth-century romance, cyclicity was accompanied by a change from verse to prose, resulting in huge prose cycles, possibly intended more for private reading than public performance, and very popular, judging from the number of surviving manuscripts.

The fashion for cyclical romances may have begun with Robert de Boron, who mentions in his *Joseph* four other branches of the Grail story which he hoped to 'assembler'. A prose cycle of his works, consisting of a *Joseph*, *Merlin* and the *Didot Perceval*, relates the early history of Arthur and the Grail, and Perceval's winning of the Grail, and ends with a 'death of King Arthur' section, apparently based on Wace's *Brut*. Although the early thirteenth-century prose *Perlesvaus* continues the tradition of Perceval as Grail-winner, another huge prose cycle, the *Lancelot-Grail*, has Lancelot's son Galahad successfully completing the adventures of the Grail. The Vulgate Cycle, as the latter was known, was composed between 1215 and 1235 by clerics of Champagne and consists of three central works: the *Lancelot* proper, the *Queste del Saint Graal* and *La Mort le roi Artu*. Later authors added to the beginning of the cycle an *Estoire del Saint Graal* and a *Merlin* and its continuation, thus filling in the pre-history of the Grail. The *Lancelot* proper (sometimes referred to as the *Prose Lancelot*) is a reworking of the early thirteenth-century non-cyclic *Lancelot do lac*, with additions based on Chrétien's *Charrete*. It relates Lancelot's early life, his creation of a chivalric identity and his falling in love with Guinevere. Mainly courtly in tone, the *Lancelot* at first presents the adulterous relationship as the inspiration behind Lancelot's socially useful feats of prowess. However, in the episodes leading up to the Grail quest, ethical and spiritual factors are emphasized, and Lancelot, though still the best knight in the world, is seen as morally compromised. Nevertheless, Lancelot is still a hero in the *Queste*, where he comes closer to the Grail than the far-too-worldly Gawain, but it is his virgin son Galahad, accompanied by Perceval and Bohort, who experiences the mysteries of the now eucharistic Grail.

The *Queste* is a didactic romance consisting of allegorical adventures, the symbolic significance of which is revealed to the questers by hermits, some of whom appear to be Cistercian monks. It is no longer worldly prowess that guarantees success, but rather those virtues extolled by the Cistercians: virginity and humility. Yet it is not a monk but the knight Galahad (a type of Christ) who heals the Maimed King and brings the adventures of the Grail to an end. This is chivalry's finest hour. Other knights, on the other hand, return to Arthur's court having suffered various degrees of failure and humiliation, thus setting the tone for the *Mort Artu*, the romance to end all romances. In a tightly woven, psychologically realistic plot reminiscent of the *peripeteia* of Aristotelian tragedy, we witness the gradual disintegration of the Arthurian world, resulting from the discovery of the adultery between Lancelot and Guinevere. While the work is somewhat critical of its characters (Mordred's treachery, Morgan's plotting, the lovers' uncontrolled passion, Gawain's thirst for revenge after the accidental killing of his brothers, Arthur's excessive concern for honour), there is also sympathetic treatment of them as victims of fate, Fortune, bad luck and conflicting values, producing the moral ambiguity at the heart of this fascinating work.

The complex plotting of the Vulgate Cycle, with its interlacing of adventures treating first one hero, then another, is also characteristic of another huge romance cycle: the Prose *Tristan*. This work (which formed, along with the Vulgate Cycle, the source for Malory's *Morte Darthur*) has survived in a series of compilations for which we have two named authors, Luce del Gat and Hélie de Boron. While the verse *Tristan*s concentrated on love and its social and psychological effects, the prose is a chivalric romance, which links the hero with Arthur, Lancelot, Guinevere and even the Grail quest.

The love episodes in the prose *Tristan* are much enhanced by the insertion of lyric songs into the prose narrative. This technical innovation was first popularized by Jean Renart in the early thirteenth century in his *Roman de Dole*, and is also found in Gerbert de Montreuil's *Roman de la Violette* and in the *Lai d'Aristote*. However, unlike the *Tristan* these works are in narrative verse and the generic shift to lyric is therefore not so clearly marked.

Verse romance was not totally eclipsed by the great prose cycles of the thirteenth century, and several Arthurian works imitating Chrétien's biographical narratives (some of which have Gawain as their hero) attest its continuing appeal. Jean Renart's romances, on the other hand, foresake the Arthurian *merveilleux* in favour of realism and observed detail of everyday life. *L'Escoufle* (c.1200), a *roman d'aventure* whose plot is reminiscent of *Floire et Blancheflor* (see page 10), contains a description of a young child rare in contemporary literature. *Guillaume de Dole* is a story of false accusations against the heroine and identification by means of a birthmark (the rose of its alternative title, *Le Roman de la Rose*). This work is, despite its implausible plot (used also by Gerbert in his *Violette*), noted for its psychological *vraisemblance*.* *Galeran de Bretagne*, usually attributed to Renart, is based on Marie de France's *lai Le Fresne*. However, the masculine viewpoint is reflected in the title, for whereas Marie's story is named after the twin daughter abandoned by a mother afraid of being accused of adultery, Jean's romance is named after the man who falls in love with her, yet nearly marries her sister instead. Again, this romance displays the mixture of courtly sophistication and bourgeois realism characteristic of Jean's works. In contrast, his much shorter *Lai de l'ombre* concentrates on the wooing of a lady by a knight gifted in courtly eloquence and can be read as a mirror of polite courtship. However, having been alerted by the prologue to the element of luck in all human activity, we are perhaps being encouraged to view ironically the knight's literally throw-away gesture of casting the lady's ring to her reflection in the well, which

---

* verisimilitude

convinces her of the sincerity of his love. Could this not be a humorous comment on the superficiality of courtly manners, the shallowness of the lady and the opportunism of the knight?

This subtle questioning of courtly conventions links the *Lai de l'ombre* with another thirteenth-century *lai*, the *Chastelaine de Vergi*, whose plot echoes Marie de France's *Lanval*. It begins with a courtly situation often found in lyric poetry: a knight is in love with a lady (possibly married), who grants her love only on condition that their affair remain secret. The knight, however, is forced to reveal their love to the Duke of Burgundy in order to clear himself of false accusations made by the duchess, a medieval Potiphar's wife. In a series of tragic no-win situations, in which first the knight then the duke finds himself with conflicting loyalties, the secret is gradually disclosed until the duchess is able to taunt the chatelaine with knowledge of it, resulting in the eponymous heroine's death from a broken heart. On the evidence of its prologue and epilogue, the narrative is an *exemplum* of the disastrous consequences of indiscretion; it could also be read, however, as a critique of poetic ideals of love, which prove impracticable when the lovers are placed in the more 'realistic' world of narrative, where action can undermine emotion, and voyeuristic or envious third parties intrude on personal love idylls.

Another text which places a hero more suited to the lyric or idyllic romance in situations which require action rather than emotion is the thirteenth-century *chantefable, Aucassin et Nicolette*. This unique example of its genre, in alternating prose and assonanced verse, may be a parody of courtly romance, exaggerating the inability of a male lover, such as Lancelot, to function in epic or more 'realistic' situations. Since Aucassin is hardly a Lancelot, however, and more like young Floire in *Floire et Blancheflor* (see page 10), its humour probably derives from the ironic gap between the hero's behaviour and the expectations created in the audience by the author's use of traditional heroic epithets and literary situations. The heroine, Nicolette, is generally presented as a more active, resourceful character than her beloved Aucassin, even disguising herself as a *jongleur*, a feature she shares with other medieval heroines.

Gender issues or violence against women are the subjects of several thirteenth-century non-Arthurian works. The short prose tale entitled *La Fille du comte de Pontieu* depicts the shame felt by the heroine after being raped by robbers in front of her husband, and her subsequent punishment by her father for trying to kill her spouse. After several exotic adventures involving shipwreck and bigamy, the original couple are reunited. The 'feminine' virtues of modesty and passive suffering are again rewarded in the *Manekine* of Philippe de Rémi, sire de Beaumanoir (*c*.1275), whose heroine cuts off her hand in order to dissuade her father from incest. Having survived his attempts to burn her, and the false accusation by her mother-in-law of giving birth to a monster in her husband's absence, she is eventually reunited with her husband and penitent father when her hand is miraculously restored to her in Rome. The moral is a Christian one about faith in God and reflects a general sense of justice found in the other medieval works, including epics, where the traditional motif of the falsely accused wife is exploited.

Violence against women is also the theme of *Philomena* (possibly by Chrétien de Troyes, but extant only in the thirteenth-century *Ovide moralisé*), the Ovidian story of rape by a brother-in-law who cuts out Philomena's tongue in order to silence her. She, however, informs her sister of the dreadful deed by producing an embroidered cloth depicting her rape and mutilation, and the sisters take their revenge by killing the man's son and serving the child up to him at dinner. There is a variation on this classical motif in the late-thirteenth-century *Roman du chastelain de Couci et de la dame de Fayel* by a certain Jakemes. Here a husband takes revenge on his adulterous wife by cooking her lover's embalmed heart. She, having partaken of it, dies grief-stricken like the Châtelaine de Vergi. Thus the tragic ending, relatively uncommon in the twelfth century (except in the verse *Tristans*), becomes more frequent in later romance, perhaps because of the spirit of scepticism which begins to undermine the optimism of the twelfth century.

The social construction of gender is the subject of Heldris of Cornwall's *Roman de Silence*, whose heroine is brought up as a boy because inheritance by women is banned in her country. Despite her successful disguise as knight and *jongleur*, to the extent that the queen Eufemie tries to seduce her (also reacting like Potiphar's wife to rejection), *nature* eventually triumphs, and it is Silence's femaleness that enables her to trap Merlin, prove her innocence and marry the king. However, while this text, like Chrétien's *Perceval* and like *Guillaume d'Angleterre* (sometimes attributed to Chrétien), demonstrates that *nurture** cannot suppress nature, the fact that Silence is convincing as a man, and that Silentia can become Silentius simply by the substitution of the suffix *us* (which in Old French means habit or custom), does suggest that masculine and feminine characteristics are largely learned and socially constructed. Similarly, in Robert de Blois's *Floris et Liriopé* Floris is disguised as a girl when he woos and wins Liriopé. The unnaturalness of this process, however, is implied by the fact that their son is the ill-fated Narcissus. Yet in *Yde et Olive* the heroine who impersonates a man in order to flee her father's incestuous advances, and is then forced to marry a woman, is 'rewarded' by being given a sex-change by God (cf. Blanchandine in *Tristan de Nanteuil*).

French vernacular literature of the twelfth and early thirteenth centuries was dominated by two major genres, epic and romance, whose conventions were renewed, reworked and questioned by successive practitioners. While these genres continued to be popular in the later Middle Ages, authors began to develop and favour other types of literature, notably theatre, historiography, didactic treatises and lyric poetry, and these will be the subject of the next chapter.

---

* upbringing

Further Reading

John Fox, *The Middle Ages*, vol. 1 of P.E. Charvet's *A Literary History of France* (London: Benn/New York: Barnes and Noble, 1974).

Alan Hindley and Brian Levy, *The Old French Epic: An Introduction* (Louvain: Peeters, 1983).

Roberta L. Krueger, *Women Readers and the Ideology of Gender in Old French Verse Romance* (Cambridge: Cambridge University Press, 1993).

Pierre Le Gentil, *La Littérature française du moyen âge* (Paris: Colin, 1968).

Roger S. Loomis (ed.), *Arthurian Literature in the Middle Ages: A Collaborative History* (Oxford: Clarendon Press, 1959).

Lynette Muir, *Literature and Society in Medieval France* (London: Macmillan, 1985).

Eugène Vinaver, *The Rise of Romance* (Oxford: Clarendon Press, 1971).

See also the Further Reading list at the end of Chapter 2.

The Middle Ages: Later Developments

KAREN PRATT

While the political stability and economic prosperity of twelfth-century France continued until the end of the thirteenth century, enabling French literature and culture to flourish further, the worsening political situation in the fourteenth and fifteenth centuries became the object of increasingly critical treatment by writers. Among the most significant historical events in the fourteenth century were the setting up in Avignon of a rival papacy to Rome in 1309, the Black Death in the middle of the century and the demise of the last Capetian king, Charles IV, in 1328, resulting in Edward III of England's claim to the throne of France and the beginning of the Hundred Years War in 1337. It is traditional to blame the war, which continued well into the fifteenth century and was accompanied by the internal struggles between the houses of Burgundy and Orléans, for the 'waning' of the Middle Ages: a period of 'decadence' characterized by a fascination with death. However, even in its so-called 'death throes' the Middle Ages still produced some fine literature, notably the poetry of Villon, one of the first authors to have his work published in print. The French language continued to evolve during this period, some critics using the term 'Middle French' to describe the language of works dating from the late fourteenth and fifteenth centuries.

Life and Art: History and Romance

Historiography, one of whose aims in the twelfth century was to trace the history of peoples back to their pseudo-classical origins (the British are presented in Wace's *Brut* [see page 13] as descendants of Aeneas's grandson Brutus and thus linked with the Trojans), soon favoured more recent history and eyewitness evidence. This is the case with Wace's *Roman de rou* (1160s) on the history of the Normans and Benoît de Sainte-Maure's continuation of it in his *Chronique des ducs de Normandie* (*c*.1174). The Anglo-Norman regnum also produced two other significant national histories: Gaimar's *Estoire des Englois* (1135–40) and Jordan Fantosme's *Chroniques* (*c*.1180), while the history of the Crusades was treated by Ambroise, Villehardouin and Robert de Clari, the latter two attempting to explain the ignominious sack of Constantinople in 1204. While many of these works claimed to present historical truths, chronicles like the anonymous *Histoire de Guillaume le maréchal* (*c*.1220) and Jean Froissart's chivalric history of the Hundred Years War (*c*.1400) were also exemplary narratives, providing their audiences with models of chivalric and courtly behaviour.

The *Vie de Saint Thomas* (*c*.1170) by Guernes de Pont-Sainte-Maxence is an early example of a vernacular saint's life which shares many features with historiography, especially an emphasis on the veracity of eyewitness evidence, and this trend continues in the *Histoire de Saint Louis* completed in 1309 by Joinville, the king's friend. This is a saintly biography as much as a history, and anticipates the *Mémoires* of Philippe de Commynes (1489–98) in its personal, intimate knowledge of the monarch in question, though the later chronicler treated his subject, Louis XI, with more objectivity and less uncritical devotion than Joinville.

As well as histories, another source of role models for the late medieval reader was romance, which continued to be rewritten in imaginative ways. (See also pages 17 to 22.) The adventures of Alexander the Great were reworked in an early fourteenth-century chivalric romance, the *Voeux du paon*, which gave rise to several continuations and other works in which knights make vows to birds, soon to be copied by real-life oath-swearing by the likes of Edward I of England. Indeed, examples of life imitating chivalric art become a feature of the later Middle Ages. Thus the Order of the Garter is said to derive from the chivalric 'Ordre du Franc Palais' which appears in the *Perceforest*, an immense fourteenth-century romance presenting the Alexander material as a pre-history for Arthurian chivalry.

Respect for tradition is again in evidence as the legend of the Seven Sages of Rome, combined with motifs from the epic and the *roman courtois*, is adapted in the mid-fourteenth-century prose romance *Berinus et Aigres*. Similarly, Philippe de Rémi's *Manekine* (see page 21) served as the source for the much less gruesome *Roman du comte d'Anjou* by Jehan Maillart (1316), another example of a heroine being supplanted by a hero in the new title. By the fifteenth century, however, more emphasis is placed on psychological investigation rather than exciting action in the prose romances of Antoine de la Sale. The *Petit Jean de Saintré* (1456), written in old age, tells of a young man's education by an older woman, his initiation in love, followed by her despair at his departure to make a chivalric reputation, and her betrayal of him with a lascivious abbot. Critics identify in this work the beginnings of the modern French novel.

Medieval Theatre: The Sacred and the Profane

While much early literature, and the later histories, epics and romances, were commissioned by royal and ducal courts, or flourished in the monasteries, cathedral schools and universities, the bourgeoisie became an important source of patronage in the thirteenth century, especially for theatrical productions. Nowhere was their influence more marked than on the plays produced in Arras, which was, around 1200, a prosperous wool town.

The beginnings of medieval drama are difficult to identify, but it seems that in the early Middle Ages popular theatre was joined by a new type of play which developed out of the Church liturgy; elements of the Easter and Christmas mass were embellished into tropes or miniature dialogues and sung antiphonally by two parts of the choir. Later these embryonic Easter and Nativity plays were taken out of their liturgical contexts, allowed to develop more fully, and performed within churches or just outside their west doors by priests wearing costumes, and gradually the Latin of the mass was replaced by the vernacular. The earliest play in Old French, though with Latin stage directions, is the mid-twelfth-century *Adam*, based on the biblical account of the Fall (including the killing of Abel by Cain) and followed by a procession of prophets foretelling Christ's harrowing of Hell. The different sections of the play are linked typologically, with Adam prefiguring Christ and the original sin committed by Eve being implicitly redeemed by the Virgin's role in the incarnation. The play is notable for its portrayal in feudal terms of the relationship between the first couple and God, and for its characterization of Eve, whose willingness to admit her fault lends her greater dignity than the self-pitying Adam.

While the Bible and the liturgy were early sources for medieval drama, it was hagiography that provided the subject-matter for the first miracle play to be produced in Arras: *Le Jeu de Saint Nicolas* by Jean Bodel, a member of the Confrérie des jongleurs et des bourgeois d'Arras and author also of lyric poetry (including an auto-biographical *Congé*), *fabliaux* (see page 30) and an epic, the *Chanson des Saisnes*. The *Jeu* (*c*.1200), performed perhaps on 5 December (the eve of the Feast of St Nicholas), shows the saint's ability to protect treasure being tested by a Saracen king, who is eventually converted to Christianity. Bodel's play is remarkable for its juxtaposition of literary scenes reminiscent of the epic or hagiography with scenes reflecting observed reality, for it switches between pagan wars in foreign lands and the familiar Arras tavern, where the pagan messenger stops for a drink on his way to fetch reinforcements, and where the thieves who are planning to steal the treasure gamble and drink. Bodel thus combines a serious Christian message with entertaining comic tavern scenes, and the audience watching the play, perhaps performed in the round, would not easily have overlooked the relevance to their own lives of this conflict between good and evil.

Bodel's introduction of comic realism into French drama was influential on at least two later playwrights, the anonymous author of *Courtois d'Arras* (early thirteenth century), a dramatic and at times comic adaptation of the biblical story of the Prodigal Son, and Adam de la Halle's *Jeu de la feuillee* (c.1276). The latter (by another bourgeois cleric of Arras known also for his lyric poetry, music and an epic, *Le Roi de Sicile*) is the first wholly comic play to have survived. It is a dramatization of a lyric *congé*, a farewell poem, presenting a character called Adam (an authorial persona not necessarily to be equated with the playwright) whose avowed aim is to leave his wife and the pleasures of Arras in order to resume his clerical studies in Paris. The play contains satire on the people of Arras and their vices or follies (the *feuillee* of the title being probably a pun on folly), somewhat in the manner of a Cambridge Footlights Revue. After a supernatural episode which anticipates *A Midsummer Night's Dream*, in which fairies curse and bestow gifts on Adam and his colleague, everyone repairs to the tavern, including Adam, whose chances of leaving Arras appear slim. The bourgeois clerics who saw their own anxieties and foibles reflected in the play were thereby asked to ponder whether man's freedom really is limited by supernatural powers as represented by the fairies and Fortune's wheel, or whether man is merely a victim of his own weakness and fleshly desires.

Adam's *Jeu de Robin et Marion* (possibly written for the Count of Artois while he was with him in Sicily and therefore a less 'bourgeois' project) is another experiment in theatre and genre, an embryonic comic opera, in which the lyric *pastourelle* and the *bergerie* have been given dramatic form. The traditional attempt by a knight to seduce (in some cases rape) a young shepherdess is here parodied, with the knight being wittily rebuffed by Marion, who misunderstands, possibly deliberately, the sexual undertones of his courtly language. There then ensue pastoral entertainments (some musical), during which Marion teaches her rustic boyfriend Robin how to treat a shepherdess like a lady. The juxtaposition of *courtoisie* and everyday village life creates most of the humour in the play, along with the recognition that, despite their differing methods, shepherd and knight share the same goals where women are concerned.

In Adam de la Halle's experimentation with genre, satirical presentation of life in Arras and ideological questioning of the conventions of courtly poetry, humour plays a vital role. However, much medieval theatre has a more serious religious message to convey than Adam's secular entertainments. The Parisian Rutebeuf's *Miracle de Théophile*, for example, is an entirely serious drama about a medieval Faust who sells his soul to the devil but is saved by the Virgin Mary. Nevertheless, like the early *Jeu de Saint Nicolas*, later passion plays and lengthy *mystères* (in their attempt to portray the whole of religious history from the Fall to the redemption of man) contain scenes of comic realism involving flawed characters with whom the audience can identify. Thus we find, juxtaposed with Christ's Passion, Roman soldiers grumbling, playing cards and falling asleep while the body is 'stolen', carpenters moaning about the cost of nails as they build the cross, or comic *diableries* with devils dragging the damned off to the Mouth of Hell.

Just as serious drama was often entertaining, so comic theatre could be satirical (though many of the farces display the cynical morality of the *fabliaux*). In the fifteenth century an evening's secular theatre would probably have consisted of a *sottie* (fool's antics and topical jokes to warm up the audience), a *sermon joyeux* (a parodic sermon on a risqué subject), a serious morality play and finally a farce. The finest of the 150 or so surviving late-medieval farces is *La Farce de Pierre Pathelin* (*c*.1465), which has bequeathed to us the expressions 'pateliner' and 'revenons à nos moutons'.* It portrays the classic situation of the duper duped, while also satirizing village lawyers, hasty judges, doctors and greedy, gullible tradesmen. Verbal irony and the clever exploitation of linguistic ambiguity, on which much of the humour depends, make this more of a comedy than a farce, one likely to have been written by a Parisian legal clerk and performed by members of the Clercs de la Basoche.

---

* to smooth-talk; let's get back to the subject

'Plaire et Instruire': Gender Politics and Mirrors for Princes

Throughout the Middle Ages authors seem to have been aware of Horace's dictum on the aims of literature: to be of use and to delight (*prodesse et delectare*). Writers of epics, saints' lives, histories and romances allude to this dual function in their prologues; even the most morally uplifting tales are not denied their entertainment value, while the *fabliaux* (short, frivolous, bawdy tales in verse or prose) are supplied with apparently serious morals for our consideration. Some of these stories depict the vices and foibles of the clergy or the lower classes, yet the lessons drawn are often practical and cynical rather than moral. In the case of the many *fabliaux* that portray the triumph of clever, lecherous wives over gullible husbands, the moral is overtly anti-feminist, thus placing them within a long tradition of misogyny stretching back to Ovid and St Jerome. What we have to judge, though, is how seriously these texts would have been taken.

A key work in the medieval debate about women was the *Roman de la Rose*, begun by Guillaume de Lorris in the 1230s and completed by Jean de Meun in the 1270s. Though some critics think that Guillaume's part was already intended to be read ironically and with moral censure, most believe that his *Rose* was a serious courtly dream allegory, an art of love depicting a young man's attempt to pluck a rose, symbolic of his beloved. The dreamer/lover/narrator is aided in his conquest by personifications of courtly virtues within himself, or of aspects of the lady's personality. However, when Bel Acueil, the welcoming disposition of the lady, is imprisoned by Jealousy in a tower, the lover despairs of ever winning the rose, and with his lament Guillaume's part ends. Jean then hijacks the narrative, and characters introduced by his predecessor (Lady Reason spurned earlier, Ami, who offers encouragement and advice, and Cupid, the god of love, whose arrow had struck the Lover) reappear to lecture Amant at length on a variety of topics.

Jean has produced a Mirror for Lovers, an encyclopaedic compendium of knowledge, which traditionally offered the reader models of behaviour. But how exemplary is Jean's *Rose*? Reason is rejected by Amant in favour of the cynical advice of Ami on how to seduce women: an anti-feminist lecture, the worst excesses of which, however, are placed in the mouth of a jealous husband. Similarly, the *vieille* guarding Bel Acueil suggests that women should use their charms to exploit men while they can, thus reinforcing the misogynistic message. The Lover is helped to storm the castle by Love and Religious Hypocrisy (cue for satire on the mendicant orders) and with the approval of Nature (who is reproducing human beings in her forge according to Neoplatonic principles of creation). Nature, in her confession to her chaplain Genius, discusses the influence of the planets on man's free will; natural and scientific phenomena such as the seasons, optics and dreams; and man's refusal to obey her. Genius then evokes in his sermon a utopian Golden Age now lost, criticizes Guillaume de Lorris's love garden, and contrasts it with a more Christianized, pre-lapsarian paradise where man's obligation is to propagate the species without sin. The conquest of the lady, clothed earlier in courtly horticultural metaphors, is now skimpily clad in religious (some may say sacrilegious) imagery, as the lover, in the guise of a pilgrim with his sturdy staff and pouches, penetrates the narrow sanctuary and, applying a certain amount of force, plucks the rose. Here the erotic dream ends.

Jean's continuation of Guillaume's *Rose* may have set out to reveal the lust lying beneath the surface of courtly mystification or he may have seen the comic, almost pornographic potential in his predecessor's work. Perhaps he wished to underline the sterility of courtly representations of love (very rarely do women become pregnant in twelfth-century texts, except in the *lais* of Marie de France), opposing them to Genius's more natural approach to procreative sex. The bawdiness of the ending seems, however, to belie any serious moral intent. What is clear is that medieval readers could not agree either on the ethics of Jean's contribution or on his attitude to the misogyny expressed by his characters. Conflicting views were voiced in the late fourteenth century during the *Querelle de la Rose*, in which Christine de Pizan (perhaps the first French feminist) attacked Jean for his misogyny and the Chancellor of the Sorbonne, Jean

Gerson, accused him of cynical immorality. His defenders, however, claimed that it was wrong to attribute the opinions of fictional characters to the author and that Jean's *Rose* was an ironic and consequently moral work.

The *Rose* is not the only work whose seriousness and didacticism are difficult to judge. There is a whole tradition of anti-matrimonial literature (to which Jean's *jaloux* contributes) in Latin and the vernacular, which presents husbands as the long-suffering victims of their wives' deception, nagging, extravagance, insatiable sexual appetite, and ability to beat them in any argument. Given that these women share with their clerical creators the ability to manipulate linguistic ambiguity, it is ironic that the overt message conveyed by these texts is misogynist. Such ambivalence is detectable in several *fabliaux*, Jean Le Fèvre's *Lamentations de Matheolus* (*c.*1380), Eustache Deschamps's *Miroir de mariage*, the prose *Quinze Joies de mariage* (an ironic parody and matrimonial equivalent of the joys/sufferings of the Virgin Mary, *c.*1420) and some of the *Cent Nouvelles nouvelles* (1460s), based loosely on Boccaccio's *Decameron*. Some poems denigrating women, such as the *Blasme des fames* and *La Contenance des fames*, occur in manuscripts along with defences of women like *Le Bien des fames*. Similarly Le Fèvre's *Lamentations*, translated from a Latin source, is accompanied by a retraction, supposedly more favourable to women, the *Livre de Leësce*. However, these defences can be as ironic as their anti-feminist counterparts, and may be no more than rhetorical exercises at putting the opposite point of view – a talent practised by poets in their *jeux-partis* (debate poems – see page 36).

It is to Christine de Pizan, writing around 1400, that we owe two unambiguously sincere defences of the morality of women: *L'Epistre au dieu d'amours* and the *Cité des dames*. In both works she refutes the clerical misogyny of Ovid and Jean de Meun by invoking her own experience of women and by citing examples of good women drawn from classical and biblical literature: the Virgin Mary, virtuous saints, female warriors, leaders and scholars (cf. Eustache Deschamps's near-contemporary *Neuf Preuses*, a female equivalent of the Nine Worthies). Appropriating clerical tools in order to subvert them, Christine retells well-known stories as selectively and partially as her male predecessors had done, thus managing even to rehabilitate Eve and Medea. In some respects a pioneer feminist (though her views on the social and political roles of women were not very progressive), she concluded 450 years ago that women would only be properly represented if they were to take up the (traditionally phallic) pen.

Not all medieval works treating women were intentionally humorous or obviously anti-feminist. Robert de Blois's *Chastoiement des dames* (c.1250) offers 'helpful' advice on table manners and warns against peering into a neighbour's house as one walks by. The Chevalier de la Tour Landry tells a cautionary tale in order to dissuade his daughters from becoming martyrs to love, and the *Ménagier de Paris* (1393) offers detailed help on household management for his 15-year-old, bourgeois wife, including spiritual instruction and practical hints on how to please her husband.

More weighty advice of a political and ethical nature was proffered in the Middle Ages to rulers, in the form of Mirrors for Princes. Robert de Blois's *Enseignement des princes* (mid-thirteenth century) and Philippe de Novarre's *Doctrinal sauvage* are early verse examples of this popular genre. Philippe's prose *Des Quatre Tenz d'aage d'ome*, written by the ex-soldier, diplomat, priest and poet at the age of over 70 (he died in 1262), conveys moral and practical teaching within a work both encyclopaedic and personal. Worth noting are his thoughts on childhood and old age, and his warning against educating girls to read and write, unless they are going to become nuns. Guillaume de Deguilleville's *Le Pèlerinage de vie humaine* (early fourteenth century) is also a semi-autobiographical moral treatise, but in the form of a dream allegory, in which the spiritual progress of the narrator is depicted alongside satire on monastic orders (a common theme in the Middle Ages). In 1389, Philippe de Mézières adopted the form of the dream allegory in his *Songe du vieil pèlerin*, written as a mirror for the young King Charles VI, who is offered the Mosaic mission of leading France to a better future. It depicts Truth, the Queen of Heaven, visiting different countries and judging the quality of their currency, symbolic of the moral and political state of the nation in question. Philippe is thereby able to attack the schism in the Church and to examine the parlous situation of the different estates (chivalry, clergy and the people) in France after the battles of Crécy and Poitiers and the effects of the Black Death. Having satirized the judicial and tax systems, his solution is a Ship of State built of the three estates with a mast representing Holy Church. Warning against reading romances about Lancelot, Philippe ends with the hope that a new military order will be established.

Defeat at Agincourt elicited similar criticism of France later in the century from Charles VI's secretary Alain Chartier, better known for his *Belle Dame sans merci*, but the author also of the dream allegory *Le Quadrilogue invectif* (*c*.1422). Here France and the three estates are given voice, with France's torn cloak symbolizing the dire situation she finds herself in. Each estate blames the others for her distress, and they all blame their leaders. Alain, however, offers no solution, merely allowing the situation to speak for itself.

Elderly statesmen were not the only people to produce moral and political treatises in the later Middle Ages. Christine de Pizan, active at the courts of Orléans and Burgundy after her widowhood in 1390, wrote, besides her defences of women and lyric poetry, several didactic works including a life of Charles V, *Le Livre des fais et bonnes moeurs du sage roy Charles V*, commissioned by Philip the Bold, Duke of Burgundy, and intended as a mirror for the Dauphin; a political work, *Le Livre du corps de policie*, adapted from John of Salisbury's *Polycraticus*; a *Livre de paix*; a work on military matters, *Le Livre des fais d'armes et de chevalerie*; and a poem on Joan of Arc.

Serious political and religious messages could also be conveyed humorously via animal allegories, the most famous being the stories about Reynard the Fox and the horse Fauvel. Entertainment was the priority of the earliest tales about the rival barons Renart and Ysengrin the wolf composed by Pierre de Saint-Cloud (*c*.1175) and based on the Latin *Ysengrimus* and various fables. As in the *fabliaux* and later farces, we meet the theme of the trickster tricked, for the cynical, lecherous, violent fox does not always triumph. The humour is largely scatological; in animal guise, universal vices and foibles rather than individuals or institutions are ridiculed, and courtly, chivalric or epic situations are parodied. Nevertheless, priests, monks, pilgrims and peasants are the butts of the humour, and the potential for social satire was soon realized as further branches were added to the *Roman de Renart* (another example of cyclicity) and the material was appropriated by later authors. Thus the fox in the Parisian poet and playwright Rutebeuf's *Renart le bestourné* represents the hypocrisy of the influential and much-hated mendicant orders, while Noble the lion reflects the king, who had fallen under their influence to the detriment of poets dependent on royal patronage. Furthermore Renart appears as the devil incarnate in *Renart le nouvel* (*c*.1288), and by the time *Renart le contrefait* (*c*.1327) was produced, raucous laughter had almost entirely given way to moral and social didacticism.

In the second decade of the fourteenth century, Renart is joined by another vehicle for socio-political satire, the horse Fauvel, whose name incarnated vice – Flatterie, Avarice, Vilenie, Variété (inconstancy), Envie, Lâcheté – and gave us the expression 'to curry favour'. Gervais du Bus's *Roman de Fauvel* is a political and moral satire, Fauvel the king (compare the late thirteenth-century *Couronnement de Renard*) being served at court by personifications of vices reminiscent of the courtly *Rose* allegories. Having been denied Fortune as a bride, Fauvel marries Vaine Gloire, and the work finally disintegrates into nonsense and a carnavalesque *charivari* symbolic of worldly decadence and the reign of Antichrist. This popular work was continued in 1316 by Raoul Chaillou de Pestain, who incorporated lyric poems of a satirical nature, so that the manuscript of this compilation, with its coloured illuminations, Latin and Old French verse, musical notation and the narrative proper, provides a fine example of medieval multimedia entertainment with a moral aim.

While it was once argued that the epic and romance were composed for different audiences, and that an aristocratic public would not have appreciated the bourgeois realism and anti-courtly satire of the *fabliaux* and beast epic, critics today now accept that the tastes of medieval audiences were wide. *We* seem more likely to be shocked by the mixture of the profane and the religious, the comic and the didactic, than our medieval ancestors were.

The Poetic 'I'

As we have seen, much medieval literature (romances, histories, epics, plays and didactic treatises) was composed in verse, and many narratives from the *Roman de la Rose* onwards were written in the first person. However, although poets no doubt drew on their own experiences, first-person poetry is not necessarily personal or sincere, but may well be conventional, with authors as different as Adam de la Halle (creator of a character Adam in the *Jeu de la feuillee*), Guillaume de Lorris and François Villon adopting personae through whom they could explore situations, express a point of view (not necessarily their own), and display their rhetorical skills by recombining traditional topoi or commonplaces in a new way.

Many of the conventional motifs exploited by northern poets were already to be found in Occitan love poetry (see page 9) and in the other types of lyric practised by the troubadours, namely humorous, parodic or satirical poetry and political, religious or crusading songs. In addition there were works by some female *trobairitz* who expressed the woman's viewpoint, though poetry in the female voice was also written by men, and it was the *chanson de toile* (love songs supposedly sung by women at their spinning) which was arguably the first genre to appear in northern France. From the late twelfth century onwards (Chrétien de Troyes's lyrics *c*.1180 were, like his romances, very early examples of the genre), other lyric forms were adopted by *trouvères* such as Conon de Béthune, Guiot de Provins, the Châtelain de Couci, Gace Brulé and Thibaut de Champagne (the grandson of Marie). These included the dawn-song (lovers parting at dawn, warned by a watchman), the *pastourelle*, *jeux-partis*, crusading songs and of course the *grand chant courtois*. The lyric *congé* as it was practised in Arras by Bodel, Baude Fastoul and Adam de la Halle combined a farewell to one's friends with criticism and satire of one's enemies. Thus some lyric genres could include topical, even personal, information, though this was more difficult to introduce into *trouvère* love poetry, which had become less sensual and more stereotyped since leaving southern France. This ever-increasing artificiality and rhetorical sophistication culminated in the fifteenth century in the highly stylized poetry of the Grands Rhétoriqueurs.

From the thirteenth century onwards, new lyric forms such as the *ballade, rondeau* and *virelai* predominated and the sung lyric was joined by the *dit*: verse to be recited like a dramatic monologue. Rutebeuf was the author of several *dits*, reminiscent of Latin goliardic poetry, and presenting the narrator and his fellows as victims of poverty, the seasons, human weakness (for gambling and drink) and even marriage (*Le Mariage Rutebeuf* and *La Complainte Rutebeuf* being two more anti-matrimonial poems in the anti-feminist tradition). Another exponent of the *dit* form and an accomplished lyric poet and musician was Guillaume de Machaut (1300–77). He popularized the *ballade, rondeau* and *virelai* forms as well as composing several *dits*, which combine allegorical figures with characters taken from real life. In *Le Jugement dou roy de Behaigne* the poet/narrator takes the case of a jilted knight and a grieving widow to his real-life patron the king of Bohemia (surrounded by allegorical courtiers) for judgement as to who is more deserving of pity. The knight wins, but in the *Jugement dou roy de Navarre* (c.1349), despite the poet's attempt to defend the decision, allegorical ladies citing *exempla* prove that the widow is more to be pitied. This latter work is notable for the description of the Black Death in its introduction, exemplifying the mixture of realism and fantasy found also in Machaut's *Remède de fortune* and *Voir dit*, both first-person love narratives containing fixed-form poems and/or letters to express the protagonists' emotions.

A more realistic poet than Machaut was Eustache Deschamps (1346–1407), who composed over 1,000 ballads and the first art of poetry in French, *L'Art de dictier* (1392), in which he claimed that poetry was musical without needing musical accompaniment. His poems are often humorous and ironic, treating down-to-earth subjects like food, the weather, illness and poverty with the eye of a keen observer. Another amateur poet and the composer of a first-person love *dit*, the *Espinette amoureuse* (1369), was Jean Froissart. He also wrote a chivalric romance, *Méliador* (1384), into which he incorporated poems by his patron, Wenceslas of Bohemia. Fixed-form poems likewise appear in the *Espinette*, which describes the narrator's meetings with figures from classical legend, his travels to England and his attempts to woo his lady on his return to France – none of which was necessarily autobiographical.

First-person poetry in the female voice is represented by Christine de Pizan, whose widowhood made her love lyrics particularly poignant. Yet however personal her poetry may seem, it too was influenced by traditional themes and a desire to hone her rhetorical skills within the fashionable forms of the *virelai*, *rondeau* and *ballade*, the latter sometimes organized into narrative sequences depicting the birth and death of love, and with some poems even written in the male voice. Despite her (purely conventional) treatment of adultery, she emerges as a strong advocate of marital love and mutual respect, consistent with her championing of women in her didactic 'defences' (see pages 32–3).

Alain Chartier too wrote conventional *ballades* and *rondeaux*, but is best known for his *Belle Dame sans merci* (1424), which provoked a *querelle* reminiscent of the *Rose* controversy. This is the first-person account of the poet's encounter with a lover whose service and wooing have no effect on his lady's heart, for she wishes to remain free, rejecting love as an arch-deceiver. Here is an example of the lady, largely silent in lyric poetry, voicing her opinions and insisting on her freedom to choose, however loyal and persistent her lover may be. However, the narrator later learns of the lover's death and warns women against treating their suitors in this way. Criticism of 'la Belle' and her creator resulted in Chartier's riposte, the *Excusacion envers les dames*, which defends the lady's position, yet ends (like many defences by men) by casting doubt on the seriousness of the whole enterprise. Thus Chartier challenges the masculine conception of courtly love, while nevertheless portraying a lady who lacks Christian mercy.

As with Christine de Pizan, so Charles d'Orléans's (1394–1465) personal experiences (widowerhood and imprisonment in England for twenty-five years after Agincourt) must have influenced his prolific poetic output, yet again much of the love sentiment and many of the expressions of longing and separation are traditional. Experience is generalized as he employs allegory to convey inner psychological turmoil. On his return to France he spent his later years in Blois, describing court festivities in his favourite poetic form, the *rondeau*, and presiding over poetry competitions. It was at one of these competitions that Charles set the first line of a poem made famous by François Villon: 'Je meurs de soif auprès de la fontaine.'*

This paradox, though not of his invention, neatly epitomizes the lyric poetry and poetic persona of François de Montcorbier, known as Villon, who attended the University of Paris in the 1450s, was accused of robbery and murder, was imprisoned, but escaped hanging on several occasions and disappeared from view around 1462. His legacies to us are some fixed-form poems, ballads in 'underworld' jargon and two narrative *dits*: *Le Lais* (1456) and *Le Testament* (1461). The former written supposedly on the departure of Villon from Paris (cf. the Arrageois *congé* – see page 36) contains humorous bequests to friends and enemies. The *Testament* is a mock will and testament, apparently uttered by the narrator/testator on his deathbed. Thus the long tradition of pseudo-autobiographical, first-person *dits*, with fixed-form poems inserted into them, reaches its comic apogee in Villon's *Testament*, in which the poet mockingly adopts the persona of the *amant martyr* à la Chartier, while bequeathing ballads and other satirical legacies to his 'heirs'.

From his poetry we gain a vivid picture of fifteenth-century Parisian life, especially the student and underworld milieux. Love (or rather sex), death, poverty and old age are the major themes treated, all linked by a strong concern with justice: social justice in the case of the poor, the moral justice of the authorities who sit in judgement on the likes of Villon, and God's justice, the ultimate arbiter. In the meantime, the testator pronounces judgement on friend and foe (for 'Qui meurt, a ses loix de tout dire'†) and teases, mocks and ridicules as he dishes out his bequests (many of which cast aspersions on the beneficiary's sex-life). Few, apart from his mother, escape Villon's wit and irony, not even the narrator himself. However, his descriptions of the misery of the underclass, and the

---

* 'I am dying of thirst beside a spring.'
† 'He who is about to die has a right to spill the beans.'

ravages of time so graphically evoked by the Belle Heaumière in her double portrait of herself as an attractive young woman and unappealing old prostitute, cannot fail to move us, even if they are juxtaposed with cynical advice about 'making hay while the sun shines'. Moreover, Villon's *Ballade des pendus*, in the voice of corpses hanging from a gibbet, challenges passers-by to question our right to judge criminals, for we shall all be viewed as sinners at the Last Judgement. Villon's linking of crime with social deprivation no doubt recommended him to Brecht, who incorporated several of his ballads into his *Threepenny Opera*.

In Villon's poetry all authority is challenged, including that of the classical and biblical *auctores*, and of proverbial wisdom. Thus the *Testament*, highly rhetorical, subversive, in constant dialogue with itself, other texts and imaginary interlocutors, treating serious issues in an ironic, humorous way, exploiting, renewing and overturning literary tradition, provides us with a fitting epitaph for the dying 'Middle Ages'.

Further Reading

Richard Axton, *European Drama of the Early Middle Ages* (London: Hutchinson, 1974).

Pierre-Yves Badel, *Introduction à la vie littéraire du moyen âge* (Paris: Bordas, 1969).

Anne Berthelot, *Histoire de la littérature française du moyen âge* (Paris: Nathan, 1983).

R. Howard Bloch, *The Scandal of the Fabliaux* (Chicago: Chicago University Press, 1986).

Grace Frank, *The Medieval French Drama* (Oxford: Clarendon Press, 1954).

Daniel Poirion, *Littérature française: Tome 2, Le Moyen Âge, 1300-1480* (Paris: Arthaud, 1971).

See also the Further Reading list at the end of Chapter 1.

CHAPTER 3

The Renaissance (1500–1610)

VALERIE WORTH-STYLIANOU

In the 1490s, under Charles VIII and Louis XII, the French were fighting to secure territories in Italy. The Italian Wars, which continued intermittently until 1559, can be seen as the herald of the French Renaissance, bringing Frenchmen into direct contact with the cultural supremacy of their neighbours for whom the rebirth of the arts and literature along a classical model was already well established. Throughout the sixteenth century French writers and artists sought to equal or surpass the Italians, and Italy remained the favoured destination of noblemen, whether for diplomatic embassies, studies or cultural travel.

Within France, François Ier (1515–47), and his son Henri II (1547–59), sought to impose firm government, particularly in response to the threat of religious dissidence after the Protestant Reformation in Germany and, closer to home, the establishment of a Protestant city-state in French-speaking Geneva. Whereas François Ier was relatively sympathetic to moderate reformers early in his reign, in 1534 the Affaire des Placards (the posting of bills against the Mass through Paris, and even on the door to the king's bedchamber) marked the shift to a climate of repression. Henri II was an even more staunch defender of the Catholic faith, instituting the *chambre ardente* to pursue heretics. There followed three successive reigns of kings each without an heir, including a period of minority rule under Charles IX, which seriously weakened France. The rivalry between leading noble families escalated as religious and political tensions became confused, and from 1562 to 1594 France suffered an almost uninterrupted sequence of civil wars, the Wars of Religion, with the Massacre of St Bartholomew (1572) being only the most infamous episode in a long catalogue of atrocities. Between the assassination of Henri III (1589) and the coronation of Henri IV (1594), France had no recognized monarch, while different factions, supported by various foreign powers, fought for their claimants to the throne. Little wonder that Henri IV and his minister Sully sought above all to restore stability and peace, and to plug some holes in the royal coffers. Henri had himself abjured his Protestant faith to take the crown, but in 1598 the Edict of Nantes assured the Protestant minorities freedom of worship and some military strongholds – a privilege that was to be challenged over the next century and ultimately revoked in 1685.

In the field of literature, the French Renaissance is distinguished by the enthusiastic reception of new models and the desire for experimentation. The Edict of Villers-Cotterêts in 1539 marked the adoption of French as the official language for legal documents, in place of Latin. Yet over the rest of the century many more works were published in Latin than in the vernacular, and the suitability of French as a medium for serious writings was still often contested. Significantly, most of the outstanding writers of the French Renaissance were deeply interested in linguistic experimentation, from Rabelais's hilariously improbable lists of neologisms to Ronsard's serious advice on adapting classical borrowings to French versification. The rise of printing – the first press was established in Paris in 1470 and by 1515 there were some hundred presses in a major centre like Lyons – had a profound impact on the development of the vernacular. Not only could all sorts of text be far more widely and speedily disseminated, but by the 1530s there were comprehensive studies of the relationship between Latin and French, such as the bilingual dictionaries and comparative grammars of Robert Estienne. It was a small step to the study of French usage in its own right. Ronsard's last revisions of his immense poetic corpus in 1584 already show the concern for linguistic propriety and precision traditionally associated with the following century. Du Bellay's visions of a renewal of the French language, expressed in the *Défense et illustration de la langue française* (1549), were to be largely realized before the end of the century.

Quests for Truth: Prose Writings before 1560

In the prologue of Rabelais's *Gargantua* (1534), a chronicle of giants blending erudition and farce, levity and profundity, the narrator urges the readers 'par curieuse leçon et méditation fréquente, rompre l'os et sugcer la sustantificque mouelle'.* The metaphor of the text as a bone from which the reader can suck the juicy marrow encapsulates a common attitude to reading in the first half of the sixteenth century. Texts are treasure houses, but the reader must actively break into them to extract their essence and, to use another commonplace Renaissance metaphor, digest their contents. Rabelais's injunction is surrounded by playful, deliberately contradictory allusions to the need for deeper interpretations yet also to the dangers of elaborating codes of allegorical reading which may distort the original meaning of the text. The alert reader must negotiate a path between 'under' and 'over' reading.

Similar issues lie at the heart of humanist scholarship, from which most Renaissance fiction and poetry cannot be divorced. In late fourteenth- and fifteenth-century Italy, scholars had devoted their lives to hunting out 'lost' copies of Latin and Greek manuscripts and re-establishing and commenting on the texts of classical works. Their conclusions were frequently at variance with the previously received tradition of the classics, and humanist readings were necessarily revisionary and thus a challenge to established academic authorities. Furthermore, the close contact with classical, generally pre-Christian writers meant that students of the *literae humaniores* (Greek and Latin) came to share the classical preoccupation with the dignity and responsibility of man, rather than the medieval Church's theocentric view of the universe. When we use the term 'humanism' (coined in

---

* 'through thoughtful reading and frequent reflection to break open the bone and suck the juicy marrow'

the eighteenth century) to designate Renaissance thought,* we are referring both to renewed philological interest in the classics and also to a broad system of values which placed man at the centre of its enquiries. The leading French humanists of the early sixteenth century wrote predominantly in Latin, then the lingua franca of Europe. But various scholars made incursions into the vernacular, particularly when they wished to win the ear of Renaissance princes, such as François Ier. Despite the latter's extensive patronage of arts and letters – in particular creating university chairs for *lecteurs royaux* in Hebrew, Greek and Latin (1530) – his own readings were confined to the vernacular. Thus Guillaume Budé wrote his advice to the young monarch, the *Institution du prince* (1516), in French. The most celebrated humanist of northern Europe, Erasmus – Dutch by birth, but styling himself *peregrinus* (the traveller) – necessarily adopted Latin to reach a wide readership, but his works were soon translated into other languages. For example, his *Adages* (1500–36), a collection of some 4,000 classical sayings with extensive commentaries, influenced many French prose writers, not least Rabelais.

To understand French prose fiction of the earlier sixteenth century we need to remember that it is often the meeting point of humanist and popular traditions. The clear best-seller was a chivalric romance, the Spanish *Amadis de Gaule* cycle (1508), in the translation by Herberay des Essarts (1540–6). The tale of the archetypal noble warrior who champions the causes of good and justice in improbable adventures before winning his beloved is a direct descendant of the medieval romances (see also pages 7–22 and 25–6). Rabelais's first two giant chronicles – *Pantagruel* (1532) and *Gargantua* (1534) – unmistakably parody chivalric romances, with the birth, childhood, education and military testing of the hero interspersed with episodes such as the miraculous escape of Pantagruel's friend Panurge from a roasting by the Turks, or the slaughter meted out to the band of attackers by a single monk, Frère Jean. Yet they also address such weighty humanist issues as the education of the prince, the 'just' war, the efficacy of prayer and the value (or otherwise for Rabelais, an ex-monk) of monasteries. *Gargantua* ends with an elaborate account of the Abbey of Thélème, built for Frère Jean at the end of the

---

* For the quite different use of 'humanism' to refer to the twentieth-century view of the human subject, see page 228.

Picrocholine War. It is, however, founded on the antithesis of traditional monastic values. The only rule for its inhabitants (men and women) is 'Fays ce que voudras',* and the name Thélème is derived from the Greek for 'will'. On one level, the episode could be read as Rabelais making an optimistic statement about the nature of free will (the subject of heated theological debate). On another, more sinister level, though, Rabelais makes much of the walls protecting the Thélémites from hostile intruders and devotes a whole chapter to a poem vilifying those forbidden entry.

Chivalric romances recede in Rabelais's later books, the *Tiers Livre* of 1546 and the *Quart Livre* of 1552 (the so-called *Cinquiesme Livre* of 1564 is probably not by Rabelais), but still Rabelais searches for the elusive truth with a blend of popular, often vulgar humour and erudite irony. Both books use circular structures with no predictable ending: in the *Tiers Livre* a series of consultations with respected and less respectable authorities as to whether Panurge should marry is inconclusive; a voyage alternating between maritime adventures and visits to imaginary islands in the *Quart Livre* ends – surely one of the best jokes on the reader in French literature – with the crew in the middle of nowhere, and Panurge listing euphemisms for the excrement with which he is covered. Rabelais implicitly questions man's capacity to arrive at destinations or clear answers; but along the way there are abuses to be satirized (greed, formalistic devotion to the outer observances of Catholicism, hypocrisy), and laughter is an essential of the spirit of *Pantagruélisme* which he recommends as 'certaine gayete d'esprit conficte en mespris des choses fortuites'.†

Rabelais's love of the excessive and monstrous, coupled with his predilection for scatological humour, earned him an unsavoury reputation in subsequent centuries. But more recently critics have been concerned not only with the more serious questions which his work addresses, but also with his outstanding qualities as a writer. Since the seminal work of Bakhtin, the 'carnival' proportions of the Rabelaisian universe have come to the forefront. The abundance of popular farce and the fixation with lower bodily functions can be seen as a challenge to authority and rigidity. The *Quart Livre* makes great play of the hostilities between the representatives of Carnival

---

* 'Do what you will.'
† 'a certain joyful state of mind based on a disregard for matters of chance'

(bellicose, plump, furry sausages, phallic in shape yet of female gender) and the monster of Lent (a shadowy, unnatural and cadaverous form of gigantic proportions). The tone of the episode is lightened, though, by the mock heroic framework and the discursive voice of the narrator. In this part of his tale, as in many others, Rabelais makes language both the subject and the object of his writing. Here he is interested in twisting common metaphors to describe Lent, and using farcical etymologies to summon up armies to fight the Andouilles. Elsewhere his work is interspersed with incredible and often unwieldy lists (such as the games Gargantua plays on wet days), extravagant puns and tongue-twisting neologisms. Through all four books runs an investigation into the nature of language and the relationship between words and physical reality. Some such episodes end in farce or bathos, but the Prologue to the *Tiers Livre* in particular, through the comparison of the narrator with Diogenes (doomed continually to roll his barrel to the top of the hill), anticipates modern writers' anxieties about the potential emptiness and futility of discourse.

Such concerns notwithstanding, Rabelais's main appeal lies in his humour, his exuberant style and his teasing play with ideas. Character and psychology, mainstays of later novelists, are sketchy in the extreme; quite simply, Rabelais's giants and their companions are required to think and act, not to feel. However, a contemporary of Rabelais's produced one of the earliest psychological novels. Modelled on Boccaccio's *Fiammetta*, Part I of Hélisenne de Crenne's *Les Angoisses douloureuses* (1538) is a cautionary tale, narrated in the first person by a wife who cannot subdue her immoral and adulterous passion; Parts II and III hand over the narrative to two male narrators as her lover embarks on adventures in the purest vein of chivalric romance. While the *histoire tragique* did not take a hold in France until 1559, when Pierre Boaistuau and François de Belleforest adapted the Italian model of Bandello (1554), two earlier collections also show an ability to analyse the workings of the heart and mind. The *Contes amoureux*, published in Lyons (*c.*1537) under the name Jeanne Flore, present seven tales celebrating love and desire. Unlike Hélisenne, Flore unambiguously defends the claims of passion.

The themes of love, adultery and marriage form the mainstay of the seventy-two tales of the *Heptameron*, the collection by Marguerite de Navarre, sister of François Ier (published posthumously in 1558). Having commissioned a translation of Boccaccio's *Decameron* in 1545, Marguerite chose a similar framework: ten characters brought together by a natural disaster pass their time telling tales. The stories range from brief farcical tricks to the long tale of the desperate passion of Amadour for the chaste and married Floride. Equally significant, and Marguerite's own contribution to the genre, are the discussions by the story-tellers after each tale. The five men and five women exchange sharply differentiated views on the moral, religious and psychological issues raised by the stories. Consensus is neither sought nor imposed, but the *Heptameron* leaves us with the impression that human relationships are fragile, and chastity and love only ultimately possible through the grace of God. The female story-tellers, particularly Parlamente, tend to argue most effectively, and the free exchanges between the sexes remind one of the role played by women in the court setting of Castiglione's dialogue *The Courtier* (1528, French translation 1537). Castiglione and Marguerite share an admiration for the Neoplatonic, idealized view of male–female relationships. Book III of *The Courtier* argues that the presence of women civilizes men, leading them to higher intellectual and spiritual planes, while several discussions in the *Heptameron* examine – albeit with reservations – spiritual or Platonic love (*parfait amour*) as an experience bringing humans closer to the love of God.

In such ways prose fiction contributes to Renaissance discussions on the status of women. The same topos had of course been endlessly debated through the Middle Ages (see pages 30–3), but the *Querelle des femmes** in sixteenth-century France was given renewed interest by the dissemination of fifteenth-century Italian Neoplatonist writings, notably Ficino's commentary on Plato's *Symposium*, a dialogue on the nature of love. The poet Symphorien Champier introduced Neoplatonism to the vernacular in his *Nef des dames*, a defence of women (1503). Others combined it with traditional catalogues of women's virtues, from the translation of the influential Latin treatise by Henri Agrippa (*Précellence du sexe féminin*, 1537) to

---

* debate over women

the late blast of cannon shots in honour of women by François de Billon in his *Fort inexpugnable de l'honneur féminin* (1555). The issue of Neoplatonism as a justification for the respect and idealization of women at court led to a short but heated exchange between poets in the 1540s. Bertrand de la Borderie made his *Amie de court* (1541) expose her Machiavellian manipulation of admirers in her ruthless search for the best (richest) husband. Antoine Héroët countered by an account of the true nature of Platonic love (*Parfaite Amie*, 1542), while Charles Fontaine changed the focus of the debate to a satire against court life in his *Contr'amie de cour* (1543). Rabelais, as ever, had an apt comic response to the debate in the discussions over Panurge's projected marriage and fear of cuckoldry in *Le Tiers Livre*. Most memorable is the largely anti-feminist doctor Rondibilis, who advises Panurge that women are driven mad by their wandering, lustful wombs, the wild animal within them! Given that the *Tiers Livre* was dedicated to the learned, chaste Marguerite de Navarre, we can surmise that Rabelais did not share Rondibilis's position.

The alternative view, that women have rational minds and a duty to cultivate them, is expressed by the poetess Louise Labé in the prefatory letter to her *Oeuvres* of 1555, as she urges women to 'eslever un peu leurs esprits par-dessus leurs quenouilles et fuseaus'.* Such positive views are particularly characteristic of Lyonnais circles (Flore, Labé, the poet Scève). Another Lyonnais, Claude de Taille-mont, vigorously defends the female intellect in his *Champs faez* (1553) – a blend of ornate allegorical description, discussions on love, and interpolated tragic tales – as the hero is led by Minerva, goddess of wisdom, to Eumathe, a paragon of beauty and learning.

Not all Renaissance prose fiction raised such grave issues, however, and other collections of *nouvelles* owe more to the medieval *fabliaux* tradition of the short comic story. If such tales have a pronounced oral quality, we should remember that books were regularly read aloud to groups of listeners, whether at court or in village taverns. Philippe de Vigneulles's version of the *Cent Nouvelles nouvelles* (1515) are a case in point, both depicting and playing to the assembled drinkers who want to be cheered up by new stories. Bonaventure des Périers goes further in his *Nouvelles Récréations et*

---

* 'raise their minds a little above their distaffs and spindles'

joyeux devis (published posthumously, 1558), making language and particularly puns the subject-matter of a number of his ninety short tales. The Prologue invites the reader to live well and rejoice (*bene vivere et laetari*), rejecting higher purposes. Yet there is the suggestion, also present in other *conteurs*, that laughter is a means of escaping momentarily from the darker sides of life. The relationship between reality and fiction is also probed by writers who choose to present the oral sources for their material as a guarantee of their authenticity. Noël du Fail's *Propos rustiques* (1547) hover between a nostalgic record of the behaviour of Breton peasants, lovers and priests, and a gently ironic awareness of the insufficiencies of the arcadian myth.

All such attractive fictions run quite counter to the austere Calvinist view of literature. Earlier humanists, such as Erasmus or Thomas More in England, had accommodated both Christian and pre-Christian, devotional and imaginative writings. In France, Guillaume Briçonnet, Bishop of Meaux, and Lefèvre d'Étaples, professor at the Sorbonne, were two of the leading figures in a spiritual revival which produced literature of a reflective, mystical and often Neoplatonic vein, such as Marguerite de Navarre's long poem, *Le Miroir de l'âme pécheresse* (1531). But Calvin, despite – or perhaps because of – his humanist training, perceived literature as at best a dangerous distraction (the *Amadis* romances were banned from Geneva), and at worst an instrument of the devil. He was himself a man of phenomenal logical and organizational powers and effectively set up the Church-state of Geneva between 1541 and his death in 1564. His main work, the *Institution de la religion chrétienne*, originally published in Latin (1536) but then revised and translated into French (1541), provides a comprehensive, highly structured exposition of the tenets of Protestant faith. Calvin was suspicious of mystical forms of inner piety, and condemns the vague Neoplatonism of court circles in his *Excuse aux Nicodémites* (1544), urging crypto-Protestants at the French court to stand up and be counted for their true beliefs. His taste for spiritual meditation was bound to the scriptural, with the poet Clément Marot's paraphrases of the Psalms (1539–43) being adopted in Geneva, and set to music.

Calvin's most vicious attacks on literary figures were reserved for those he believed had profaned the sacred through irreverent laughter, in particular Rabelais and Des Périers. It is a characteristic of Calvinist writing that ambiguity is eschewed; good and evil, truth and falsehood are antithetical certainties in a confession of faith articulated around such oppositions as the Fall/redemption, Adam/ Christ, man's sinfulness/God's grace. The religious positions of Rabelais and Des Périers, on the contrary, are much harder to disentangle, for they write allusive fiction, not doctrine or propaganda, and, crucially, both are influenced by a Greek master of irony, Lucian (second century AD). Rabelais's giants may sometimes fulfil the serious Erasmian ideal of the humanist Christian prince, and Calvin would no doubt approve the spirit – if not always the vulgarity – of Rabelais's satire of the reactionary theologians of the Sorbonne (then the powerful Faculty of Theology), but he is brutally out of sympathy with the confidence with which Rabelais allows man to question our interpretation of God's revelation. As for Des Périers, Calvin condemns as blasphemous the four short dialogues of his *Cymbalum Mundi* (published anonymously in 1537). They open with a provocative portrait of Mercury, messenger of the gods on earth – a traditional allegory of Christ – yet protector of thieves and liars. The human quest for truth, according to Des Périers, seems doomed, distorted as it is by quarrelsome and vain philosophers and theologians seeking public applause. Such cynical pessimism anticipates the mood of writers later in the century.

Renewed Traditions and New Visions: Poetry and Poetics

The poet Joachim Du Bellay's (prose) manifesto, *La Défense et illustration de la langue française* (1549), argues forcefully the need for aspiring poets to make a clean break with the French models of the preceding generations, and look instead for inspiration to the great poets of Rome, Greece and (with some envy) Italy. In a sense the advent of the Brigade, later known as the Pléiade – the group of seven young 'stars' dominated by Ronsard and Du Bellay, under the tuition of the humanist Dorat – does mark a watershed in French poetry. On the technical level, new poetic forms derived from classical models (odes, sonnets, *hymnes*) come to replace popular medieval ones (*rondeaux, ballades*); the literary language is enriched with neologisms drawn from Greek, Latin and Italian; and versification is reshaped as the twelve-syllable Alexandrine rivals the decasyllabic line. In terms of subject-matter and poetic sensibility, the Pléiade achieved new depth and vision, particularly in cycles of love poems and in philosophical poetry, and the Pléiade poet Jodelle wrote the first 'classical' French tragedy, *Cléopâtre captive* (1552). Yet we must beware taking at face value Du Bellay's dismissal of native tradition, for the differences between the Pléiade and their pre-decessors were often ones of emphasis and perspective. On matters such as rhetoric or national pride, they shared more ground than Du Bellay might acknowledge.

In the early sixteenth century, poetry was still commonly classified as a sub-branch of rhetoric – the art of persuasion through the expressive powers of language. Thus a treatise embracing rhetoric and versification was published by Pierre Fabri in 1521, entitled *Le Grand et Vrai Art de pleine rhétorique*. Both early and later Renaissance poets valued the technical mastery of style, but what changed was their perception of the relationship of style to subject-matter, and how far both are shaped by the twin concerns of inspiration and imitation. The Grands Rhétoriqueurs poets of the turn of the century, such as Jean Marot and Jean Bouchet, tended to accord priority to formal excellence, and their works are characterized by technical complexity, elaborate allegorization and clever word-play. Clément Marot, following in their footsteps but also renewing popular French forms, won much applause for his light touch and wit (as well as, on occasions, his more vulgar humour), displayed in his *Épîtres* to friends and patrons. He could, though, turn his humour to more serious ends, as in *L'Enfer* (published 1541), a satirical denunciation of the Châtelet prison where he had been sent for failing to observe Lenten fasting rules. His love poetry was also much admired, being set to music by many of the leading composers of the day. Yet Du Bellay specifically cautioned young poets against imitating Marot's poetry, caricatured as frivolous and unlearned, for the Pléiade saw rhetoric as an art deriving from imitation of the best classical models, and destined to express higher truths. Both Ronsard and Du Bellay admired the Rhétoriqueur Jean Lemaire de Belges, whose popular prose work *Les Illustrations de Gaule et singularités de Troie* (1511–13) bolstered national pride through the legend that the first Gauls were descended from the Trojans, and who argued for a closer harmony between France and Italy in *La Concorde des deux langues* (1511–13), a combination of prose and verse. Among the ambitious aims of Du Bellay's *La Défense* is the wish to promote a national renewal of French poetry, and Ronsard's epic, *La Franciade*, although unfinished, develops Lemaire's Trojan myth.

It may seem paradoxical to the modern reader that the Pléiade poets wanted to innovate through a programme of imitation, but, imbued with humanist culture, they saw classical texts as a source of inspiration rather than fixed models to be reproduced slavishly. A poet's learning gave his work authority, and lent him a dignity denied to mere *rimeurs* or hacks. His status was further enhanced by the diffusion of Neoplatonic ideas, which represented the poet as a kind of prophet, whose inspiration (*fureur*) granted him privileged insights into divine truths. A year before the *Défense*, the *Art poétique* of Sebillet (1548), an admirer of Marot, already set poets in the line of Moses, the prophets, Orpheus and Homer. Du Bellay, in reaction, played down the role of inspiration, to give priority to imitation; but in 1555 Peletier's *Art poétique* – reflecting in part the early achievements of the Pléiade – presented imitation and inspiration as working in harmony. The fullest exposition of the Platonic myth of inspiration was provided by Pontus de Tyard's prose dialogue, the *Solitaire Premier* (1552). Ronsard also explores the theme in many poems, particularly his philosophical *Hymnes* (1555–6, 1563). The *Hymne de l'automne* opens with a description of his election by the Muses, as he learns 'à bien déguiser la verité des choses/ D'un fabuleux manteau dont elles sont encloses'.* Significantly the poet is not to reveal the naked truth, but reverently cloak it in the riches of his verse. The Pléiade ideal of poetry is both aristocratic and elitist:

---

* 'to disguise well the truth of matters/Beneath a fabulous cloak in which they are enfolded'

written by the inspired and learned few for a similarly minded audience.

In practice, poets tempered the ideal to suit reality. Few could afford not to seek patrons – and Ronsard fought hard to be recognized as the official court poet of Charles IX. Hence *pièces de circonstance* flourish, and the Renaissance court poet was a public servant on call for royal entertainments, triumphal *entrées* and the like. For Ronsard, the celebration of the Valois monarchy and court dignitaries did not, however, have to eclipse the poet's wider vision. The *Hymne de la justice* (1555) concludes in praise of the statecraft of Henri II and the Cardinal de Lorraine after some 500 lines interweaving pagan and Christian myths of the Fall of man and the establishment of justice, and an exploration of the complex relations between God, nature and destiny. Even when explicitly composing royal (Catholic) propaganda for Catherine de Médicis in his series of poems known as the *Discours des misères de ce temps* (1562–3), Ronsard can combine satire of the Protestants with an original and extended allegory of the chaos wrought by the classical monster *Opinion* (*Remonstrance*, 1563). In so doing he also confutes Protestant criticisms of the Pléiade's 'pagan' predilection for mythology.

Command performances infiltrate even that apparently most intimate of genres, the love poem. For example, Jodelle's *Les Amours* (published posthumously in 1574) include a sequence of three sonnets written on behalf of a lesbian lady to her lover. In assessing Renaissance love poetry – undoubtedly the genre which retains the widest appeal today – we need to look for the moving or aesthetically pleasing *representation* of experience rather than post-Romantic sincerity. Imitation of classical and Italian poets, especially Petrarch's love poems to Laura, the *Canzoniere*, was a common feature, but did not prevent the poet finding his or her own voice. Before the Pléiade – and admired by them – the Lyonnais poet Maurice Scève wrote the first extended French sequence of love poetry, *Délie* (1544), in which 449 *dizains* are grouped under fifty emblems and proverbial mottoes. The direct visual power of the emblems complements the allusive, often abstract language of the poetry. Scève presents the archetypal Petrarchan dilemma of unrequited love for a distant, idealized woman (in this case married to another man), which leads to conflicting feelings of hope/despair, love/anger, expressed through elemental clashes such as the perennial image of the icy fire, as the mistress's eyes both burn and freeze the lover. An ironic apprehension of the nature of his suffering is counterbalanced by Scève's Neoplatonic intuition that he and Délie share a communion of souls which will outlive this mortal life. Where Scève's collection is dominated by the shades and the moon (Délie = Diana, goddess of the moon and the underworld), Pernette du Guillet, commonly believed to be the source of his passion, responds in her *Rimes* (1545) with serenity and an acceptance of spiritual love, calling Scève 'mon jour'.*

Two later Lyonnais poets were known instead for their strong depiction of passion and erotic desire. Claude de Taillemont, in his *Tricarite* (1556), shares all Scève's admiration for his beloved's virtue, but with voyeuristic delight includes twenty-four *blasons* detailing her physical charms from head to toe. Louise Labé's brief collection of twenty-four sonnets and three elegies (*Oeuvres*, 1555), on the contrary, explodes the Petrarchan myth of the faithful man eternally serving his chaste mistress. She adopts the voice of the woman who has given way to love and been abandoned, only to feel more strongly the pain of unanswered passion. Labé's language appears simpler, less loaded with mythological allusions than Ronsard's or Scève's, but the directness cleverly underlines the ironic disjuncture between women's capacity for true feeling and the stereotyped Petrarchan code in which male poets heartlessly woo them.

Ironic treatment of the Petrarchan mode is not the exclusive preserve of women poets. Admittedly the earliest Pléiade collections of love poetry, Du Bellay's *Olive* (1549) and Pontus de Tyard's *Erreurs amoureuses* (1549), are fairly stilted if well-crafted reworkings of Petrarchan commonplaces, but in the first of his three major cycles of love sonnets, *Les Amours* (1552–3), Ronsard dares to mark his distance from the Italian master. Cassandre may be a sublimely beautiful, noble lady, distant and virtuous, Ronsard's love may be unreturned, but the very spectacle of her beauty often brings joy rather than Petrarchan despair, as the poet experiences the 'doux venin'† of love. Furthermore, erotic desires can be fulfilled in the

---

* 'my daylight'   † 'sweet poison'

poet's imagination at least, as he identifies himself with Greek gods renowned for their sexual conquests.

Dreams and reality appear closer to coalescing in Ronsard's *Continuation des amours* (1555), addressed to a country girl, Marie. The collection marks the transition from the high-flown, erudite literary style of *Les Amours* (even contemporaries had to resort to a commentary to understand some of the mythological allusions!) to Ronsard's *beau style bas*,* an artfully simple imitation of Greek and Latin bucolic poets. Cassandre's beauty was represented by comparisons with precious jewels or majestic landscapes, but for Marie Ronsard chooses flowers, milk and honey. The underlying message is an epicurean appeal to Marie to enjoy life while she can – not what Petrarch expected of his chaste Laura.

Ronsard's final love cycle, the *Sonnets pour Hélène*, is very different, being written over twenty years later (1578). No longer the leading court poet, smarting at the success of younger men like Desportes – whose three sets of *Amours* (1572–3) had polish and fluency, but no deeper emotional pulse – Ronsard is prepared to ironize Petrarchism, love, his mistress Hélène and, not least, himself. If he admires Hélène's youth, beauty and virtue, he does not hesitate to remind her that she too will grow old and then will marvel over the famous poet Ronsard's love for her. He can smile bitterly too at his own folly in pursuing love when grey-haired, and – a supreme reversal of Petrarchan tradition – choose to abandon the chase when he knows he cannot win.

The *Hélène* cycle is all the more powerful in that Ronsard returns to traditional Petrarchan topoi and conceits, but deployed in an ironic way. Others did so too, following different paths. Catherine Des Roches, a bluestocking of Poitiers society who firmly rejected proposals of marriage, wrote an exchange of sonnets between Sincero, a caricature of the Neoplatonizing lover, and his mistress Charite (*Oeuvres*, 1579). Sincero's sonnets parody fashionable modes of compliment, while Charite wittily exposes the insincerity of such conventions. Du Bellay develops the Petrarchan sonnet in a completely unprecedented and ironic direction in his two collections *Les Antiquités de Rome* and *Les Regrets* (published 1558). Both record not

---

* 'beautiful low style'

the experiences of love, but his impressions of Rome, where he had spent three long years. *Les Antiquités* illustrate the crumbling of the humanist dream: Rome is but a decaying monument to its former glory. *Les Regrets* are a longer sequence (191 sonnets) and more complex, moving from the poet's nostalgic regrets for his distant homeland (expressed in terms reminiscent of the absent lover), to increasingly sharp satire of the corruption of Rome, the papal court, and even individual popes and cardinals. Throughout, despite initially claiming to lack high poetic inspiration, Du Bellay displays a gift for turning the stock elements of Petrarchan poetry to new ends. In fact the straightforward imitation of Petrarchism was fairly short-lived in France. To the fertile Renaissance imagination, variations on a theme were always more interesting than mere reproductions of it.

The theatre is another field in which the Pléiade sought to break with native, popular tradition in favour of the imitation of classical models. At the start of the sixteenth century, mystery, miracle and morality plays were still widespread, as were uncomplicated *soties* and farce. However, by the 1540s students at humanist colleges were performing serious dramas composed in Latin verse. This practice, together with renewed interest in some of the theoretical writings of Horace and Aristotle and the plays of Seneca and the Greek tragedians, led to the emergence of French classical tragedy. (Despite humanist interest in Plautus and Terence, comedy received less attention.) Renaissance French tragedies have often suffered from anachronistic comparison with the masterpieces of Corneille and Racine. The Renaissance authors did not necessarily envisage the staging of their plays, certainly not to a public audience, and their interest is primarily in the stirring of emotions through fine, sustained verse. Hence set pieces (monologues, *récits*) alternate with the lyrical reflections of a chorus; dramatic action and psychological development are secondary. Garnier's *Hippolyte* (1573) concludes with an awesome account of the gory death of the hero, but the tragedy has been expected ever since the monologue by Égée's ghost in Act I. Garnier's version of the myth (indebted to Seneca's play) emphasizes Hippolyte's virtue and chastity, and provides neo-Stoical warnings on the dangers of the passions.

In *Saül le Furieux* (1572), Jean de la Taille has a more Aristotelian concern, as he makes clear in his prefatory *Art de la tragédie*: his is the hero of middling virtue, partly but not wholly deserving of his fate. *Saül* is one of the more psychologically compelling of Renaissance tragedies, with its moving study of Saul's madness, and his grief at the death of his sons. The nature of kingship, obedience to God and divided families were all traditional subjects, but they had particular contemporary resonances in the Wars of Religion. Although most playwrights opted for classical plots – an interesting exception is Montchrestien's dramatization of the death of Mary Queen of Scots in *La Reine d'Écosse* (1601) – they often included debates on matters of state of interest to their age.

Protestant dramatists were more obviously didactic in their use of familiar stories (from the Old Testament) to remind their contemporary audiences of eternal truths. Unlike the humanist tragedies, de Bèze's *Abraham sacrifiant* (1550) was definitely written for performance, and retains a popular element of satire in Satan disguised as a monk. It is also noticeable that Protestant playwrights, such as de Bèze, des Masures in his *Tragédies saintes* on the life of David (1563) or Rivadeau in *Aman* (1566), cultivate a simpler literary style. Rhetorical flights of the imagination were perceived as a threat to the pure truth of the Word.

Shifting Perspectives on a World in Turmoil: The Baroque

Where the literature of the earlier sixteenth century was frequently illuminated by the optimism and confidence of humanism, the last generation of French Renaissance writers fall under the shadow of the Wars of Religion, and their writing is, not surprisingly, characterized by uncertainty and pessimism. The rise in fragmentary forms and incomplete works, the fascination with irregularity and shifting perspectives, and the first real attempt to capture all the layers of the self in Montaigne's *Essais* (1580–95) make the period seem strikingly modern. Yet the hyperbolic, even bombastic style in which poets in particular explore these preoccupations may jar on the reader attuned to the elegant understatements of French classicism. Literary critics have followed art historians in labelling such a style the baroque (derived from the Portuguese *barroco*, a pearl of irregular beauty) – even if there is still debate about how far before and beyond 1570–1600 the term should apply (see page 67). Baroque themes, equally, defy attempts to impose rigid chronological limits, but the later sixteenth century certainly sees a particular, self-conscious interest in instability and mobility, metamorphosis and disguised identity, death and decay.

Life offered more than enough first-hand experiences of violence, tragedy and strange prodigies, and reality and fiction could be oddly indistinguishable. Various genres include tales whose status hovers between anecdotal reports and pure invention. The novel attracted little attention before d'Urfé's *Astrée* (1607–27), but the *nouvelle* continued to flourish, especially shorter collections in which each tale is given maximum dramatic and emotional impact. Increasingly, writers turned to the tragic tale, generally ending in bloodshed and evoking terror or horror. Four of the five stories related in Jacques Yver's *Printemps* (1572) are in this mould, as are Habanc's *Nouvelles Histoires tant tragiques que comiques* (1585) and Poissenot's *Nouvelles Histoires tragiques* (1586). Poissenot's earlier collection, *L'Été* (1583), combines stories with the various reminiscences and conversations of the three story-tellers. This mixed genre had the attraction of accommodating shifting perspectives, through which ideas could be voiced without drawing didactic conclusions. Noël du Fail's *Contes et discours d'Eutrapel* (published 1585, but composed from c.1550) are another attractively hybrid collection, with no main narrative framework.

It is typical of the later Renaissance that writers should favour a form akin to the anthology, which allows information to be loosely compiled rather than organized. Unlike in late medieval encyclopaedic works, diversity no longer suggests the rich repository of an ordered nature; rather, it signals writers' uncertainties about imposing values and hierarchies. The title of Tabourot des Accords's *Bigarrures* (1583–90) makes a virtue of his combination of *contes*, local folklore and discussions of language and literature. It took an author with an imagination (and *esprit gaulois*) similar to Rabelais's to see the comic, labyrinthine potential of such *pots-pourris*. Béroalde de Verville's *Le Moyen de parvenir* (*c*.1610) purports to be a banquet uniting some 400 distinguished and less distinguished classical figures (Socrates, Nero), near-contemporaries (Luther, Ronsard) and anonymous guests (L'Autre, Le Premier Venu), who exchange tales, anecdotes and comments on a multitude of subjects. The author augments the sense of disorder by claiming that the present work is a corrupt manuscript which has confused the speakers' words and a commentary on them. Language becomes intoxicatingly self-generating, as text/commentary have no necessary point of conclusion, and the reader is caught between admiration, amusement and bewilderment.

In their formal shape, Montaigne's *Essais* (1580–92, posthumous edition 1595) also deliberately undermine pre-established generic classifications. Many of the early chapters read like slightly whimsical humanist commentaries on classical quotations or familiar moral (or military) conundrums. But increasingly Montaigne made the quotations or points at issue the pretext, and the record of his own discursive thoughts the essential text. Unlike Béroalde, Montaigne achieves this fusion while keeping his authorial voice distinctive and dominant. He could hardly do otherwise, for the *Essais* become the record of his life and thoughts, subject to indefinite expansion as he incorporates new reflections upon the existing text. However much we may be interested in Montaigne's views on subjects such as cultural relativism (I.23, I.31, III.6), education and books (I.25, I.26, II.10), illness and death (I.20, II.3, III.13), we find that the real delight of the *Essais* is the discovery of the mind of Montaigne the man – a discovery which we make alongside himself. Montaigne is diffident about presenting himself as a worthy literary subject, yet he becomes aware that the true record of a life, however humble, may help others to know themselves, for 'chaque homme porte la forme entière de l'humaine condition' (III.2).* The difficulty – and excitement – of his task lies in his sophisticated awareness of paradoxical pressures: the desire for sincerity must grapple with the

---

* 'every man bears the entire form of the human condition'

artifice inherent in all attempts to express ourselves through language; the self is both ever-shifting and yet possessed of a quintessential constant, or 'forme maîtresse' (III.2). It is not the least of Montaigne's achievements that he explores such complex issues in an engagingly informal, lively style, allowing the reader to believe that through the writing he or she knows the author himself.

The *Essais* stand out as one of the great landmarks of French literature, attracting very differing but never indifferent responses – and never convincingly imitated. Their individual quality is highlighted by comparison with several of the contemporary genres which they partly resemble. Published autobiography, to the Renaissance, equalled the memoirs of military or political figures, a genre increasing in popularity towards the end of the century, with works such as the *Commentaires* of the military commander, Blaise de Montluc, appearing the year of Montaigne's death (1592), or the *Mémoires* of Marguerite de Valois, sister of Henri III. Both Montluc and Marguerite construct an *apologia* for their own public conduct, but Montaigne concentrates on the private, claiming in his preface 'Mes défauts s'y liront au vif, et ma forme naïve.'* In the memoirs tradition, fast-moving and precise narrative is foregrounded; in the *Essais* it is episodic and usually secondary to the interpretations to which it gives rise. If we prefer to look at the *Essais* as digressive moral reflections, they have a natural precursor in Erasmus's *Adages* (see page 45), but a useful comparison can be drawn closer to Montaigne's time with the *Discours politiques et militaires* (1587) of the Protestant gentleman François de La Noue. The latter tackles moral, political and military subjects, and some chapters share common ground with Montaigne (education, reading, the duties of a subject). But where Montaigne uses 'public' subjects to examine the values and moral conscience of the individual, La Noue maintains a gaze turned steadily outwards. Concerned at the plight of France, he is less interested in individuals than in social groups, and tends to talk in broad categories. The clarity of his views is matched by the linear structure of the *Discours*, whereas Montaigne's chapters (and indeed his syntax) meander sinuously to accommodate doubts, parentheses and correctives.

---

* 'My faults will be clearly read in the *Essais*, and my true nature.'

It is as the archetypal man of doubt, or sceptic, that Montaigne was read in the seventeenth century, and he had a profound influence on the work of the religious apologist Pascal (see pages 90–1). Certainly the long chapter entitled the 'Apologie de Raymond Sebond', from setting out to defend a medieval proof of God from the observation of nature, turns into a powerful attack on the power of reason; ultimately, belief in God is seen to depend on faith alone. Fideism has a long-established tradition within Christianity, but Montaigne is more interested in exploring the weaknesses in any dogmatic philosophical position rather than expounding religious doctrine – a task he prudently claims to leave to the theologians, finding the study of man and the lessons of human experience more congenial. One of Montaigne's admirers, Charron, was also to be hijacked by the *libertins*. His *De la sagesse* (1601–4), largely an ordered compilation of Stoic and sceptic ideas drawn from the *Essais* and other contemporary thinkers, establishes a moral code for human behaviour. The overall context of the work situated this code within a Christian neo-Stoic framework, but individual chapters, read in isolation, make the case for the suspension of judgement, apparently authorizing a dangerous divorce between religious belief and moral behaviour.

If we look to the *Essais* as a reflection of the preoccupations of the late Renaissance, we may be surprised that Montaigne rarely accords the Wars of Religion more than a passing reference. Perhaps he feels they are too close for balanced judgement, and in any case examples from history or other contemporary civilizations (such as the cannibals of the New World) prove equally illuminating of human conduct. In passing up the chance to comment at length on history in the making Montaigne is untypical of his age, for much of the writing of the times offers committed reflections on political or religious themes. The tendency towards absolutism had progressed under the earlier Valois monarchs, but was increasingly questioned as the civil wars eroded royal authority. After the Massacre of St Bartholomew (1572), writers felt a particular sense of urgency to define the extent and abuses of royal authority. The unpublished treatise against tyranny by Montaigne's friend Étienne de la Boétie,

Discours de la servitude volontaire (*c.*1552), was seized upon and circulated by Protestant propagandists (1574) for its renewed topicality. The previous year, François Hotman's *Franco-Gallia* had argued against absolutism, and even in favour of deposing a bad monarch, on the basis that it was the assembly of the people which invested the king with authority. From Geneva, de Bèze, in his *Du droit des magistrats sur leurs sujets* (1575), took a similar stance, seeing the king as the supreme magistrate, but subject to natural and divine law. Jean Bodin, on the other hand, provided one of the most influential early apologies for absolutism in his *Six Livres de la république* of 1576 (*république* = the state). Although maintaining that absolute power rested with the individual ruler, and dismissing the notion of a contract between ruler and ruled, Bodin did distinguish between tyranny and good kingship.

Political debate took a new turn with the contested succession of Henri IV in 1589. The meeting of the States-General in 1594 saw the circulation of the *Satire Ménippée*, the work of six moderate Catholics who chose to publish it anonymously. Its success, both immediately and even once the cause of Henri IV was won, was largely due to its clever form. Seven speakers all defend their own candidates for the throne, but whereas the first six naively reveal their selfish motives, the final speech, for the Third Estate, is a moving appeal for Frenchmen to support their hereditary king. There is none of the confusion of voices we observed in prose fiction of the late Renaissance, but the work is a satirical masterpiece, with sharply differentiated parodies of the styles of the Italian cardinal legate, the soldier of fortune, etc. – in contrast to the sober sincerity of the last speaker.

The most emotional reactions to violence and religious upheavals are undoubtedly those of poets. On the one hand there is a rise in devotional poetry, the individual's attempts to bring his or her fears and hopes before God. On the other hand, several poets perceive through the immediate disorder the larger patterns of history, and express these within an epic framework. Both groups share a desire to move the reader, not least through powerful visual imagery. Indeed, Georgette de Montenay, a poetess of Huguenot sympathies, adapted the emblem genre to (rather didactic) meditational poetry in her *Emblesmes ou devises chrestiennes* (published 1571). The twelve *Sonnets sur la mort* (posthumous, *c.*1597) and the *stances* of Sponde, a Protestant who later converted to Catholicism, evoke a graphic sense of the struggle between body and soul, between this life and the world to come. The tight structure of the sonnets, the skilful use of antithesis and rhetorical appeals to the reader, convey the urgency of Sponde's meditations. The opposition of life and death is also central to the much longer sequence (434 sonnets) by Chassignet, *Le Mespris de la vie et consolation contre la mort* (1594). At its simplest, earthly life is depicted as *paraître*, eternal life as the true *être*. But in conveying the vanity and inconstancy of this world, Chassignet paints paradoxically vivid tableaux of the transient, and death is apprehended in its full, even horrific, physical reality rather than simply as a passage to eternal consolation. Gabrielle de Coignard also unites the physical and metaphysical in her devotional *stances*, odes and sonnets (published posthumously, *Oeuvres chrétiennes*, 1594). Her imagery is often derived from Petrarchan love poetry and can border on the erotic.

Striking concrete descriptions and the concentration on single instants of experience are two widespread characteristics of baroque poetry. They shape the epics of du Bartas and d'Aubigné no less than the devotional sonnets of Sponde and Chassignet. The Pléiade had hailed the epic as the supreme poetic form, a lasting monument to national glory, yet, ironically, where Ronsard's attempted epic had foundered those of two Protestants met with success. However, du Bartas's *Première Semaine* (1578) is not primarily partisan, whereas d'Aubigné's *Les Tragiques* (composed post-1577, published 1616) set out to record and interpret the Protestant cause. Both writers share a large-scale vision, du Bartas describing the creation of the world (at once a literal account of the seven days of Creation and an inventory of the natural wonders known to Renaissance man) and d'Aubigné spanning the history of mankind from the Fall to the Apocalypse. Du Bartas is a polymath, encyclopaedic, readily admitting digressions, and matching his enthusiasm for the vast diversity of creation with an exuberant style (including a host of neologisms). D'Aubigné proposed a more obvious crescendo of styles through the seven books of *Les Tragiques*: from satire of his opponents to the martyrology of the faithful and finally the ecstatic vision of union with God. Yet some of the most moving passages occur early in the work, for example the image of France as the mother torn apart by the civil wars, while the last books never miss the chance to caricature the enemy even when anticipating the salvation of the elect. Antithesis is central to d'Aubigné's conception of history, as so often in the Calvinist view of human destiny.

Taken as a whole, *Les Tragiques* confidently asserts that the true Church will finally win the struggle between good and evil, but d'Aubigné is poignantly aware of the damage wreaked by the civil wars. He is, after all, recording the tragedy of his generation. It follows that the Massacre of St Bartholomew is a crucial episode in the poem: it is presented with a baroque play of perspectives and taste for the spectacular, as the Protestant leader Coligny, lodged among the elect of heaven, looks down on the historical event of his own assassination. In such tableaux d'Aubigné self-consciously exploits the full armoury of rhetorical and prosodic devices to play on the reader's emotions. Although not published until 1616, *Les Tragiques* is one of the last great texts of the Renaissance, vigorous, combining controversial reworkings of classical and biblical sources, and above all ambitious in the poet's universal scale of vision.

Further Reading

E. Berriot-Salvadore, *Les Femmes dans la société française de la Renaissance* (Geneva: Droz, 1990).

T. Cave, *The Cornucopian Text: Problems of Writing in the French Renaissance* (Oxford: Clarendon Press, 1979).

A. Goodman and A. MacKay (eds), *The Impact of Humanism on Western Europe* (London and New York: Longman, 1990).

T. Greene, *The Light in Troy: Imitation and Discovery in Renaissance Poetry* (New Haven: Yale University Press, 1982).

H.-J. Martin and R. Chartier (eds), *Histoire de l'édition française. Vol. 1. Le livre conquérant: du moyen âge au milieu du XVIIᵉ siècle* (Paris: Fayard, 1989: first edn 1982).

G.-A. Pérouse, *Nouvelles françaises du seizième siècle: images de la vie du temps* (Geneva: Droz, 1977).

C.B. Schmitt and Q. Skinner (eds), *The Cambridge History of Renaissance Philosophy* (Cambridge: Cambridge University Press, 1988).

A. Tournon, M. Bideaux and H. Moreau, *Histoire de la littérature française du XVIᵉ siècle*, (Paris: Nathan, 1991).

H. Weber, *La Création poétique au seizième siècle* (Paris: Nizet, 1955).

CHAPTER 4

The Seventeenth Century (1610–1715)

VALERIE WORTH-STYLIANOU

When in the early nineteenth century the adjective 'classique' was applied not only to works of antiquity but also to the literature of seventeenth-century France, the Romantics were both paying homage to what Perrault had termed in 1687 'le siècle de Louis XIV', and yet also seeking to set a seal on the past and escape its dominance. Even in the twentieth century, French writers have been alternately drawn to and repelled by their neo-classical heritage. Traditionally associated with clarity of thought, elegantly and economically expressed – 'Ce que l'on conçoit bien s'énonce claire-ment', said Boileau* – neo-classicism would apparently preclude the wanderings of the imagination, the untamed lyrical outbursts of the soul. There is some truth in all myths, and, overall, the seventeenth century did set a premium on rational arguments and the precise use of language, but not at the expense of stirring the emotions of the reader or spectator, nor to the exclusion of all experiments with form and genre. For tragedians Racine declared that 'la principale règle est de plaire et de toucher'.† Prose writing, for its part, was less circumscribed by reference to Latin or Greek models, and so the novel in particular enjoyed a peculiar freedom. As critics have looked with increasing interest at the possibility that the period 1610–60 was still characterized by baroque tendencies rather than

---

* 'That which is well thought out is clearly expressed.'
† 'The most important rule is to please and to move.'

being a simple precursor of French classicism, works and ideas which do not conform fully to the supposed classical ethos can be better appreciated alongside the undisputed masterpieces of the age of Molière, Pascal and Racine.

Debates about the French language were no longer, as in the Renaissance, the preserve of the scholarly elite. Polite society became intensely, even obsessively interested in 'le bon usage'. The salons hosted by distinguished noblewomen – the most famous being that of the Marquise de Rambouillet – made delicacy and wit the marks of a pleasing mind, as even male language was refined for aristocratic female company. Literary salons abhorred pedantry and dogmatism, but the foundation of the Académie française in 1635 by Louis XIII's minister Richelieu created a privileged forum for more prescriptive criticism. Protected by royal patronage, the Académie had the task of safeguarding the purity of French language and literature both through its own publications (the first *Dictionnaire de l'Académie* eventually appeared in 1694) and its published comments on other writers. The Académie's existence signals an increasingly formalized link between literary creation and the predominance of *doxa* acceptable to monarch and advisors. Yet the triumph of Pierre Corneille's play *Le Cid* (1637) in the face of the Académie's strictures is evidence that the Académie was not all-powerful. None the less, as the century progressed most poets and tragedians accepted that literary elegance required a syntactic and lexical purity which would have been foreign to the Pléiade poets a century earlier. Thus all of Racine's eleven tragedies draw on a vocabulary of only some 3,000 words – an extreme example of the gulf that developed between the literary idiom of court/polite society and general usage.

Inevitably the literary history of the seventeenth century remains that of a privileged minority, for even if literacy levels rose among the bourgeois, the aristocracy remained the core of the literary and theatre-going public. Historians have demonstrated that the reign of Le Roi Soleil had darker economic and social consequences for the workers and peasantry, but such concerns are only rarely dwelt upon by those writing from within and for aristocratic circles. The dominance of the personality of Louis XIV is unsurprising when we remember that he reigned for seventy-two years (1643–1715), and his death was indeed the end of an epoch, for he was succeeded by his great-grandson. On the accession of Louis XIII in 1610 the civil wars and the collapse of royal authority were a recent memory, but by 1715 French absolutism had become entrenched. Cardinals Richelieu and Mazarin, advisers to Louis XIII and XIV respectively, were primarily concerned to quell the ambitions of the nobles and raise the status of the king. Yet the Frondes (1648–53) – a series of uprisings by the Paris Parlement and then some of the princes – left the young Louis XIV with an indelible image of the indignity of being forced to flee from Paris for his own safety. Once he assumed personal control of affairs of state (1661), he sought to remove power from the hands of the nobles, and, together with his minister Colbert, had France governed by a network of administrative officers, drawn mainly from the bourgeoisie. Many of the latter bought noble titles, but the members of this *noblesse de robe* were often despised for their lack of birth and envied for their new wealth by the traditional *noblesse d'épée*.

For the latter, increasingly deprived of real political power, there remained the dual occupations of attendance at court and seeking distinction in Louis's self-aggrandizing military campaigns abroad. The court of Versailles, though the foremost European model of formal elegance and sumptuous taste, gave pause for thought to some minds, and was soon to be sharply criticized in the memoirs of the Duc de Saint-Simon. Even as the century drew to a close, Fénélon's novel *Télémaque* (1699), written for the Dauphin's son, made oblique criticisms of Louis XIV's reign, including the sombre warning that the most pernicious fault in government is 'une autorité injuste et trop violente dans les rois'.*

Freedom and Rules: Poetry and Prose (1610–60)

Looking back on the poetic achievements of the two preceding generations, Boileau in his *Art poétique* (1674) highlights the movement from disorder to regularity. The famous couplet

---

* 'an unfair and unduly harsh authority wielded by kings'

Enfin Malherbe vint, et le premier en France,
*Fit sentir dans les vers une juste cadence**

recognizes the significant contribution of Malherbe as poet and critic, but obscures the continuing presence of alternative voices, particularly those now loosely identified as *libertins* poets. Malherbe's early work shows some of the energy and forceful imagery associated with the baroque (for example the *Larmes de Saint-Pierre*, 1587), but once he had won the favour of Henri IV in 1605, he sought above all to raise the grandeur of poetry in celebration of the monarchy. His political aim was not essentially different from that of Ronsard, but their poetics were radically opposed. Where Ronsard had prized the poet's inspiration and visionary powers (see pages 53–4), Malherbe set the greatest store by his formal control. Clarity of thought, detailed attention to the rules of versification and the harmonious ordering of sounds are, for him, the hallmarks of the poet's art. In his own poetry and his influential (though unpublished) criticisms on Desportes, Malherbe waged war on hiatus, enjambement, foreign borrowings and extravagant imagery. His quip to his friend and fellow poet Racan that they would be remembered as 'deux excellents arrangeurs de syllabes'† is, though, unfair to his poetic range, which as well as formal celebrations of political events includes gravely sonorous paraphrases of the Psalms.

An authority to be reckoned with in the salons, Malherbe was not without his critics. Marie de Gournay, the adoptive daughter of Montaigne, fought fiercely to uphold the richness of Pléiade poetry against what she saw as the insipidity produced by Malherbe's cull of the French language (*Traité de la poésie*, 1619). Régnier, nephew of the defamed Desportes, also looked to the linguistic vigour of Pléiade models in his *Satires* (published posthumously, 1613), which cut down to size such types as court fops and third-rate poets. Less aggressive but equally significant in his assertion of independence is Théophile de Viau, probably the most widely read poet right through the seventeenth century (his *Oeuvres*, 1621–6, being regularly republished after his death). Théophile maintained

---

* 'Finally Malherbe came, and was the first in France/ To lend to poetry a true/accurate sense of rhythm'
† 'two excellent orchestrators of syllables'

that each poet should choose his own path, and his was far removed from Malherbe's by both inclination and practice. An epicurean thinker, who looked to nature (rather than God) as his guiding principle, Théophile associates moral *libertinage* with sensual pleasure, especially in his witty love poems. His descriptions of nature show a fascination with detail rather than grander structures, and vignettes are rendered striking by original images, sometimes verging on the surreal. The ability to surprise the reader by unpredictable shifts of the imagination is also characteristic of the poetry of another *libertin*, Saint-Amant, who took a particular interest in the Italian form of the *caprice*, a poem moving cleverly between different tones and genres. He delighted in choosing unexpected, even trivial subjects (such as a melon or pipe) as a starting point for whimsical or burlesque pieces. In the place they accord to personal sensibility Théophile and Saint-Amant are appealingly modern. Yet Saint-Amant's definition of the purpose of poetry ('Le principal but de la poésie doit être de plaire')* was quite in tune with the value his age put upon public taste as the arbiter of literary achievement.

In the increasing refinement of the literary use of prose, it was the consensus of cultured opinion which counted. Montaigne's *Essais* (see pages 60–2) had already set the gentleman of leisure, the *honnête homme*, above the pedant or word-spinning lawyer. In the first half of the seventeenth century the good usage of polite society was opposed to the jargon-laden 'galimatias' of *parlements* and universities. The grammarian Vaugelas, whose *Remarques sur la langue française* (1647) represent an intriguing attempt to resolve disputed points of usage, takes as his authority 'la façon de parler de la plus saine partie de la Cour',† where overt displays of scholarly erudition or professional specialization were judged to be in extremely bad taste. Serious subjects could be, and were, debated, but in a form accessible to the intelligent layman. Thus Saint François de Sales's *Introduction à la vie dévote* (1609) was as successful for its harmonious, attractive prose style as for its subject-matter (showing spiritual devotion in a light acceptable to the *honnête homme/femme*).

---

* 'The principal aim of poetry must be to please'
† 'the way the soundest part of the court speaks'

One of the most famous works of philosophy also opens with an invitation to the non-specialist reader. 'Le bon sens est la chose du monde la mieux partagée',* says Descartes in his *Discours de la méthode* (1637). The appeal to universal reason, the anecdotal use of the first person to record his search for new principles, indeed the very choice of the vernacular and not Latin for his treatise, all contribute to the public interest aroused by the *Discours*. It was also a work which, by its insistence on a return to first principles, obviated the need for a tedious study of Aristotelian scholasticism, the school of philosophy which had dominated Western thought since the Middle Ages. Descartes started instead from what we know intuitively, and which he therefore believed to be beyond doubt: our ability to think proves our existence (the famous *cogito, ergo sum*); we can conceive of infinite perfection, and since we could not imagine what we do not know, God must have given us this intuition, and therefore exists. The Cartesian God is the Creator who, having established the universe, only intervenes in the miracles recorded in scripture, but otherwise leaves the world to run as a machine. Although Descartes believed his philosophy was a refutation of sceptics who questioned the very existence of God, Church authorities were alarmed at the idea of a mechanistic universe. Unwittingly, Descartes had prepared some of the ground for the Enlightenment's deist view of 'God the watchmaker'. It was not until the latter end of the century that Malebranche, an Oratorian theologian, revised some of the tenets of Cartesian thought to make them more theologically acceptable. In various works (1674–1712), which were widely read, he argued that it is the active will of God which ensures the continued existence of the universe through time, and the figure of Christ who is the cause of divine grace.

In the mid-seventeenth century, salons were at least as interested in Descartes's view of man as in his physics or metaphysics. The treatise on *Les Passions de l'âme* (1650) extends his mechanistic model to human behaviour. Descartes proposes that the passions which assail us are not pernicious in themselves, only when they are excessive, and excess can be checked by human reason. This is an optimistic contribution to a debate which enthralled his age: the

---

* 'common sense is the most evenly shared quality in the world'

relationship between our passions and our reason. The novel provided one of the main testing grounds for infinitely modulated positions on the subject, and the dissection of human behaviour, based both on the examples drawn from literature and on real-life experience, was a central preoccupation of many a social gathering. Since women hosted salons and were avid readers of novels, love was often seen, even by male writers, from the female perspective: the woman's own psychology, or the conditions she imposed upon her lover during the prolonged ritual of courtship. The 'Bible' of lovers for most of the century was the long pastoral novel L'Astrée by Honoré d'Urfé (published in instalments 1607–27). Although it is nominally set in fifth-century Gaul, with Druids, shepherds and shepherdesses, the panoply of characters have the delicacy of feelings and expression so admired by d'Urfé's own society. Astrée is the archetypal précieuse sévère, unbending in her high moral standards, Céladon the ideal lover, devoted to her wishes and desiring only to win back her love and trust. Yet alongside the Neoplatonic framework (chaste love elevated almost to the status of a religion) the novel has a strangely erotic vein. Céladon may be officially barred from Astrée's presence, but such is his longing for her that he disguises himself as a shepherdess and enjoys the most intimate glimpses of his unsuspecting mistress.

Most novels of the rest of the century owe a debt to L'Astrée, whether they are written in imitation or reaction. The formula of young lovers, separated by a series of misfortunes or misunderstandings which indefinitely postpone the (inevitable) happy ending, was adopted by writers of heroic romances. These are the successors of the medieval romances and of the Amadis cycle beloved of the Renaissance (see page 45), in which knights in shining armour battled against dragons and magicians to win their princesses. Gomberville's Polexandre (1629–37) set the trend for epic-length, swashbuckling adventures in pseudo-historical settings. The eponymous hero was virtuous and fearless in his tempestuous journey around the world to find the beautiful Alcidiane. He represents the aristocratic ideal, but – unlike, say, the heroes of Corneille's tragedies of this period – he is liberated by the powers of imagination and fiction from the political constraints of the real world. If Gomberville prided himself on good style (he avoided the contested conjunction *car* through all five volumes of *Polexandre*), La Calprenède could hardly owe the enormous success of his marathons (*Cassandre*, 1642–5, and *Cléopâtre*, 1647–58) to his inflatedly heroic style and hyperbolic clichés. But contemporaries enjoyed being dazzled by the extraordinary feats of the heroes and the exotic, historically remote settings (Persia and the world of Caesar respectively). One distinguished devotee, the letter-writer Madame de Sévigné, perhaps shared the sentiments of those today caught up in 'soaps': whatever the stylistic defects, the characters and the bursts of fast action had her hooked!

The foremost woman writer of the heroic novel, Mlle de Scudéry, was generally more interested in the analysis of sentiment than in the clash of swords. Her main works (*Le Grand Cyrus*, 1649–53, and *Clélie*, 1654–60) had the added interest of being *romans à clefs* – there is a thinly disguised portrait of herself as Sappho in *Le Grand Cyrus*. A leading salon hostess, identified with the rise of *préciosité* (the cult of extreme refinement of language and sentiment), Mlle de Scudéry made her characters discourse on the intricacies of love just as their readers might. Her celebrated map of love in *Clélie*, the *Carte de Tendre*, represents the byways of the moral experience of love, as the lover negotiates a path between such dangers as violent passions and inconstancy before reaching the blissful 'Terres Inconnues' in which 'Tendresse' reigns supreme. Other novels followed this allegorical mode, and one example, Tallemant's *Le Voyage de l'île d'amour* (1663) and *Le Second Voyage de l'île d'amour* (1664), was successful not only in France for the remainder of the century, but also in an English version by Aphra Behn, and is one of the earliest examples of secular literature translated into Russian in the eighteenth century.

Both their hyperbolic style and the *invraisemblance* (lack of verisimilitude) of the plots made pastoral and heroic novels an irresistible target for parody. Even as *L'Astrée* was nearing completion, Sorel depicted a comic hero, Lysis, led astray by reading too many pastoral romances and suffering burlesque misadventures when disguised as a shepherd (*Le Berger extravagant*, 1627). And if exotic princesses could afford to spend their days analysing the slightest change in sentiment, Furetière showed in his *Roman bourgeois* (1666) that they provided a dangerous model for the daughters of the bourgeoisie, who should have had their minds on more immediate and practical issues. The depiction of non-aristocratic classes is a common feature of comic novels, and allows scope for satire as well as parody, as in Tristan l'Hermite's short work *Le Page disgracié* (1643). Furetière is remarkably unsympathetic to his bourgeois world, depicted in all its petty, rather grubby detail as obsessed with money and hypocritical in its moral standards (one unmarried heroine even becomes pregnant, a circumstance unthinkable in *L'Astrée* or *Clélie*). Scarron, on the other hand, in his *Roman comique* (1651–7), shows a Rabelaisian verve in his farcical accounts of the horseplay of a troupe of itinerant actors. While he frequently indulges in burlesque imitations of heroic style, the interpolated stories revealing the mysterious backgrounds of his characters allow us to be drawn into a world of disguise and suspense which may sometimes emulate rather than parody romance. But he never permits the reader to enjoy the willing suspension of disbelief for too long, for he delights in shattering our illusion that this is the voice of an omniscient narrator recounting a true tale.

The comic writings of both Scarron and Furetière show an interest in the relationship between pure fiction, *vraisemblance* (veri-similitude) and *le vrai* which was also evident in the work of some contemporary dramatists. One such author, Cyrano de Bergerac (himself subsequently the historical subject of Rostand's play of 1897), also produced a novel which was an unusual blend of science and fantasy. Notorious for his *libertin* views, Cyrano used the highly original framework of a voyage to the moon and then the sun (*Les États et empires de la lune*, published posthumously, 1657, and *Les États et l'empire du soleil*, 1662) to create a range of characters, some of whom deny the existence of God and the immortality of the soul. Others provide piquant critiques of man's assumed supremacy in the universe, as well as exposing the relativist basis of our social and political values. Cyrano's work, which has only recently received the critical attention it deserves, demonstrates the extreme liberty of form and thought which the novel could afford in the mid-seventeenth century.

The Theatre Comes of Age (1610–1715)

A bare forty years saw the composition of nearly all the dramatic works which now rank as the masterpieces of French neo-classical theatre, from Corneille's *Illusion comique* (1636) and *Le Cid* (1637) via Molière's whole major repertoire (from *Les Précieuses ridicules*, 1659, to *Le Malade imaginaire*, 1673) to Racine's *Phèdre* (1677). It was a period in which literary critics, writers, patrons and spectators all recognized the power of the theatre, and both comedy and tragedy truly came of age. The Pléiade and fellow poets had revived humanist interest in Greek and Roman drama, but their plays – few in number compared with the seventeenth-century dramatic corpus – were read only by an intellectual elite (see pages 57–8). By the mid-seventeenth century in Paris, *honnêtes gens* regularly saw plays performed, whether at the public theatres, in private performances at an aristocratic house, or at court. The bourgeoisie and some of the lower ranks of society also frequented the public theatres, standing in the pit (*le parterre*).

Early in the century Paris boasted two permanent theatres, each with its own company and regular authors. The Hôtel de Bourgogne became famous for its tragedies, while the Théâtre du Marais was better known at first for comedies and later for machine plays. Hardy was an early example of the professional playwright, producing an estimated 600 to 700 works for the Hôtel de Bourgogne, of which only some thirty-six were published. They provide fascinating evidence of the dominance of baroque trends before 1630. Tragicomedies (serious subjects with a happy outcome) and pastorals co-exist with tragedies and comedies; Hardy does not concern himself with the unities of time, place and action, or the principles of *vraisemblance* and *bienséance* (propriety); and action, even of a violent kind, is common on stage – as in the rape and murder of two girls in *Scédase*. The growing popularity of the tragicomedy was such that another contemporary dramatist, Jean de Schélandre, revised his tragedy *Tyr et Sidon* (1608) as a tragicomedy (1628).

Accustomed to the twists and turns of lovers' fortunes in the novel, spectators looked for similar excitements on stage, and one of Pierre Corneille's earliest works, *Clitandre* (1632), could not have disappointed them, with its disguises, treachery, an attempted rape and a villain's eye gouged out before a (relatively) happy ending. In retrospect we can detect precursors of neo-classical regularity, such as Théophile de Viau's *Les Amours tragiques de Pyrame et Thisbé* (1623). It may seem strange that a *libertin* poet should have respected the unity of time, but the concentration here adds to the sense that nature and fatal passions (rather than moral forces) have conspired to cause the lovers' doom. Love, in a benign guise, was the focus of the popular pastoral genre, in which the unities of time, place and action were respected as early as Mairet's *Silvanire* (1630). The same author's *La Sophonisbe* (1634) is generally recognized as the first regular tragedy. Based on the work of the Roman historian Livy, it shows characters acting with consistent nobility and dignity, as Sophonisbe is torn between her duty to her country and her love for its conqueror.

The early career of Pierre Corneille – a very independently minded author – both mirrors the general shift towards regularity and yet demonstrates the lasting attraction of some characteristics which might be termed baroque. Although his reputation now rests mainly on his tragedies, he first established himself as a writer of elegant comedies, of a type new to France. The plots revolve around the obstacles separating young lovers, but it is the refined and clever dialogues which most pleased contemporary audiences. In some cases Corneille gives characters unusual traits which raise the comedy to piquant satire (Amarinte in *La Suivante*, 1633–4, makes sharp observations on the undeserved good fortunes of her social superiors) or expose psychological depths (the hero of *Le Menteur*, 1644, is almost pathologically incapable of telling the truth). The confusion of reality and illusion is stunningly exploited in *L'Illusion comique* (1636), a tragicomedy, where the audience, together with the hero's father, falls under the spell of a magician as the life of the hero is enacted before us, and then finally telescoped with his performance as a tragic actor. A popular contemporary of Corneille, Rotrou, also exploits dramatic illusion with a play within a play, but in a very different vein. His tragedy *Le Véritable Saint Genest* (1645) presents an actor who is himself overwhelmed by the play he is performing (a mockery of the martyrdom of Adrian); Genest's sudden conversion to Christianity leads to his being condemned to death.

Both Corneille and Rotrou are masters of the unexpected change of pace, the increase in dramatic tension, and playing on the audience's emotions. It was these same qualities which helped ensure the success of *Le Cid* (1637). Despite the complaints of censorious critics (led by Chapelain and Scudéry) about the essential immorality of Chimène's continuing love for the man who has just killed her father in a duel, Corneille conceived tragedy to be uplifting. What we witness in *Le Cid* is the love between two noble souls, separated by an unforeseen circumstance and newly conflicting duties. The struggle between the pursuit of *gloire* (the hero's honour and public reputation) and the claims of private emotions is central to Corneille's three other most celebrated tragedies, *Horace* (1640), *Cinna* (1641) and *Polyeucte* (1643). Horace so sternly puts his loyalty to Rome above all else that he kills his sister Camille for valuing love more than patriotism. Cinna is only able to reconcile his love for Émilie and his duty towards the man she hates, the Emperor Auguste, because the emperor shows exceptional *générosité*. Polyeucte must choose between Christian faith and human love, his wife Pauline between her loyalty to her husband and her love for the Roman Sévère. The victory of moral duty is the mark of the true hero or heroine, arrived at by relentless self-scrutiny, and fuelled by a sometimes boundless egotism. Parallels have been made between the Cornelian triumph of the will over the passions and Descartes's confidence in the power of reason, but for Corneille's protagonists there is a price to be paid, and before the conclusion is reached the audience have shared the deep emotions of the characters.

Corneille perceived excellent drama and subject for debate in the relations between ruler and subject and the workings of state. Contemporaries often saw echoes of the political turmoils of their own age (for example, the hero of *Nicomède*, 1651, was thought to be modelled on Condé), but Corneille was primarily interested in broader political and human issues. If the just and clement ruler can be admired, like Auguste at the end of *Cinna*, some of Corneille's best subsequent works depict the Machiavellian ruler looking only to his own political interests. *La Mort de Pompée* (1643–4) sees Ptolomée governed by *raison d'état*, unlike his adversary Caesar. In *Rodogune* (1645) Corneille achieves a particularly energetic depiction of evil in the figure of the ruthless queen, Cléopâtre, who will sacrifice the life of either of her sons to take revenge on Rodogune. His last play, *Suréna* (1672), hinges on the monarch's almost irrational fear of his subject Suréna, who has secured him so many victories in the past.

Although Corneille continued to be recognized as one of the leading playwrights, after the notable failure of *Pertharite* (1651) his fortunes were mixed, and he retired from the theatre until 1659. In some cases audiences found his plots, often drawn from obscure historical episodes, too complex. Furthermore, public tastes were changing. The Frondes had led to a wave of political cynicism, and other playwrights were leaving the high political debates in which Corneille excelled for the suspense afforded by romanesque elements of disguise, mistaken identities and the pathos of ill-fated love. Thomas Corneille, Pierre's younger brother, achieved the box-office success of his generation with *Timocrate* (1656), which was based on an episode in a novel of La Calprenède. The plot stretches *vraisemblance* to its limits by making the hero assume a double identity (unknown to the audience) until the final act. Apart from their exploitation of suspense and surprise (not unlike those of a good modern thriller), plays such as *Timocrate* or *Camma* (1661) conform to the aesthetics of the heroic novel in their depiction of love, a noble sentiment deserving of fine analysis. Pierre Corneille had never believed the love interest alone was enough to sustain a tragedy, yet the success of an author such as Quinault is due precisely to his mastery of *galanterie* and the attendant psychology of passions.

Astrate (1665) is centred on what could be a Cornelian dilemma: Astrate and the queen love each other, but discover that a political enmity separates them. Quinault, however, accords scant interest to politics; the audience's emotions are totally engaged by the pathos of the lovers' discovery.

The passions displace politics as the focus of the tragedies of Racine, but, with the partial exception of *Alexandre* (1666), love is rarely treated in a heroic fashion. Racine's protagonists may be rulers of mighty kingdoms, but they are rarely able to subjugate their personal passions. In *Andromaque* (1668), the king, Pyrrhus, would follow the dictates of his heart and marry his prisoner, Andromaque, rather than the princess to whom he is betrothed. He meets Andromaque's resistance with cruel blackmail, threatening to hand her young son over to his political enemies. Audiences were riveted by the depiction of raw emotions – love, anger, jealousy – yet aware that such characters violated the accepted codes of noble behaviour. Where Corneille had sought to arouse *admiration* or awe in his audiences, Racine evokes the Aristotelian response of pity and (to a lesser extent) fear. The rise of Racine coincides with a growing awareness among writers in other genres of the essential weaknesses of mankind, and a questioning of the power of human reason – what the critic Bénichou succinctly termed 'la démolition du héros'.* The audience watches, terrified and powerless. In some cases (such as *Britannicus*, 1669) we see clearly what the characters do not, and our pity is compounded by an ironic awareness of the impending tragedy. In other cases – arguably the most moving – characters possess a lucid realization of the horror of their situation, and admit their guilt. From the first act of *Phèdre* (1677) Racine moves us to compassion for the heroine's hopeless and incestuous passion for her stepson, precisely because she herself hates the dark forces which govern her. Phèdre is morally aware, yet unable to assert her will.

Such a pessimistic vision may derive in part from Racine's education by the Jansenists, a group of Catholics sharply opposed to the Jesuits in the stress they placed upon the fallen nature of man and our inability to achieve good save, exceptionally, by the grace of God. Although Racine broke away from his Jansenist mentors, almost half

---

* 'the destruction of the hero'

of his plays show the weakness of man at the mercy of fate or the gods. Where Pierre Corneille had drawn his plots largely from the annals of Roman history, Racine excelled in his reworkings of Greek mythology. His supernatural is not a benevolent Christian deity, but rather the Ancient Greek notion of an implacable Fate (*La Thébaïde*, 1664, *Andromaque*) with amoral or jealous gods (*Iphigénie*, 1674, *Phèdre*) – or the vengeful God of the Old Testament (*Athalie*, 1691). Even when the innocent are spared, we are made aware of how precarious their escape was, and that further bloodshed and tragedy will be part of the inevitable pattern of human destiny.

The power of Racine's plays is due in large part to the concentration on the forces of destruction, a concentration aided by his exceptionally tight dramaturgical control. Unlike Corneille, Racine usually presents well-known myths or historical figures, and his works were initially controversial precisely for their relative simplicity. The Preface to *Bérénice* (1670) offers his fullest apology of the art required to 'faire quelque chose de rien'.* Racine redirects our attention from action to *re*action, as the whole play revolves around the painful separation of Titus and Bérénice, with no external events to propel the tragedy. The stately grandeur and regularity of Cornelian declamation give way to a more natural patterning of the Alexandrine, so that at moments of heightened intensity interjections, exclamations and unfinished utterances convey the characters' inability to master events. The work of some other dramatists of the 1670s suggests that Racine's aesthetic of simplicity provided a new model. Thomas Corneille's *Ariane* (1672) and *Le Comte d'Essex* (1678) have simpler plots and a greater concentration on the tragedies of the respective heroine and hero than his earlier works, and indeeed Pierre Corneille's *Suréna* is often considered distinctly Racinian. The younger playwright Campistron also emphasized the psychology of suffering, in *Andronic* (1685), whose hero is similar to Britannicus, and *Tiridate* (1691), where the incestuous passion of the main protagonist strongly recalls the moral torments of Phèdre.

Yet when Racine returned to the theatre with *Esther* (1689) and *Athalie* (1691), after an absence of twelve years, tragedies had a serious rival in the new genre of the *tragédie en musique*, or opera.

---

* 'make something from nothing'

Quinault, for example, had confined himself to writing libretti for Lully's music, choosing serious subjects such as *Cadmus et Hermione* (1673, the first *tragédie en musique*), *Thésée* (1675) and *Atys* (1676). Racine undertook a bold dramaturgical experiment, combining the spoken word and music in the introduction of choruses, on the Ancient Greek model. Originally commissioned by Madame de Maintenon to be acted by the girls at the convent of St Cyr, both plays show Racine's sense of the dramatic to be undiminished. The choruses mean that the action is continuous throughout the tragedies. The result in *Athalie* is a particularly strong sense of urgency, culminating in the secret coronation of Joas and the defeat of the queen. The denouement is one of the most obviously theatrical in Racine's repertoire, with a curtain rising at the back of the stage to reveal to Athalie (and the audience) a concealed army of Levites. It demonstrates that Racine, who had been the director and producer of his own troupe as well as their playwright, fully appreciated the value of selective on-stage action and visual effects.

The importance of good acting and staging is paramount in the comedies of Molière, who claimed to be loath to publish his early success *Les Précieuses ridicules* (1659) because the text would be bare without the 'ornements' of performance. Molière was a playwright and director but also, according to contemporaries, an outstanding comic actor, and he himself performed the leading comic roles in his plays (Arnolphe, Orgon, Sgnarelle, Monsieur Jourdain, etc.). After early years in the provinces writing and performing short farces, he returned to Paris to share a theatre for several years with an Italian troupe, and was influenced by the acrobatics, mime and rapid improvisation characteristic of the commedia dell'arte. The farce tradition never disappears from his writing, but his output between 1659 and his death in 1673 also includes five-act comedies of manner in verse (starting with *L'École des femmes*, 1662), *comédies-ballets*, one *comédie héroïque* and contributions to court entertainments, including a collaboration with Pierre Corneille and the musician Lully (*Psyché*, 1671).

Having won the favour of Louis XIV early in his career, Molière was frequently called upon to provide new works for the court, often at worryingly short notice, as the skit *L'Impromptu de Versailles* (1663) reminds us. Spectacles combining music and dance with acting were especially popular. *Le Bourgeois Gentilhomme* (1670), depicting the hilarious attempts of Monsieur Jourdain to ape the nobility, shows how cleverly Molière could blend contemporary fashion (the interest in things Turkish) with his own comic genius, as Monsieur Jourdain is happily duped into believing that he has become a 'mamamouchi' in the final balletic extravaganza. Some *comédies-ballets*, such as this, were transferred unchanged to Molière's Paris theatre, the Palais-Royal. In the case of *George Dandin* (1668), a tale of the hapless marriage of a rich peasant farmer to the flighty daughter of impoverished country nobles, the play was performed with musical *intermèdes* and ballet, and achieved a great success at Versailles. However, for subsequent public performances only the three acts of the prose comedy were retained, probably for reasons of economy. On the other hand, Molière's last work, *Le Malade imaginaire* (1673), is an elaborate combination of music, drama and speech which shows Molière moving towards *opéra comique*; initially conceived for the court, this work in fact opened at the Palais-Royal.

One of Molière's greatest achievements was the fusion of two previously distinct comic traditions: popular farce and the polite comedy of manners and character favoured in the 1630s and 1640s. A number of his major works provoked controversies, partly from jealous rivals, but also because they implicitly redefined the boundaries of comedy. Like the sophisticated Latin playwright Terence, Molière did not see laughter and the barbed satire of society and social types as incompatible. Critics of *L'École des femmes* claimed that Arnolphe was inconsistent: ridiculous in his obsession with avoiding cuckoldry, yet admirable in his spontaneous generosity towards an old friend's son. Molière's mouthpiece in *La Critique* (1663), his one-act riposte cleverly imitating a salon discussion, responded that 'il n'est pas incompatible qu'une personne soit ridicule en de certaines choses et honnête homme en d'autres'.* It is a formula that allowed Molière to create characters in a broadly credible social setting, yet with exaggerated character traits that produce laughter. When *Tartuffe* (1664) fell foul of the authorities for

---

* 'it is not incompatible for a person to be ridiculous in some matters and to behave like a gentleman in others'

its provocative satire of a religious hypocrite who gains the confidence of a gullible bourgeois, Molière fought to prevent the work being banned, and in his letter to the king stole the moral high ground arguing 'Le devoir de la comédie [est] de corriger les hommes.'* Even if the circumstances invite us to see it as a case of special pleading, many of Molière's plays provided his audiences with food for thought.

His later monomaniacs – Harpagon in *L'Avare* or Argan in *Le Malade imaginaire* – are sufficiently fantastical and close to farce for the *honnêtes gens* of the audience to be able to laugh at their obsessions without disquiet; the interest of these plays resides rather in Molière's subtle variations upon the play within a play, as the characters are made to cross the boundaries between their deliberate play-acting and the unconscious adoption of roles. Yet the definition of comedy in *La Critique* as a 'miroir public'† implies that in other cases the audience may find the comic resemblance too close for comfort. This is true for the aristocratic salon setting of *Le Misanthrope* (1666), in which Alceste's crusade for honesty is ludicrously inappropriate, yet the *coquette, prude* and foppish marquis are all shown up in their true colours. Equally, bourgeois women's pretensions to learning and wit are ridiculed with little mercy in *Les Femmes savantes* (1672).

Le Misanthrope is often thought of as a problem play, along with *Don Juan* (1665). Both have potentially disquieting denouements (Alceste's decision to leave Paris society, Don Juan's descent into Hell). Furthermore, both plays sometimes make us laugh *with* rather than *at* characters whose morals we cannot approve (Célimène the coquette and the *libertin* Don Juan), and the *raisonneurs* are ambiguous (Philinte in *Le Misanthrope*) or ludicrous (the servant Sgnarelle in *Don Juan*). The challenges posed by these works of the mid-1660s were not directly taken up by comic playwrights of the following generation. It is Molière's later, more obviously comic monomaniacs that provided the model for his closest successor, Régnard, who excelled in farcical portraits, such as the compulsive gambler (*Le Joueur*, 1696) or the absent-minded man (*Le Distrait*, 1697). However, other comic writers of the end of Louis XIV's reign

---

* 'The duty of comedy [is] to correct men.'
† 'public looking-glass'

used satire to make more outspoken criticisms of their society than Molière had done. Well before Beaumarchais, Lesage showed a valet and maid outwitting their unpleasant masters (*Turcaret*, 1709): an unscrupulous financier, a self-centred Baronne, and a faithless Chevalier have become the unsteady props of an amoral social order, and there is no room for the ambiguity of, say, *Le Misanthrope* as we laugh at their downfall. With Lesage the theatre as a forum of harsh social criticism has come fully of age.

Classical Tastes and Dissident Voices: Poetry and Prose (1660–1715)

The Duc de la Rochefoucauld defined society as the 'commerce particulier que les honnêtes gens doivent avoir ensemble'.* Devoting one of his *Réflexions diverses* (published posthumously, 1731) to the subject, he suggests that society is necessary, but its survival requires a careful balancing act: between our own desire to speak and others' desire that we should listen to them; between polite tolerance and boringly flat conformity; and between honesty and the respect for others' feelings (cf. Molière's *Le Misanthrope*). Such fine distinctions informed many salon discussions and much of the literature which emanated from them. In another *Réflexion*, La Rochefoucauld singles out for praise the 'bon goût qui sait donner le prix à chaque chose',† yet he sees it as a quality which few people possess wholly. Salon society thrived on civilized disagreements. Individual and even dissident voices drew attention to stylistic points of debate and to the contradictions and counter-arguments which could threaten the validity of a general truth. This was the ideal forum for writers to try out their works on a receptive audience prior to publication. Racine read acts of new tragedies to such gatherings, La Rochefoucauld there refined his *Maximes*, and La Fontaine, though only on the fringes of court, enjoyed the hospitality and encouragement of the salon of Madame de la Sablière. The Chevalier de Méré's *Conversations* of 1668 (between himself and his friend the Maréchal

---

* 'particular society which people of good birth/breeding must share'
† 'good taste which knows what value to place upon each thing'

de Clérambault) and the Jesuit Père Bouhours's *Entretiens d'Ariste et d'Eugène* (1671) provide models of the light, graceful tone of conversation befitting an *honnête homme*, treating subjects such as language and taste, but shying away from the pedantic erudition of scholars or the affectations associated with *préciosité*.

While Méré may seem a little too eager to believe in the consensus of opinion of a social elite, the correspondence of Madame de Sévigné (written *c.*1646–96) provides a privileged insight into the real dealings of the aristocracy in private, as well as at salons and court. She writes to a range of friends and relatives, offering lively accounts of public events (the trial of Fouquet) and court scandals (the calling off of La Grande Mademoiselle's marriage), but also of her own social life (sermons, plays, a visit to a spa). She expresses her views freely, and her personal feelings are intimately revealed in her endless letters to her absent daughter, Madame de Grignan, which might be seen to constitute a narrative and analysis of (unrequited) love. Madame de Sévigné frequently protests her distaste for her letters being made public, yet she knew they would be passed around circles of friends, and she is a more conscious stylist than she would admit. Her portraits of key figures stand out, but never approach the scurrilous nature of those drawn by her cousin Bussy-Rabutin, another keen letter writer, who was exiled for seventeen years for the scandalous anecdotes and thinly veiled references to his contemporaries in his fictional work, the *Histoire amoureuse des Gaules* (1665).

In less sensationalist vein, other writers also cultivated the personal portrait, particularly within the genre of memoirs. Like Madame de Sévigné, her friend the Cardinal de Retz disclaimed all literary pretensions, and his *Mémoires* were published only post-humously (1717), yet they are an example of highly polished writing. Providing a (subjective) justification of the cause of the Frondeurs, they contain vivid portraits of leading figures (Anne of Austria, Richelieu, Condé), judged with the eye of a moralist who saw only too well the human weaknesses which beset the best-intentioned of men. The brilliant portraits of Saint-Simon are memorable chiefly for their acid criticisms and merciless exposure of the weaknesses of Louis XIV (shown as a mediocre king and self-centred man) and many of his courtiers. Saint-Simon began assembling his material in 1694, but only completed his work between 1739 and 1749; yet his accounts bring to life the closing years of the reign of Louis XIV, as he uncovers the secret motives and passions governing characters' behaviour. His *Mémoires* do not claim to offer moral instruction, but they illustrate the decadence of the French aristocracy, which Saint-Simon saw as a direct consequence of the rise of the *noblesse de robe*.

Hierarchies, power, treachery and ambition are common subjects in the *Fables* of La Fontaine, but precise references to identifiable political figures are eschewed. Instead La Fontaine provides cameos of an animal (and sometimes human) world in which the law of the jungle generally prevails. The wolf eats the lamb, the naive donkey is made a scapegoat. Occasionally the large, proud and powerful discover that even they are not as safe as they thought – the lowly reed bends in the wind while the mighty oak is broken, and a gnat can drive a lion mad – but this does not signal a universal reestablishment of moral order, simply an ironic reversal of perspectives. La Fontaine may have dedicated his first six books of fables (1668) to the 6-year-old Dauphin, but he avoids moral didacticism, surprising his adult readers by making simple prose tales (drawn largely from Aesop) into sophisticated poetry which requires that we remain constantly alert. The adoption of the *vers libres* allows him to play with different tones and registers, and he is a master of ironic understatement or the ambiguous moral. The later fables (Books VII–XI, 1678–9; Book XII, 1694) are inspired by less conventional models (especially the Indian philosopher Pilpay), and some offer more sustained comments on serious issues: a satire of the Cartesian model of a mechanistic animal world ('Les Deux Rats, le renard et l'oeuf'), a touching and personal eulogy of love ('Les Deux Pigeons'), or, in the last fable, an attempt to weigh up the relative values of an active life in the world against the claims of solitude. In Boileau's *Art poétique* of 1674, which sought to establish the essential principles of poetic composition by describing the best of contemporary practice (and criticizing the worst), the fable is not even considered as a genre. By the time of La Fontaine's death twenty years later, from being a slight salon form it had given rise to one of the most enduringly popular of all seventeenth-century works.

Although Boileau's *Art poétique* deals primarily with works in verse (including tragedy and comedy), the values which it enshrines also correspond to many of the priorities of salon writers of prose genres. Upholding the examples of the best writers of classical Greece and Rome, Boileau believes reason and the desire to achieve the truth must guide the artist, who should toil to achieve an apparently natural precision of style ('des pensées vraies et des expressions justes':* *Préface*, 1701). He accompanied his own elegant and witty treatise (we should not forget that throughout his career he was also the author of excellent *Satires*) with his translation from the Greek of Longinus's *Traité du sublime*, a work on powerful literary expression. The aesthetics of Longinus correspond closely to Boileau's own: a quest for natural, simple expression combined with maximum emotional impact on the listener or reader.

Longinus's and Boileau's horror of bombast, prolixity and the mediocre are shared by writers of maxims and aphorisms. To be successful, a maxim must be striking, yet seem to confirm an essential truth; it must also be concise and elegantly expressed. Apart from published collections (such as the *Maximes et pensées diverses*, 1678, of the salon hostess Madame de Sablé), aphorisms are scattered through the works of such diverse authors as La Bruyère, Madame de Lafayette, Pascal, La Bruyère and the Cardinal de Retz, as though the concentrated form of expressing a universal truth became ingrained in the thinking of the age. Few, however, could sustain the incisiveness of La Rochefoucauld's *Maximes*, first appearing in 1665 and polished in successive editions (until 1678). In a largely random ordering of some 500 maxims, he scrutinizes the values of human society (*honnêteté*, *gloire*, etc.) and the relationship between the conscious mind and subconscious forces. The picture which emerges is unflattering in so far as it shows us prey to self-interest, passions and fortune. This moral pessimism may be the cynicism of an ex-Frondeur, or a calculated attack on human pride which would believe itself capable of achieving virtue (La Rochefoucauld deliberately isolates from the field of his enquiry those touched by

---

* 'accurate ideas and precise expression'

religious grace). Yet the *Maximes* are not a work of unmitigated bleakness. They show how our *amour-propre* (rather like the selfish gene) contributes to the survival of society; our motives may be tainted, but the effect of *amour-propre* upon our conduct may be positive as well as negative. And La Rochefoucauld's symmetry, concision and irony make the *Maximes* anything other than dogmatic, for it is left to the reader's intelligence to unravel such elliptical formulae as 'Il y a des héros en mal comme en bien'.*

The climate of moral pessimism and the relentless examination of the gulf between human intentions and actions also came to dominate prose fiction of the 1670s. Long heroic novels went out of fashion, superseded by the *nouvelle*, a short story often in a recent historical setting, in which action and characters were governed by a respect for *vraisemblance* similar to that recognized by playwrights. Indeed, the *Lettres portugaises* of Guilleragues, published anonymously in 1669, were long thought to be genuine. The heroine of these five letters, a Portuguese nun, is overwhelmed by her passions and despair as she contemplates her lover's desertion. Other writers cultivate a more controlled, objective narrative voice in deliberate counterpoint to the intense emotions of the characters. Saint-Réal's *Dom Carlos* (1672) underplays the baroque theatricality afforded by the incestuous and adulterous love of Dom Carlos and his murder at the hands of his father, King Philip II, for the author opts to concentrate on the psychology and fatal inevitability of passion. The title *Les Désordres de l'amour* chosen by Madame de Villedieu (1675) corresponds to her sober and penetrating analysis of the sufferings attendant upon unhappy marriages and clandestine passions.

Her *nouvelles* bear striking similarities to the most famous short novel of the period, Madame de Lafayette's *La Princesse de Clèves* (1678), the account of a young girl's desperate attempts to remain faithful to the husband she respects but does not love in the face of an adulterous passion. The particular strength of Madame de Lafayette's work is the close analysis (with minimal apparent authorial commentary) of the Princesse's painful states of mind and feeling: love, shame, jealousy and the search for inner peace. The novel raises moral issues which readers debated hotly: was the

---

* 'Evil has its heroes just as goodness does.'

Princesse right to confess her love for Nemours to her husband? Should she have married Nemours after her husband's death? The fact that the Princesse, unlike almost all the other Renaissance courtiers who provide the backdrop to the novel, resists passion does not lead to any Cornelian celebration of the will and reason. For we are aware both that the Princesse's exemplary public behaviour is not matched by her tumultuous private feelings, and that her final sacrifice is achieved at tremendous cost.

Madame de Lafayette, like La Rochefoucauld, has been thought to betray a Jansenist austerity in her unheroic treatment of her characters' moral endeavours. It is true that both writers frequented Jansenist circles, but neither wished to bring theology explicitly into their portrait of human behaviour. For Pascal, however, it is the appeal to religious truths, conceived within a Jansenist framework, which alone can make sense of the human condition. The *Lettres provinciales* (1656–7), arising from the Jesuit attack on Arnauld, a leading Jansenist, appeal initially to the reader's common sense. Pascal simplifies theological discussions of the nature of divine grace so that even the provincial *honnête homme* of the title is persuaded the Jesuits are wrong. From this it is a short step for the skilled satirist to move the reader to indignation at the abuses inherent in the Jesuits' casuistry and to outrage at their misplaced emphasis on human reason in place of simple love of God. With the *Lettres provinciales*, Pascal made theological debate topical and even entertaining, yet, as a layman who himself had moved in worldly circles before his second conversion (1654), he wanted to bring doubting minds and careless *libertins* (like his friend Méré – see pages 85–6) to a fuller recognition of the urgency of metaphysical questions. His projected apology for the Christian religion was cut short by his early death (1662), but he left some 800 fragments, varying in length from several words to continuous paragraphs of finely articulated argument.

Strangely, the appeal of the *Pensées* from their first appearance (1670) to the present lies largely in the power of the fragment form. Like the maxim, it is graphic, universal and challenging. The simple concision of 'Condition de l'homme. Inconstance, ennui, inquiétude' sums up an essential of Pascal's argument, the 'misère de l'homme sans Dieu', to be counterbalanced by his revelation of the 'grandeur de l'homme avec Dieu'.* A kind of centrifugal design brings all the strands of Pascal's arguments (psychological, scientific, philosophical, scriptural) together in a common theological purpose, but his analysis of human nature particularly stands out. He had the gift of appealing to the *honnête homme* on his own ground (for example, inviting him to wager on the existence of God), while delivering a message intended to shake the very foundations of his complacency.

Bossuet, tutor to the Dauphin and then Bishop of Meaux, demonstrates that some Jesuits also did not flinch from delivering unpalatable truths, albeit in sweetened form. His sermons (most preserved only in drafts) remind his audiences of the vanity of ambition, the need to keep death ever before our gaze. Congregations flocked to enjoy the eloquent appeal to their emotions, so much so that Bossuet was sometimes moved to warn them not to confuse hearing a sermon with attending a play. Yet his celebrated *Oraisons funèbres* (1666–87), on the deaths of leading figures, have an undoubted theatrical appeal. Delivered before the court, they combine pomp and solemnity with moments of touching simplicity, particularly the oration on Henriette d'Angleterre. When reviewing the life of one such as Condé, whose fortunes and morals had been mixed, Bossuet had the more delicate task of balancing eulogy and criticism – a task aided by his confidence in divine providence which, he claimed, led Condé ultimately to piety.

Bossuet is also significant for his stand with the *Anciens* in the literary debate known as the *Querelle des Anciens et des Modernes*. The central issues concerned authority and style. Charles Perrault launched the challenge that his age was at least the equal of the golden age of Latin literature in his long poem *Le Siècle de Louis XIV* (1687). Where Boileau, Bossuet, La Bruyère, La Fontaine and Racine (among others) defended their admiration of classical models and the power of poetry, the *Modernes*, represented by figures such as Fontenelle, Saint-Évremond and Perrault (author of the *Parallèle des anciens et des modernes*, 1688–97), championed a clean break with the past in the name of progress. Over and above the polemics, the *Modernes* clearly stood for a new age in which scientific enquiry

---

* 'Condition of man. Inconstancy, boredom, anxiety' . . . 'misery of man without God' . . . 'greatness of man with God'

would displace traditional models, and poetry would be rivalled by prose (see page 95). And what could be perceived as the straitjacket of classical style would be cast off to make way for flights of the imagination (Perrault was himself the author of numerous fairy-tales) and the expression of *sensibilité*.

The period 1680–1715 is thus characterized by a conflict between the official face of order, absolutism and orthodoxy, and a critical spirit of enquiry which was part of what the critic Hazard has defined as 'la crise de la conscience européenne'.* Even La Bruyère, whose *Caractères* (1688–96) build up to a resounding praise of divine providence and a harsh satire of freethinkers (in the chapter 'Des esprits forts'), is uncomfortably aware of the hollowness of much of the social order he observes. In over a thousand fragments, a form adopted for its immediacy and versatility, he pens both humorous and caustic portraits of social types (obsequious courtiers, the coquette, tax farmers who have made scandalous profits). Some of his characters resemble Molière's later monomaniacs – eccentrics more dangerous to themselves than to society – but he also perceives chilling inequalities, including the poverty of peasants, and raises issues of social justice to be taken up by the Enlightenment.

Other writers made their doubts and questions the central issue of their work. Fénélon, tutor to the Duc de Bourgogne, published his novel *Télémaque* (based on the imaginary adventures of Ulysses' son) surreptitiously in 1699, but still earned the disfavour of Louis XIV for his criticisms of bad kingship and aggressive warfare. Fontenelle's extremely popular *Entretiens sur la pluralité des mondes* (1686) had the bland appearance of a civilized salon discussion about the possible existence of life on other planets. However, the work not only popularized the Cartesian notion of a mechanistic universe, but also raised the spectre that, if the universe is infinite, Christianity may not possess the unique truth (an idea also implied earlier in Cyrano de Bergerac's *L'Autre Monde* – see page 75). The privileged position of Christianity came under attack from a different wing as the (Latin) writings of the Dutch philosopher Spinoza infiltrated France. Spinoza challenged the general belief (upheld by such men as Pascal and Bossuet) that the Bible was an infallible historical document, and

---

* 'the crisis in European thought'

although he claimed to use reason in defence of religion, he opened
the way for more radical sceptics. Bayle, a Frenchman who lived in
the relative safety of Holland, not only attacked superstition in his
Pensées sur la comète (1682–3), but went on to hint at rational
objections to religious belief in his monumental *Dictionnaire critique
et historique* (1697–1706). Although many of the entries seem
unexceptionable, in the massive apparatus of footnotes Bayle finds
space for his doubts, notably concerning the presence of evil in the
world. The *Dictionnaire* was quickly to become the sceptics' Bible,
admired by Voltaire and other *philosophes*. Bayle's relentless spirit of
critical enquiry is summed up by the maxim, worthy of any neo-
classical writer, 'les erreurs pour être vieilles ne sont pas meilleures'.*

---

* 'errors are no better for being old ones'

Further Reading

P. Bénichou, *Morales du grand siècle* (Paris: Gallimard: 1948).

R. Briggs, *Early Modern France: 1560–1715* (Oxford: Oxford University Press, 1977).

J. DeJean, *Tender Geographies: Women and the Origins of the Novel in France* (New York: Columbia University Press, 1991).

P. France, *Politeness and Its Discontents: Problems in French Classical Culture* (Cambridge: Cambridge University Press, 1992).

C. Gossip, *An Introduction to French Classical Tragedy* (London: Macmillan, 1981).

E.J. Kearns, *Ideas in Seventeenth-Century France* (Manchester: Manchester University Press, 1979).

M. Lever, *Le Roman français au XVIIe siècle* (Paris: Presses Universitaires de Paris, 1981).

C. Lougee, *Le Paradis des Femmes: Women, Salons and Social Stratification in Seventeenth-Century France* (Princeton, NJ: Princeton University Press, 1976).

J. Mesnard (ed.), *Précis de littérature française du XVIIe siècle* (Paris: Presses Universitaires de France, 1990).

M. Moriarty, *Taste and Ideology in Seventeenth-Century France* (Cambridge: Cambridge University Press, 1988).

CHAPTER 5

The Eighteenth Century (1715–1820)

ANGELICA GOODDEN

'Le grand siècle, je veux dire le dix-huitième siècle',* said the Romantic historian Michelet. How can its claims be upheld against those of the seventeenth century, so brilliant in its dramatic production, or the nineteenth, so impressive in its novelistic *oeuvre*? Not, it seems clear, by pointing to its poetic achievement: Jean-Baptiste Rousseau, Saint-Lambert, Delille and Watelet are for most modern readers merely names, though André Chénier is recognized as belonging to the first rank, the greatest French poet between Racine and Romanticism. By seeing it as an age of prose, then; but not as a prosaic age. (The century which saw the writing of Prévost's *Manon Lescaut*, Voltaire's *contes*, Rousseau's *La Nouvelle Héloïse*, Diderot's *La Religieuse* and Laclos's *Les Liaisons dangereuses* can scarcely be called that.) The novel, it is conventionally said, 'rose' in the eighteenth century, but so too did vivid short stories and scintillating prose dialogues. And if the tally of great serious dramas is meagre, the same cannot be said of comedy: largely freed from the constraints of rhyme, it was able to explore both the intricacies of human psychology and the social conditions of a changing world.

When Louis XIV died in 1715, Philippe d'Orléans became Regent. The joyless rigidities that had marked the closing years of Louis's reign were replaced by a mood of insouciance which the literature of the time reflects: the Regency spells verve, moral flexibility and a

---

* 'the great century, I mean the eighteenth century'

touch of dare-devilry, a stylishness that sometimes displaces substance and an openness to new experience.

Civilization could come to seem excessively polished, though, and the development of culture a potential threat to inner repose. The exaltation of nature (always an ambiguous word in the eighteenth century) is in some respects to be set against the contemporary promotion of Enlightenment, a movement aimed at highlighting and enhancing intellectual progress in a world often darkened by bigotry and superstition. Its Bible was the *Encyclopédie* edited by Diderot and D'Alembert, a work originally modelled on Chambers' *Cyclopaedia* which was designed to 'changer la manière commune de penser'.* The cult of nature was linked from mid-century on with a defence of the rights of the heart, which also entailed a concern for the welfare of one's fellow men. Such sensibility could shade into *sensiblerie*, a debased pandering to mawkish desires and self-indulgent emotional satisfactions, but in its strong sense it led to an investigation of the links between feeling and virtue of the kind Rousseau conducted in his greatest novel. Rousseau's emphasis on the sway of the heart was opposed by more worldly writers who, like their predecessors in the Regency, focused on the countervailing attractions of libertinage. But Rousseau's was the message which the Romantics heard and developed, stressing the loneliness of the individual in society, the risks of incomprehension suffered by exceptional men and women, and the compensating joy of fulfilment. Fulfilment, though, is shown by them to be a precarious and ultimately often frustrating state.

Mind, Manners and Society: The Regency

Marivaux seems to epitomize the understated elegance of the Regency, and Voltaire its playful wit; but both writers also suggest the uncertainties of human existence, seeing life as a hazardous affair as often as it is a joyous game.

The *brio* of the Regency is captured in Lesage's novel *Gil Blas de*

* 'change the usual way of thinking'

Santillane, published between 1715 and 1735. Not everything Lesage wrote was so good-humoured – his play *Turcaret* (1709) had been marked by a savage cynicism that strongly qualified its status as a comedy (see page 85) – but this huge tableau of social life has a robust vigour that precludes moral seriousness. Like most of Lesage's fiction, it is set in Spain (a country he never visited), but the mood it reflects is that of early eighteenth-century France. It tells the story of Gil's growth to manhood in a world of opportunism and chance, his roving, rapscallion life, his times of prosperity and disgrace, his political activities and finally his arrival at a tranquil old age. An episodic, sprawling work in which the narrative line is constantly interrupted by interpolated stories, it is written in the form of the pseudo-memoir – the commonest novelistic type in the first half of the eighteenth century.

One of the most engaging of the memoir-novelists apparently found it a tricky genre to handle, so accommodating in its baggy looseness that it seemed to resist completion. Neither Marivaux's *La Vie de Marianne* (1731–41) nor his *Le Paysan parvenu* (1734–5) is finished, though both attracted the attention of continuators. Marivaux is a subtler writer than Lesage, much concerned with the psychological intricacies of human conduct and motivation, and his characters often lose themselves in prolonged bouts of self-analysis that do nothing to advance the plot. Yet the lack of a closed structure perhaps simply echoes the artistic principle underpinning pseudo-memoirs: they describe a life, not a plot, and in the nature of things their first-person narrators cannot be telling a story that has ended.

The mood of Marivaux's two novels is sharply contrasting, though both are suffused with the light irony that is a hallmark of his writing. Marianne's life is the more refined (she is a countess in her fifties looking back on her youth, and tracing her social progress after an unpropitious start as a foundling), and her narrative style correspondingly more delicate: it is quintessentially feminine, a seductive filigree which belies Marianne's claim that she writes artlessly. The anecdotal tone of the narrative reminds us that Marivaux was a journalist as well as a novelist and playwright, but its unhurried charm cannot disguise the periodic *longueurs*, the most extended of which – the interpolated story of the nun Tervire – finally takes the novel over. *Le Paysan parvenu* is rather less a psychological novel or *roman d'analyse*, and has something of the picaresque gaiety of *Gil Blas*: it too describes a young man's social ascent against a background of adventure and occasional skulduggery, and it has the same down-to-earthness as Lesage's novel. But it shares with *La Vie de Marianne* an intriguingly oblique quality which contrasts with that directness. How naive, the reader wonders, was either character in his or her relations with others, and how knowingly calculating? Marivaux, looking over their shoulder, seems to point to some of the answers, but his ironic detachment means that they are only lightly suggested.

His comedies, which he evidently found much easier to complete, employ indirectness in a different way. They are largely concerned with eliciting information about the state of the protagonists' emotions, a process which involves the elaborate verbal fencing known as *marivaudage*: the game of half-statement and badinage, born in society salons, becomes a dramatic analysis of the workings of the heart whose acuteness is unsurpassed. Marivaux took most of his characters from the Italian commedia dell'arte, and wrote primarily for the Comédie-Italienne (Paris's second official theatre after the Comédie-Française), but his matchless work seems entirely his own.

There are definitively Marivaudian themes – the dissection of feeling, the instantaneity of love – even in his slightest comedies, like the delicate squib *Arlequin poli par l'amour* (1720). If the plays are often bagatelles, recalling the *Fêtes galantes* of the contemporary painter Watteau, they can be infused with philosophic or social seriousness. Personal integrity is an abiding preoccupation, and is most memorably illustrated in *Le Jeu de l'amour et du hasard* (1730) and *Les Fausses Confidences* (1737): both plays insist that relationships should be based on true inclination, and that the issue of happiness is not to be taken lightly. The play-acting and disguise may reflect the Regency's *joie de vivre*, but their intention is anything but frivolous. Marivaux bypasses the comedy of manners associated with other contemporary playwrights like Destouches, and plumbs psychological depths previously thought to be the province of serious drama alone.

If Regency literature liked to present itself as a game, there might still be a serious purpose behind it. During a period which seemed more propitious to change than the stultifying last years of Louis XIV's reign, the propagation of new ideas could be more effectively assured (so it was thought) by varying their mode of presentation. Plays, novels and *contes*, according to this logic, were better vehicles for fresh political, social and philosophical messages than tracts and treatises, because they were bound to attract a wider readership: hence the beginnings of a 'literature of thought' which reached fullest expression in mid-century. Montesquieu's *Lettres persanes* (1721) and Voltaire's *Lettres philosophiques* (1734) are representative of this philosophical trend, in the sense which the eighteenth century gave to the word *philosophe*: that which is concerned with human issues in all their diversity, rather than with narrow matters of intellectual thought. They also did much to popularize the letter-fictions which were to dominate the novel in the second half of the century.

Montesquieu was nevertheless wrong to claim, as he does in his *Quelques réflexions sur 'Les Lettres persanes'*, that it was his work which taught the art of writing epistolary novels: Guilleragues's *Lettres portugaises* of 1669 had done that, though it was believed at the time to be a collection of real letters (see page 89). But Montesquieu accurately pinpoints the facility offered by the form to digress at the writer's whim, and to embrace a variety of topics of philosophical, political and moral concern. It is less certain that he succeeds in making an artistic whole out of this baroque assemblage, despite his argument that a 'chaîne secrète' holds the work together. This 'chaîne' is the intrigue in the Persian Usbek's harem, the Eastern foil to the Western world which he and his travelling companion Rica inhabit for the length of the novel; and Usbek's despotic reaction to the sedition in his seraglio shows how imperfectly he has actually learnt the liberal lessons to which he seems to give his allegiance in France.

It is a book about cultural change and cultural relativism, in which the distancing device of foreignness enables Montesquieu to make pointed comments on the virtues and vices of Western ways. It enjoyed a popular regard among contemporaries which the didactic tone of some of Usbek's letters – on depopulation, political constitutions, economics, religion, slavery and the like – may make it hard for the modern reader to understand. (Rica, more of a worldling, writes with an altogether lighter touch.) Voltaire's *Lettres philosophiques* is a sprightlier work, both less laboured and less substantial. It too casts a critical eye on French society and culture, but this time from the outside: sending his correspondent at home letters about England, the French visitor (alias Voltaire) is in fact slyly lampooning his own country. In England, it emerges from this entertainingly biased account, nearly everything is better done than in France: the political constitution works more effectively, the religious liberalism makes more sense, and science is much further advanced. Only English literature is regrettably barbarian, its essential fault being to ignore the canons of French neo-classicism which to Voltaire were absolute. Despite constant enmity with England, English culture retained its fascination for the French throughout the century, paradoxically culminating around the time of the Revolution. The *Lettres philosophiques* was a risky broadside to fire at a touchy establishment: the chancellor Maurepas ordered its author's arrest, but Voltaire – who had already had a spell in the Bastille – escaped to Lorraine before the book could be burnt by the public executioner.

Though he might write with the most serious of intentions, Voltaire never let solemnity overwhelm his fiction: he believed the sting of ridicule and the dry mocking of irony to be a better tool for reform. But then fiction, to which he addressed himself chiefly in his middle years, did not seem to him a serious literary enterprise. He attached far greater importance to the consecrated artistic modes of tragedy and the epic; but though his attempts at epic impressed contemporaries and his drama was revered by them, modern readers have shown little taste for either. The plays, with minor exceptions such as the Othello-like *Zaïre* (a work which Rousseau thought enchanting), are now utterly dead; and one must hope that this master of irony would have appreciated the irony of being forgotten for what he assumed he would be remembered by, and judged immortal by the fiction he disparaged.

Tragedy may have died in the theatre, where the seventeenth-century model was limply recycled in the new age of prose, but it was emphatically alive in the novel. Nothing better illustrates the fact than the anguished fictional corpus of the Abbé Prévost, just as nothing better illustrates the error of seeing 'pre-Romantic' trends only in literature of the second half of the eighteenth and the early nineteenth centuries: for Prévost's works – written in the 1730s and 1740s – are permeated by the gloom and *ennui* usually associated with that label. Perhaps, in fact, such labels should be as ruthlessly discarded as the conventional wisdom which sees the first half of the eighteenth century as an age of reason and the second as one of sensibility: the two currents are mingled from the start, and establishing over-rigid symmetries and contrasts – heart and senses, instinct and reason – can only mislead.

Whatever we choose to call him, though, we must now give Prévost his due as a novelist of the first importance: after years of critical neglect, he deserves to be seen as more than the author of one minor masterpiece, *Manon Lescaut* (1731). Of course *Manon*'s claim to greatness is indisputable, and the reasons why it has worn better than Prévost's other fictions are fairly clear: it is brief (but so is the *Histoire d'une Grecque moderne* of 1740) and intriguing, and the matters it deals with are of enduring interest. The plot, which is conducted with as much nonchalance and laxity as any of Prévost's, is of far less moment than the moral issues raised: whether passion, which is involuntary, is therefore innocent (a question earlier debated in *La Princesse de Clèves* – see pages 89–90), whether love, as the readiest source of supreme happiness, is therefore the greatest good, and its pursuit legitimately humanity's primary concern, and whether intense feeling is self-justifying, exonerating individuals from the possible moral consequences of their actions under its influence. Like all of Prévost's novels, *Manon Lescaut* is full of ambiguities: we simply do not know whether or not the 'destinée' which the narrator Des Grieux recurrently and self-disculpatingly invokes is in fact merely his sexual desire, and we are altogether unsure about the sincerity of Manon's feelings for him; for she is one of the most famous enigmas in literature. We cannot be certain, as a result, whether we are being asked to condemn the lovers (as the preface implies) or sympathize with them. But most readers will feel that Des Grieux is something more than the *fripon* (rogue) Montesquieu called him, and Manon not simply a *catin* (strumpet) who will sell herself to any man who promises her luxury and pleasure.

The story is told by Des Grieux once he has lost Manon. The risky lives they led since he fell in love with her (meeting her as she was about to enter a convent to arrest her 'penchant au plaisir'), their social misdemeanours and crimes, had finally caught up with them: Manon, as the more lowly born, and a woman, was more severely punished than her lover, being sentenced to deportation while he merely suffered imprisonment. But he accompanied her to America, watched her die of exhaustion in the desert after apparently undergoing a moral conversion, and returned to France to give pleasure to his loyal friend Tiberge and restore the family name he had besmirched. We are unsure whether he has been truly 'cured' of Manon, or whether, had she been resuscitated as miraculously as Prévost's other characters regularly are, he would not simply have resumed his old ways. We may suspect, too, that the real cause of her conversion was merely the absence of the old world's temptations. There is a crucial lack of clarity in central aspects of the story, as in the novels *Cleveland* (1731–9), *Le Doyen de Killerine* (1735) and *Histoire d'une Grecque moderne*; but no work of eighteenth-century literature gives a sharper picture of material life, the role of money in human affairs, the seductions of libertinism in the hedonistic world of Regency Paris, and the unjust forces of social repression. The blurring is in the presentation of psychology and motive.

Prévost's universe is, without exception, one of black melancholy, sharp anguish and tormented passion. *Cleveland* presents in the person of the narrator-hero, an illegitimate son of Cromwell who suffers dreadful tribulations, an archetype of the *ennui* later to be explored by writers like Chateaubriand and Constant (see pages 115–17), and the type reappears – but without Cleveland's compensating stoicism – in the Doyen de Killerine's half-brother Patrice. *Ennui* was seen as a characteristically English trait (though the Dean and his family are Irish, and Killerine is Coleraine): Prévost, who translated the novels of Samuel Richardson and lived for a time in England, was much influenced by that country's literature. Nothing in contemporary English writing, however, matched the gothic gloom of his world. Prévost's novels brim with extraordinary coincidence and logic-defying circumstance; but they are compelling works which offer their reader far more than cloak-and-dagger suspense.

The brittle elegance of Crébillon *fils* is a world apart, but equally characteristic of the age. Where Prévost's canvas is sweepingly broad (the hero of *Cleveland* thinks nothing of sailing to America, where he becomes chief of an Indian tribe, and the protagonists of *Le Doyen de Killerine* cross the Irish and English Channels with as much alacrity as they leave one European country for another), Crébillon's is claustrophobically tiny: the scene of his greatest novel, *Les Égarements du coeur et de l'esprit* (1736), is confined to Paris, and to the high-society Paris of salon and boudoir. Because the novel is unfinished, it is unclear whether this restricted world will be enough to provide the wealth of experiences needed for the sentimental education of its hero, the callow young Meilcour; certainly it is an impoverished world in comparison with that of Stendhal's Julien Sorel, Balzac's Lucien de Rubempré and Flaubert's Frédéric Moreau. And yet, as Meilcour's mentor Versac tells him, the rules of the game are few enough: education consists simply in being taught how to avoid committing social gaffes and learning adroitness in erotic affairs, both areas in which the 17-year-old Meilcour needs instruction.

When the novel breaks off he is on the way to wisdom, having lost his virginity to the 40-year-old Madame de Lursay and been otherwise taken in hand by social peers. But he feels the hollowness of the *monde*'s doctrine, yearning for union with the remote beauty Hortense de Théville whom he barely knows. Perhaps she was destined to be Meilcour's moral saviour, the 'femme estimable' who restored the hero to himself: the preface, at least, hints as much.

Whatever the case, Crébillon insisted that he had written a morally useful novel, one which showed the spangled futility of *Ancien Régime* life for what it was. He was proud, too, of the artistic limitations he had imposed on himself, eschewing exotic intrigue à la Montesquieu and fantastic improbability à la Prévost. If the contrived neatness of the prose often seems too hard a surface to permit the most profound investigation of the human mind and heart, and if the determined attention to manners limits the moral perspective, Crébillon has still produced a major work. Laclos's later novel *Les Liaisons dangereuses* is crucially indebted to it.

The Discontents of Civilization: The Ages of Louis XV and Louis XVI

The satisfactions of elegant living were less equivocally argued in another work published the same year, Voltaire's poem *Le Mondain*. Voltaire, in keeping with his age, saw the pursuit of happiness, both individual and collective, as the only worthwhile goal of human striving, and its frustrations and successes are variously catalogued in his *contes*. If the dervish to whom Candide and Pangloss address themselves regards evil and unhappiness as of no account in the cosmic scheme, Voltaire regards them as centrally important in the human one. *Candide*, written in 1758 and published the following year, is a parody of many things – of what Voltaire mischievously chooses to present as the Optimistic nonsense of Leibniz (the notion that an all-powerful God could not have created a world that was less than the best possible), peddled in the *conte* by Pangloss, of the literary voyage of discovery, of the adventure-novel also disparaged by Crébillon in the preface to *Les Égarements*, of the fairytale and of the medieval quest. Like Prévost's *Cleveland*, but in knowing *faux-naïf* style, it has a hero separated from his loved one, a sentimental journey over different countries and much metaphysical speculation on the meaning of life. But its tone is pragmatic in an altogether different and characteristically Voltairean way, for it denies that misfortune can enlarge the soul or deepen the spirit. Misfortune, it concludes, should be abhorred; man should resolutely focus on what can make material life better, and so increase the stock of human happiness.

In its practicality this is a thoroughly unpoetic message; but the panache and energy that define Voltaire are at odds with the spirit of poetry. The lesson of *Zadig* (1747), *Micromégas* (1752) and *Le Monde comme il va* (1759) is also prosaically matter-of-fact: accept the world, complain at its injustices, try to right wrongs and correct deficiencies where possible, but at all costs avoid losing yourself in abstractions. Those with a taste for metaphysics and a yearning for psychological penetration will find little to satisfy them in Voltaire. Others will admire his wit, lucid intelligence and iconoclastic daring and disdain to search his fiction for qualities he never sought to put in it.

Voltaire was essentially a man of the world, the familiar of monarchs (Catherine the Great had a copy of his bust by Houdon in the Hermitage), a lover of luxury and a writer who had grown rich by the pen. He seems in all respects different from Rousseau, who died in the same year (1778) and enjoyed equal fame as a writer: Voltaire is all sociability and poise, his smile the very smile of reason, and Rousseau the clumsy misfit, the scourge of society, the champion of brute primitivism and the prophet of untrammelled sentiment. Of course, this is in some ways a misleading generalization, for Voltaire also acknowledged the power of sensibility, and Rousseau was far from belittling reason: the beginning of his *Discours sur les sciences et les arts* (1750) praises man as an intellectual being who has used his brain to overcome ignorance, and presents as strong a case as any for seeing the author as a defender of the Enlightenment. But inasmuch as Enlightenment entailed a subordination of spiritual values to scientific ones, and of moral to material impulses, Rousseau was not of it. The cantankerous hermit ridiculed in Palissot's play *Les Philosophes* (1760) may be a myth, but the individualist who found memory and imagination more substantial and reassuring than actuality is not. Rousseau created fictions, as he drafted social contracts, as a way of displacing the real world and counterbalancing its imperfections.

A largely self-taught man, he was an unsystematic but radical thinker who exerted enormous influence on virtually every field he entered. When not a political theorist he was an educationist, and the educationist was a writer of fiction too: *Émile* (1762) is a novel as much as it is a pedagogical treatise. His most important fictional work, however, appeared the year before *Émile*, and was the publishing phenomenon of the century. The letter-novel *Julie, ou La Nouvelle Héloïse* is dated, certainly, but as a monument to the sentimental revolution which the eighteenth-century novel both caused and recorded it must still be read. Goethe's *Die Leiden des jungen Werthers* and Laclos's *Les Liaisons dangereuses* are unthinkable without it; and if Rousseau, whose *Discours* of 1750 had attacked the cultivation of the arts as detrimental to moral and social wellbeing, was embarrassed to find that he had actually become a world-famous novelist, readers generously forgave his inconsistency.

Diffuse in structure, with lengthy digressions on the education of children, domestic economy, opera and the like, the book is simple in plot: Julie falls in love with her tutor Saint-Preux, conceives and then miscarries his child, but is forced by her father to marry a much older man, Wolmar, with whom she has a businesslike relationship running a country estate at Clarens and raising two sons. Saint-Preux is dispatched on various voyages to cure him of his passion, and finally comes to Clarens to act as a tutor to the Wolmar children. But Julie eventually realizes that she has been living a lie, and loses the will to live: 'le premier sentiment qui m'a fait vivre . . . s'est concentré dans mon coeur',* and so she slips edifyingly out of life after saving her son from drowning, and before she can compromise her regained virtue by yielding to love. She looks forward, however, to an afterlife in which she can adore Saint-Preux 'sans crime'.†

This is clearly a less moral conclusion than Rousseau, who considered most novels a threat to virtue, ought to have intended: appearances are saved, but only by sleight of hand. Yet a part of the immense public enthusiasm for the work rested on the belief that it upheld 'safe' bourgeois values like domesticity, fidelity and sentiment, opposing them to the corrupt ways of aristocrats and city-

---

* 'the first feeling that made me live . . . is embedded in my heart'
† 'blamelessly'

dwellers. 'J'ai vu les moeurs de mon temps, et j'ai publié ces lettres',* Rousseau proclaims in the preface, and Laclos borrowed his words for the epigraph to his scandalous novel of worldliness *Les Liaisons dangereuses*. Sensibility rules: if there is much on the torments of frustrated love, it never carries the charge of similar plaints in Prévost, for Rousseau, as his *Confessions* (see below) also make clear, actually regarded passionate love as a threat. Julie, like the Princesse de Clèves before her (see pages 89–90), professes to prefer loveless-ness in marriage because it permits the individual to live without 'inquiétude', in a state of 'repos';† passion, on the other hand, stops the business of life getting done. It was the tension between such pragmatism and the countervailing seductions of illicit romance that made the book such a thrilling read for Rousseau's contemporaries.

If it fails to engage its modern audience to the same extent, our inaccessibility to the profusions and effusions of eighteenth-century 'sensibilité' is only one reason. It is in various ways a novel of excess – excessively long, overstated, prosy and humourless, blending fiction and lecture as unsubtly as *Émile*. It is marginally less didactic than the latter work (which contains diatribes against city life, mothers who neglect to breast-feed their babies, the use of swaddling clothes, meat-eating and so on), but undermines its own moral doctrine regarding the possibility of regaining lost virtue; yet it remains an imaginative *tour de force*.

Rousseau abandoned his public literary career after the official condemnation of *Émile* and *Du contrat social* (1762) and continued to defend his soul against the corruptions of art and modern life by living off his meagre earnings as a music copyist; he marked his revolt, too, by selling all his fine linen and his watch, a particularly defiant step for a Swiss to take. His preoccupation with personal values is most finely and movingly expressed in the *Confessions* (written between 1766 and 1769 but posthumously published between 1782 and 1788), and the unfinished *Rêveries du promeneur solitaire* (1782), the former revealing his essential but frustrated sociability, his often painful ability to probe the recesses of his own consciousness, his existential guilt and his paranoia, and the latter

---

* 'I have seen the morals of my age, and have published these letters.'
† 'anxiety' . . . 'peace of mind'

suggesting, with all the gentle lyricism of resignation, both the unsettling and the reassuring effects of memory. Rousseau, anticipating Proust's Marcel, saw the stuff of remembrance as more real than present experience, and rejoiced in being able to redouble his sense of existence through its operations.

His one-time friend Diderot, less given to introspection, was more regularly certain that a social end was proper to mankind, and had offended Rousseau by making a character in his play *Le Fils naturel* (1757) remark that 'Il n'y a que le méchant qui soit seul.'* The observation is directed against Dorval, a forebear of Chateaubriand's René (see below, page 116), with whom he shares his longing for solitude, his rootlessness, his *ennui* and his incestuous love for a sister. It is part of an attempt to persuade him to stay in the world and fulfil ordinary social duties, such as those of fathering and raising children. Its moral force is somewhat blunted by the fact that it is voiced by a woman, Constance, who wants to marry Dorval, but no radical irony is intended. This is a drama with a serious message about living, and is a contribution to the stock of *philosophe* arguments in favour of productive involvement with the affairs of the world. Drama was considered to be a particularly effective tool of persuasion because it appealed directly to the senses, and so provoked thought: the philosopher John Locke's proposition in the *Essay Concerning Human Understanding* (1690) that ideas, rather than being innate, were a product of sense-impressions exerted enormous influence on eighteenth-century French thought. So Diderot developed a drama of (intendedly) humane and moralistic tenor, and one which aimed to speak to its audience directly by presenting them with ordinary characters rather than royalty and nobles.

It was an attractive theory, but its practical realization could scarcely have been less alluring. It is not that Diderot lacked a sense of the dramatic: some of his philosophical dialogues, and one of his novels, have been effectively adapted for the stage. But in writing formal drama he seems to have felt constrained by the weight of the great seventeenth-century legacy, which presses down on *Le Fils naturel* and *Le Père de famille* (1758) so heavily as to exclude innovation: the 'revolution' in dramaturgy actually leads to more

---

* 'Only the wicked man is alone.'

soliloquizing than in Racine, a proliferation of theatrical cliché (misplaced letters, climactic recognition scenes and *coups de théâtre*), hopelessly stylized language and enormous coincidence. It is all as beguiling as a sermon, virtue-mongering, solemn and rhetorically inflated. *Le Fils naturel* was originally called a 'comédie' (later Diderot described it as a 'drame' midway between comedy and tragedy), but it is benighted and begloomed by the author's obsession with propagating goodness.

He is, happily, not always so pious. The pseudo-oriental erotic novel *Les Bijoux indiscrets* (1748), a tribute to the hedonism of Louis XV's new reign, deserves little critical attention: according to his daughter, Diderot wrote this repetitive story about a bored sultan who tests women's virtue by pointing a magic ring at their pudenda and making them speak simply to prove how easy such enterprises were. But his most characteristic trait as a writer was to stir up debate (mostly posthumously, for he published little in his own lifetime apart from the dramas and dramatic theory, some early philosophical works and the *Encyclopédie*, which he edited and to which he was a main contributor). So, in the dialogue *Le Neveu de Rameau* (1762) he opposes an honest bourgeois philosopher – to whom he mischievously gives the name 'Moi' – to the iconoclastic bohemian parasite 'Lui' and makes the pair discuss ethics, aesthetics, the good life, music, education and other favourite Enlightenment themes, without letting them reach any very definite conclusions.

This is Diderot's most open-ended work; *La Religieuse* (1760) is probably his most closed, or 'monological', though the philosophical dialogue on materialistic determinism *Le Rêve de d'Alembert* (1769) runs it a close second. *La Religieuse*, a nun's compelling but gothic account of her horrific experiences in the convents where her parents have confined her against her will, raises familiar questions about the individual's right to self-determination and the perverse (and perverting) rigours of claustration, and was one of a stream of anti-conventual works written in France before the Revolution. In it Diderot shows himself to be a master of suspense, a writer of striking visual skills (he had just begun work as an art critic) and a man of sometimes unguarded feeling: 'Je me désole d'un conte que je me fais',* he reportedly told a visitor who found him in tears as he wrote. But he also seems to take a prurient pleasure in describing scenes of sadism and lesbian love, however emphatically he condemns the institutions that allegedly foster them.

The novel *Jacques le fataliste* (1773), which some regard as Diderot's masterpiece, will strike others as an overstretched conceit, a dialogue-debate on free will and determinism which is often so manneredly insistent as to repel the reader's attention. It is a self-consciously manipulative work, concerned with techniques of story-telling rather than with actually telling a story, but is most engaging when it simply allows itself to narrate. *La Religieuse* is unashamedly a narrative; *Jacques* takes pride in not being one, but the pride is perhaps misplaced.

Diderot's literary influence on contemporaries was necessarily limited to the few areas in which he chose to publish before his death. His *drame* theory appealed, rather unfortunately, to the playwright, adventurer and anti-establishment gadfly Beaumarchais, whose efforts were no more successful than Diderot's: *Eugénie* (1767) is a creaking and histrionic play about a girl who has been made pregnant by an aristocrat she mistakenly thinks she is married to, but who is actually preparing to marry someone else; *Les Deux Amis* (1770) no more compellingly describes a banker's embezzlement of a large sum of money to release a friend from temporary financial embarrassment. Neither can have given Beaumarchais's public any idea that he was capable of the comic brilliance of *Le Barbier de Séville* (1775) or *Le Mariage de Figaro* (1784), the box-office success of the century whose performance was originally forbidden by Louis XVI on account of its revolutionary tenor: for it was filled with imprecations against the nobility, inherited privilege and other favourite targets of the Fourth Estate. *Le Barbier de Séville* revealed an explosive comic talent and an unmistakable new dramatic voice of commanding authority: it has all the fizz and thrust which French comedy had lacked since Molière, and makes almost everything else written in the eighteenth century look unfunny. *Le Mariage de Figaro*, in which Figaro is about to be cuckolded by his employer Comte Almaviva (but where the resourcefulness of the female characters

---

* 'I am moved to tears by a tale I am telling myself.'

saves the day), is equally irresistible, if too tightly packed to be altogether digestible. The court, which it lampooned, loved it as much as the general public. Beaumarchais saw fit to return to the *drame* in the final play in the Figaro trilogy, *La Mère coupable* (1792), but predictably failed to ignite the same spark. The only *drame* generally agreed to have succeeded was Sedaine's *Le Philosophe sans le savoir* (1764), a play which upheld the dignity of commerce and so helped promote the internationalism of the Enlightenment. It is a vigorous work, convincing in characterization and robust in dialogue.

An infinitely less accomplished playwright than either Beaumarchais or Sedaine, Marie-Joseph Chénier, shared Beaumarchais's inclination to use the stage as a tribune for the proclaiming of Revolutionary sentiment: his tragedy *Charles IX* (1789) is a very mediocre work, but its political influence was immense. His brother André, a political moderate guillotined in the Terror, was a far greater writer, whose poetry breaks away from the flatly descriptive or narrative modes of the time and blends the classical and the modern in a startlingly original way. 'Sur des pensers nouveaux faisons des vers antiques',* he announces in the poem *L'Invention*, meaning that the encyclopaedism of the eighteenth century is to be given a far more seductive literary form than the routine verse-mongering of contemporaries like Lebrun-Pindare could achieve. Victor Hugo thought that a new poetry had been born in Chénier. The posthumously-published *Bucoliques, Elégies* and *Odes* – including political odes like the one addressed to Charlotte Corday, and 'La Jeune captive' – are the work of a great lyricist; but he also translates the historical events of his time into poetry. In him the sensibility of the eighteenth century blends with its pragmatic activism; and respect for tutelary tradition is made to harmonize with the demand of personal inspiration – imitation redefined and made into invention.

---

* 'Let us write antique verse about new thoughts.'

Libertinage and the Female Voice: Towards the New Era

Sentimental realism as represented by Marivaux and Rousseau was both attacked and refocused as the century drew to its close. The attacks came from Laclos and Sade, and the new perspective from Restif de la Bretonne. Restif's *Le Paysan perverti* (1775) and *La Paysanne pervertie* (1785), whose titles underline the debt to Marivaux, push social realism much further. Restif is the chronicler of the peasantry and the 'petit peuple',* and relishes the opportunity the novel provides for an extended examination of their rise and fall in the sophisticated world. He describes their fortunes sympathetically but with a moralist's attention to retribution and reward, punishing the excesses of libertinage which he has earlier complaisantly detailed.

Does Laclos do something similar in his epistolary novel *Les Liaisons dangereuses* (1782)? Opinions differ as to the gravity and appropriateness of the punishments meted out at the end of the work: did not Valmont really desire the death he dies after causing the Présidente de Tourvel's terminal decline, and has not the Marquise de Merteuil preserved intact the lucid intelligence she deployed to such destructive effect over the length of the book, even if she has lost her reputation and beauty? Did not the Présidente, admittedly an adulteress, deserve exoneration or a mitigation of her suffering on account of the long fight she put up against Valmont, and is not Cécile Volanges, the girl he seduces as a way of avenging himself against her mother, too young and naive to deserve the punishment she receives? Even more importantly, has not Laclos made his evil protagonists too compelling in their resourcefulness and glamour for readers easily to withhold their admiration? Is the melodramatic, retributivist justice meted out at the end – when Merteuil is struck down with smallpox, loses an eye and her court case, and is hounded out of the capital – a belated and unduly heavy-handed attempt to redress the balance which the 'esprit du mal'† pervading the narrative has upset?

We cannot be sure. For Baudelaire, it was clear that *Les Liaisons*

---

* 'common people'   † 'spirit of evil'

dangereuses was a 'livre de moraliste'*; and it is undeniable that it presents evil as destructive and sick as well as seductive. The criminal manipulation of human lives for the sake of corrupt amusement is emphatically condemned, but Laclos is too astute a psychologist to deny the fascination of the *interdit*:† as Diderot had stated earlier in the century, the magnitude and energy of evil can create a perverse kind of sublimity. We may distance ourselves from it morally, in other words, but give it a limited artistic assent.

Sade's *Idée sur les romans* (1800) does not mention Laclos, but proffers the disingenuous statement that he himself has given vice such a repellent form in his own writings because writers like Crébillon *fils* had presented it too attractively. This was the defence offered of works like *Les 120 Journées de Sodome* (written in 1785, but unpublished until 1904), in which four hugely wealthy psychopaths lock themselves in a castle with their wives and assorted sexual partners to practise various infamous acts; *Justine, ou Les Malheurs de la vertu* (1791), a ghastly extension of *Zadig*'s exploration of virtue, vice, punishment and reward; and *La Philosophie dans le boudoir* (1795), the ultimate perversion of the novel of sentimental education. Some readers of *Les Liaisons dangereuses* had particularly objected to the presentation of naked vice in the figure of a woman, even if they saw the hideousness of Merteuil's evil as palliated by its contrast with the Présidente's angelic sweetness. The popular novelist Marie-Jeanne Riccoboni took Laclos to task for precisely this, saying that his work offended her both as a woman and as a patriot. Laclos merely replied that her own books offered the alternative view of her sex.

It is worth dwelling briefly on this point, because women novelists from the early eighteenth century had presented their own, broadly consistent, picture of woman's inherent strength and her unimpeachable virtue: Laclos's (moral or psychological) error, then, lay not in having shown her as more powerful than the male – for Merteuil is clearly the dominant partner in her relationship with Valmont – but in making her so sullied by vice. The *Princesse de Clèves*-like novel by the Marquise de Tencin, the *Mémoires du comte de Comminge* (1735), has a pure heroine who is always mistress of her conduct if not of her feelings; it is the hero who is impetuously

---

* 'a moralist's book'   † forbidden

passionate, a 'jeune aveugle'* in the mould of Prévost's Des Grieux. But Madame de Tencin's decision in the later *Siège de Calais* (1739) to write fictional history means that a real examination of moral issues relating to eighteenth-century women is precluded, because history rarely deals explicitly with them.

Françoise de Grafigny's *Lettres d'une Péruvienne* (1747), a phenomenally successful novel, depicts a faithful woman, the Inca princess Zilia, and a faithless lover, the Inca ruler Aza, who forms another relationship after they are captured by *conquistadores* and shipped to Europe. She is as strong-willed and resolute as Rousseau's Julie, however, and by the end of the novel has staked her claim to economic and social freedom in France, refusing the offers of marriage made by her besotted admirer Déterville because she is eternally in love with Aza. It is a powerfully feminist work, underlining the injustice of male domination in society and the horrors of convent education, and allowing its heroine's demand for a Woolfian 'room of her own' to be fulfilled. Madame Riccoboni's *Lettres de Mistriss Fanni Butlerd* (1757) also criticizes the social prejudices that encourage one form of behaviour in men and another, more repressed, in women; and it is to be noted that the same author's continuation of *La Vie de Marianne* makes the merely inconstant Valville of Marivaux's novel into a common seducer.

The most interesting presentation of these tensions is to be found in the work of Isabelle de Charrière at the end of the century. The engagingly simple *Lettres neuchâteloises* (1784), dealing with the small and regular world of urban Switzerland, has a heroine, Marianne de la Prise, who is happy to defend and even admit her love for the German clerk, Henri Meyer, who has got a seamstress with child and so led to her dismissal from her employment. (The reader is left to decide whether the priggish and sexist Henri will ultimately marry Marianne or not.) The first half of the *Lettres écrites de Lausanne* (1786) describes how a young English lord is unable to make up his mind to pledge faith to the charming but goitrous Cécile de ***, and the second half – the haunting story of Caliste – virtually repeats the scenario: the young man's tutor, William, who is under pressure from his father to break with Caliste because she was once an actress

---

* 'blind young man'

and a kept woman, effectively kills her through his irresoluteness and vacillation. (There are also hints that William is homosexual.) The fiction of Isabelle de Charrière, who has sometimes been likened – generously – to Jane Austen, clearly anticipates the work of Benjamin Constant and Germaine de Staël in the early nineteenth century, but her focus on faithful, resolute women and weak, wavering men is barely different from the pattern set by female writing over the length of the eighteenth century.

Towards Romanticism

Charrière's style, a beautifully crafted amalgam of understatement, wit and tact, could scarcely be more different from the grandiloquent flamboyance of Chateaubriand. Not that his lush rhythms and overblown sonorities were without precedent in French literature, for the pastoral novel of 1788 by Bernardin de Saint-Pierre, *Paul et Virginie*, had anticipated them; but there is less epic orotundity in Saint-Pierre's simple story of two European children brought up by their mothers in a Mauritian state of nature, which then comes into conflict with residual 'civilized' values and ultimately leads to the young Virginie's death. Both men – who, unlike Lesage (see page 97), had actually travelled to the countries in which they set their fictions – had a taste for exoticism which opened a rich and plangent vein in the literary language.

Les Natchez (finished at the very end of the eighteenth century) was described by Chateaubriand as an 'épopée de l'homme de la nature',* but might more accurately be called an epic of the Fall. He plundered this enormous and barely readable work of its two jewels before publishing the rest, to limited acclaim, in 1826; *Atala* appeared in 1801 and *René* in 1802, and were huge successes.

Atala, the story of the Indian girl who dies after taking poison because of the conflict between her mother's last request that she remain a virgin and her love for René's mentor, Chactas, is a moving narrative of troubled passion, sumptuously written. (It was

---

* 'epic of natural man'

composed, Chateaubriand tells his reader, in the middle of the American desert among the huts of savages.) *René* describes a man gripped by 'éternelles inquiétudes',* a victim of the pre-Romantic *ennui* and *mal du siècle* whose eighteenth-century versions are displayed by Cleveland and Patrice (see pages 102–3); Chateaubriand's mellifluous prose cannot fail to seduce, but his hero's angst as he sits weeping on the edge of a volcano may strike the modern reader as more ridiculous than moving. Not that Chateaubriand himself felt much solidarity with him: like the brisk Père Souël, who declares the hero to be 'entêté de chimères',† he found his taste for solitude thoroughly unhealthy. René's obscure and unfocused dissatisfaction with the world, his longing (the classically Romantic feeling of *Sehnsucht*), eventually crystallize as he is made aware of his sister Amélie's incestuous love for him. He himself is in love with grief, finding in the pain of Amélie's confession and withdrawal to the cloister 'une sorte de satisfaction inattendue dans la plénitude de mon chagrin'.‡ 'Douleur', he decides, is delicious in its inexhaustibility, unlike earthly pleasures.

Le *Génie du christianisme* (1802) pinpoints the dangerous modern malaise of the 'vague des passions',§ a state of knowing all the *theory* of feeling without actually experiencing any of it, being old before one's time, and living – as Rousseau's Julie felt she lived – with a full heart in an empty world. In the *Défense du 'Génie du christianisme'* (1809) indeed, Chateaubriand roundly attacks Rousseau for championing this useless propensity for reverie and encouraging hordes of young men to devote themselves to aimless, unfocused solitude. Senancour's *Obermann* (1804) depicts another introspective anti-hero, a creature of the Alpine heights who is also seized by the *mal du siècle*: like René, whom Souël brusquely counsels to do his social duty, he is a man who feels rather than works, and who is therefore prey to every stray impulse of *ennui*. *Obermann* is a long threnody which lacks all the philosophical and rhetorical self-indulgence of Chateaubriand's writings: a less flamboyant work than *René* or *Atala* it is also infinitely more profound.

---

* 'eternal worries'   † 'obsessed with dreams'
‡ 'a sort of satisfaction that was unexpected in the depth of my grief'
§ 'vagueness of passions'

Pre-Romantic man, unflatteringly, presents himself as useless to the world, buried in self-preoccupation and unable or unwilling to galvanize himself into productive activity. Is he, more seriously, a threat to others as well as a burden to himself? Benjamin Constant's *Adolphe* (published in 1816 but written between 1806 and 1807) suggests that he is, at least when he precipitately decides to convert solitude into union with another, and then realizes that he is uncommitted to the new relationship. Adolphe, a gauche and emotionally inexperienced young man, sets out to seduce an older woman, Ellénore, in order to flatter his vanity and emulate a friend who is blissfully in love; but his passion cools (as Ellénore's does not), and he begins to find his mistress burdensome rather than a means of expanding his sense of self. Society intrudes, encouraging him to see her as an obstacle to his advancement in the world – a world for which he had earlier signalled his distaste – but he finds he cannot simply abandon a defenceless woman who loves him and whom he pities.

Fatally suggestible, Adolphe swings between Ellénore and the world, devoted – or so he believes – to neither, but acutely conscious of the conflicting responsibilities of emotional fidelity and social commitment. Though he has stopped loving Ellénore in the romantic sense, he cannot stop, or help, *having loved* her: the burden of the past and the weight of memory are always there to curb his individual liberty. So he never makes the final break which Ellénore, tortured by his equivocation, is wordlessly begging of him. His irresolution kills her, and commits him to a living death as he contemplates the barren expanses of freedom that surround him once she has died.

Adolphe tells his own story, and so is a partial witness. He insists that his *récit* is not an attempt at self-exoneration; but if this is true – and it is a difficult question to resolve – why does he narrate at all? His soul-searching cannot now help Ellénore, who witnessed enough of it during her life with Adolphe; it may instruct, but it can scarcely edify, his reader, who principally learns from the story that humans deserve to be treated as ends in themselves, not as means to other people's ends. As a bleak summary of *mal du siècle* in its most self-abasing form, *Adolphe* is unsurpassed.

It both resembles and stands apart from the overblown fictions of Constant's lover, Germaine de Staël: alike in its revelation of a distinctively female form of suffering in a man's world, but dissimilar in its sobriety and control. *Adolphe* is a miracle of concision and clarity; the novels *Delphine* (1802) and *Corinne* (1807) are, in contrast, swirling fogs of bombast and overstatement. A compatriot remarked that Madame de Staël generally wrote badly, but in *Delphine* wrote especially badly; and certainly it is a poorly constructed work with no discernible shape to its plot, episode after episode simply amplifying the uncomfortable nature of Delphine's relations with the society she both needs and deplores. Staël's heroines are characteristically decisive women who none the less subordinate everything to their love for an indecisive man: they are clearly meant to stand for the eternal feminine, living by and for the heart. Both *Delphine* and *Corinne*, however, show that this mode of existence can never bring strong women happiness: they are too various to find satisfaction in the heart alone, but society has little use for their talents and strengths. Or, if it does, their talents will wither under emotional pressure, as Corinne finds when she loses her poetic gifts after her lover Oswald's desertion.

Although Delphine writes that she gives herself to love as believers do to their faith, the man she adores, Léonce, finds her too individualistic to be socially reassuring: a prisoner of convention, he wants only to be married to a woman who will not be talked about. He chooses Delphine's repressed cousin Mathilde, and tries to forget his love for Delphine: Mathilde dies after a brief period of marriage, but Léonce and Delphine are not free to wed because she, in desperation, has become a nun. Friends tell her that she can have her vows annulled, which shocks the conformist Léonce; Delphine is so distraught at discovering his reaction that she goes into terminal decline.

Corinne too is destroyed by conformism, the weight of public opinion on the mind and heart of the irresolute Oswald. Corinne, he remembers his dead father saying, is too much her own woman to be a suitable wife for him: despite Oswald's passion for her, and fascination with her artistic gifts, he cannot see how this half-Italian muse would fit into the ordered regularity of English provincial life. So he marries Corinne's half-sister, the passive and child-like Lucile, but betrays his sense of guilt by immediately leaving her to go to war. Corinne, who has previously returned to Italy, dies of frustration and lovesickness, only remarking – as an echo of Constant's Ellénore – that 'Les hommes ne savent pas le mal qu'ils font, et la société leur persuade que c'est un jeu de remplir une âme de bonheur, et d'y faire ensuite succéder le désespoir.'*

It is easy to dismiss these two novels as verbose (Isabelle de Charrière called their author a 'talking-machine'), laboured and occasionally hysterical. Staël lacked a sense of proportion, and *Corinne* particularly suffers from this defect. It is so crammed with historical, archaeological, religious and geographical detail about the country in which it is principally set that the old Bibiothèque nationale catalogue classified it under 'Italy', not 'Novel'. But Benjamin Constant, an acute critic despite being a wearied lover, remarked of *Delphine* that he knew of nothing written by a woman that stood comparison with it. George Eliot observed that only in France had women had a vital influence on the development of literature, such that 'if the writings of women were swept away, a serious gap would be made in national history', and for all her grandiloquence one cannot deny the power of Staël's contribution.

Taking the eighteenth and early nineteenth centuries together, and moving from novel to play to *conte*, and back to novel again, one must still award the palm to men. But the female achievement in imaginative literature unquestionably deserves wider recognition than it has been accorded.

---

* 'Men do not know the harm they do, and society persuades them that it is a game to fill a heart with happiness and then make it endure despair.'

Further Reading

Peter Brooks, *The Novel of Worldliness* (Princeton: Princeton University Press, 1969).

Henri Coulet, *Le Roman depuis ses origines jusqu'à la Révolution*, 2 vols (Paris: Armand Colin, 1975).

Jean Ehrard, *L'Idée de nature dans la première moitié du XVIIIe siècle*, abridged re-edition (Paris: S.E.V.P.E.N., 1970).

Jacqueline de Jomaron (ed.) , *Le Théâtre en France*, vol. I (Paris: Armand Colin, 1988).

Robert Mauzi, *L'Idée du bonheur dans la littérature et la pensée françaises au XVIIIe siècle* (Paris: Armand Colin, 1960).

Jean Starobinski, *L'Invention de la liberté* (Geneva: Skira, 1964).

CHAPTER 6

The Nineteenth Century (1820–1880)

ANNE GREEN

French social and political life in the period 1820–80 was marked by dramatic changes. Regimes followed one another in rapid and sometimes violent succession. The Bourbon monarchy which had been restored after the abdication of Napoleon in 1815 lasted only until 1830: Charles X, who had succeeded his brother, Louis XVIII, in 1824, was forced to abdicate after the July Revolution of 1830. His place was taken by his cousin, the Duc d'Orléans, who accepted the throne as Louis-Philippe I. Under the July monarchy – as Louis-Philippe's constitutional, 'bourgeois' regime was known – municipalities were given the right to elect their own municipal councils, and literacy increased as every commune was obliged to provide a primary school and a teacher. Industrialization continued apace, and new roads, canals and railways transformed the country's communications. By 1846 the historian Guizot felt able to boast that France had the most stable government in Europe. But a growing economic crisis, exacerbated by a series of bad harvests, the government's financial commitment to its education programme and the long-running war with Algeria, inflamed the opposition, and Louis-Philippe was in turn overthrown in the revolution of 1848. That revolution sparked unrest throughout Europe and paved the way for radical measures such as the abolition of slavery in French colonies and the introduction of universal male suffrage. With about 97 per cent of the electorate voting for the first time, the elections held by the provisional government in April of the same year returned a moderate Assembly. But the new Second Republic was even more short-lived than the regimes which had preceded it: Napoleon's nephew, Louis-Napoleon Bonaparte, who had been voted president in 1848 by the enlarged electorate, crushed his political opponents in a swift *coup d'état* in 1851. A year later, after his overthrow of the Assembly had been approved by plebiscite, he was proclaimed Emperor Napoleon III. The great Exhibition of 1855 perhaps best demonstrates French pride in the country's industrial and commercial achievements during the wave of economic expansion that occurred in the early years of the Second Empire. The 1850s and 1860s saw the rapid expansion of the railway system, and the massive restructuring of Paris under Haussmann. Under the Second Empire, France began to pursue a more active but not always successful foreign policy: the country fought alongside Britain and Turkey in the Crimean War; in 1859 Napoleon declared war on Austria in support of Italian unification (Nice and Savoy were annexed to France under the peace terms); and there were further military campaigns in West Africa, Indo-China (annexing Cochin-China in 1862 and making Cambodia a protectorate), Syria and, disastrously, Mexico. In July 1870 Napoleon declared war on Prussia but was forced to surrender at Sedan less than two months later; the Third Republic was declared on 4 September 1870. With Paris under siege and the provisional government based in Bordeaux, peace terms – including France's loss of Alsace and part of Lorraine – were negotiated with the Germans. But in Paris, growing resentment against the government (which had moved from Bordeaux to Versailles) led to serious insurrections in March 1871, and to the setting up of a municipal government, the Paris Commune. The Commune lasted until the end of May, when troops of the Versailles government stormed the capital: it is estimated that 20,000 were killed in the massacres and fires that followed. By the end of the decade legitimist, Orleanist and Bonapartist opposition to the Republic had waned. In 1879 the government returned to Paris, *La Marseillaise* became the national anthem, and 14 July was declared a national holiday. The new Republic seemed solidly established.

Looking Inwards

The Napoleonic wars had brought many Frenchmen into contact with foreign cultures and literature. Returning *émigrés*, too, brought with them a new awareness of writers such as Goethe and Schiller, Shakespeare, Byron and Scott. Elaborating on ideas expressed earlier in the century by Madame de Staël, Stendhal (pseudonym of Henri Beyle) argued in *Racine et Shakespeare* (1823) that French writers should draw inspiration from these foreign authors rather than continuing to imitate neo-classical French literature. All the great writers of the past were romantics in their own period, he says, but as time passes their works cease to be relevant to the problems and preoccupations of later generations. For Stendhal, romanticism is 'l'art moderne', and writers must search for new literary forms to express new feelings and ideas. In numerous manifestos and prefaces, authors proclaimed this need to liberate themselves from the conventions of the literature of the past – as Victor Hugo wrote, in the preface to his *Odes et Ballades* (1826), the poet 'ne doit pas écrire avec ce qui a été écrit, mais avec son âme et son coeur'.*

In his *Confession d'un enfant du siècle* (1836), a fictionalized account of his love-affair with George Sand, Alfred de Musset describes an anguished generation of young men brought up with dreams of Napoleonic glory, but who have now been left with no fixed values and no direction. 'Tout ce qui était n'est plus; tout ce qui sera n'est pas encore. Ne cherchez pas ailleurs le secret de nos maux,'† he writes. A sense that the values of the past are gone for good and a quest for something new to put in their place are characteristic of much of the literature from the earlier part of this period. Frequently, writers describe their feelings of uncertainty and aimlessness as a melancholic disease – as, in Alfred de Vigny's words, a 'maladie toute morale et presque incurable, et quelquefois contagieuse'.‡ This *mal du siècle* with its sense of disorientation and hopelessness – and a certain melancholy relish of that anxious state – pervades much of

---

* 'must not write with what has already been written, but with his heart and soul'
† 'All that was exists no longer; all that will be is yet to come. Look no further for the secret of our ills.'
‡ 'purely moral sickness that is virtually incurable, and sometimes contagious'

the literary output of the 1820s and 1830s. Writers expressed their discontent with the present by turning inwards, seeking to find within themselves a source of inspiration which the chaotic and unstable world around them could not provide. Charles Nodier, the novelist and short-story writer whose salon became a meeting place for avant-garde writers such as Hugo, Vigny, Musset, Sainte-Beuve, Aloysius Bertrand and Pétrus Borel, as well as young painters, engravers and sculptors, drew inspiration from an internal world of dreams, and declared that poetry should concern itself with hitherto unnoticed aspects of things. The power of the imagination, the sensibilities of the individual, the intricacies of emotional torment were explored as this generation of authors searched for answers to the great philosophical questions of our place in the universe.

Above all it was in poetry that these emotions found expression. The success of Alphonse de Lamartine's four main collections of poems – *Les Méditations poétiques* (1820), *Les Nouvelles Méditations poétiques* (1823), *Harmonies poétiques et religieuses* (1830) and *Recueillements poétiques* (1839) – was largely due to their affinity with the preoccupations of his generation. They give lyrical and melodious expression to themes of human and divine love, nature, religious mysticism, idealism and despair, while often reflecting crises of faith and love in his own life. But sources in his personal experience – in particular his love for Julie Charles, who died of tuberculosis little over a year after Lamartine first met her – are muted and transformed; poems such as 'Invocation', 'L'Isolement', 'Le Soir', 'Le Vallon', 'Le Lac' and 'L'Automne' from the first *Méditations* were all inspired by his grief and despair at her death, yet this personal anguish was couched in terms whose universal resonance clearly struck a chord with his contemporaries. The impact of *Les Méditations* brought Lamartine immediate fame, and despite his later writings on politics, history and fiction and his attempts to write a great modern epic poem (of which *Jocelyn* (1836) and *La Chute d'un ange* (1838) were the only episodes completed), it was the philosophical, meditative poems of that first collection which have come to symbolize the Romantic era.

Later in the century Paul Verlaine was to reintroduce lyricism into French poetry with his own form of intensely personal introspection. His poems reflect little of the outside world; instead, they are an expression of his own emotions and sensations – often melancholy, hesitant and fearful (as in his first collection, *Poèmes saturniens*, 1866). What distinguishes Verlaine's poetry is its subtle musicality, created by refrains and repetitions, assonance, variations in verse form and in particular the continual use of the mute *e* . The poem 'Art poétique' (written 1871–3), which begins 'De la musique avant toute chose', defines his views on prosody.

Melancholy introspection took a more didactic and pessimistic turn in the poems of Alfred de Vigny. Vigny claimed to be the first French poet to express philosophical concepts in epic or dramatic form, and he helped create the myth of the 'poète maudit'* – the poet as an isolated, misunderstood individual of heightened sensibility who, through superior insight, can guide society towards enlightenment. His prose play, *Chatterton* (1835), which portrays the misery and eventual suicide of the English poet, memorably conveys this idea with an image of the poet as a sailor who climbs high above the rest of the crew to the crow's nest, and is the first to sight land and guide the vessel safely to shore. For Vigny, poetry is 'l'écho profond, réel, sincère, des plus hautes conceptions de l'intelligence, des plus mystérieuses impressions de l'âme',† and his poems often use carefully elaborated symbols to convey those impressions. Austere, isolated, visionary, frequently biblical figures (Samson, Moses, Jesus) convey the ideal of stoicism in the face of suffering and persecution, well summed up in the closing lines of one of his best-known poems, 'La Mort du Loup': 'Gémir, pleurer, prier, est également lâche . . . souffre et meurs sans parler.'‡

In the influential preface to his play *Cromwell* (1827), Victor Hugo forcefully argued the case for a renewal of dramatic form. Instead of the classical segregation of genres into tragedy and comedy, he called for a theatrical mingling of the sublime and the grotesque which would reflect, as Shakespeare's plays do, the co-existence in nature of the beautiful and the repugnant. He dismissed conventional,

---

* 'accursed poet'
† 'the real, profound and sincere echo of intelligence's highest concepts and of the soul's most mysterious impressions'
‡ 'To moan, weep or pray is equally cowardly . . . suffer and die in silence.'

noble, theatrical language as 'common', and insisted on using more supple, varied, natural language. It is worth remembering that in 1829 a performance of Vigny's translation of *Othello* could be booed off the stage by an audience brought up with classical tastes and outraged at the use of such indelicate words as 'mouchoir'.* In the *Préface de Cromwell* the classical unities of time and place were rejected on grounds of *invraisemblance* (lack of verisimilitude), while the importance of local colour to define the setting was claimed as an essential element of dramatic truth.

In *Hernani* (1830), which opened to heated controversy, Hugo successfully put these principles into practice. The hero of that play, like many others of the period, is a proud but anguished outsider whose predicament is that he has no fixed centre or identity. Dogged by fate, constantly questioning his position, and guided by codes of honour which are of dubious value in the unstable world around him, he feels himself propelled into an obscure but doomed future:

> *Où vais-je? Je ne sais. Mais je me sens poussé*
> *D'un souffle impétueux, d'un destin insensé.*
> *Je descends, je descends, et jamais ne m'arrête.*†

The one positive value in the play is the power of love, yet Hernani and Doña Sol's overwhelming passion for one another can be realized only in death.

The 1830s saw a profusion of plays such as Alfred de Musset's *Les Caprices de Marianne* (1833), *Fantasio* (1834) and *Lorenzaccio* (1834), Alexandre Dumas *père*'s *Antony* (1831), and Vigny's *Chatterton* (1835) – all of which explore the problems of their melancholy, misunderstood heroes. Hugo himself continued writing for the stage with dramas in prose – including *Lucrèce Borgia* (1833) and *Marie Tudor* (1833) – and in verse – *Le Roi s'amuse* (1832), *Ruy Blas* (1838) – until the failure of his over-elaborate *Les Burgraves* in 1843. With their manipulation of dramatic suspense, their focus on problems of

---

* 'handkerchief'
† 'Where am I going? I do not know. But I feel myself blown onwards
  By a raging wind, by a senseless destiny.
  I go down and down, and never stop.'

identity and their tragic endings, these plays combine lyricism and melodrama with deep moral seriousness.

Self-questioning, inward-looking tendencies are also evident in the psychological novels (*romans d'analyse*), which are often partly autobiographical in content. One of the most prolific authors of such novels was George Sand (pseudonym of Amandine-Aurore-Lucie Dupin). Although she was later to deny that *Indiana* (1832), her first successful novel, was based on her own experience, its theme of the unhappily married woman who defies social conventions to find love and happiness outside marriage has clear echoes in her own life. It proclaims the purifying value of love, and was the first of several of her novels from this period to assert women's right to independence. Like the romantic dramatists, Sand presents love as a passion beyond the reach of the ordinary moral laws of society. For example, in *Jacques* (1835), the husband is willing to kill himself so that his wife may be united with her lover; his suicide is a legitimate action because it removes the lovers' impediment, and the lovers bear no responsibility: 'Ils ne sont pas coupables, ils s'aiment. Il n'y a pas de crime où il y a amour sincère.'*

Eugène Fromentin's semi-autobiographical *Dominique* (1863) moves away from that romantic position as it describes how the writer-hero comes to renounce his passion for a married woman and find contentment in work, marriage and family. Yet the obvious tensions that underlie the narrator's protestations of happiness indicate ambivalence about his choice. Despite Dominique's final pragmatism, the novel's first-person narrative, with its inward-looking, meditative tone and subtle psychological analysis, is a late reflection of the Romantic tendency to introspection.

Autobiographical memoirs, in which the main interest lies in the author's emotions and responses to events rather than in the events themselves, are very much a nineteenth-century phenomenon. François-René de Chateaubriand's *Mémoires d'outre-tombe*, published 1849–50, but written between 1811 and 1841, are characterized by the memorable passages of self-revelation which lie alongside his descriptions of political events such as the beginning of the French Revolution or the fall, imprisonment and death of Napoleon. Other

---

* 'They are not guilty, they love one another. There is no crime when love is sincere.'

writers concentrate exclusively on the inner world: Eugénie de Guérin's *Journal intime* (published posthumously in 1862, but written 1834–42) and her brother Maurice's *Cahier vert* (1832–5) are both profoundly introspective. Reminiscences of childhood take on a special significance for many writers, who find a source of their adult self in their often traumatic early memories: Chateaubriand, Lamartine (*Les Confidences*, 1849), Benjamin Constant (*Le Cahier rouge*, published posthumously in 1907), Gérard de Nerval (*Sylvie*, 1854), Stendhal (*La Vie de Henri Brulard*, published posthumously in 1890) and George Sand (*Histoire de ma vie*, 1854–5) are among those who write movingly of their childhood experiences. The latter four all suffered the death of a parent when they were very young, and a sense of unresolved loss runs through their work.

Looking Outward

In 1820 only two out of five Frenchmen could read, but that proportion rose steeply after universal primary education was introduced in 1833–5. The technological innovations in printing and publishing techniques which allowed books to be produced quickly and cheaply helped to feed a huge demand for fiction on the part of the growing middle class. New newspapers started up, and in 1836 *La Presse* (under its flamboyant editor Émile de Girardin) and *Le Siècle* introduced the system of financing their publication by advertising revenue, thus enabling them to be bought by a wider public that could not afford an annual subscription. The introduction of *roman-feuilletons* or serialized novels also increased newspaper sales. Long works of cliff-hanging fiction by authors such as Dumas *père*, Paul Féval, Frédéric Soulié and Pierre-Alexis Ponson du Terrail were published in instalments in daily newspapers, encouraging readers to buy the paper regularly, and in turn creating an eager public when the novels were published in book form. Sometimes these serializations had spectacular success: during *Le Constitutionnel*'s publication of Eugène Sue's *Le Juif errant* in 1844–5, circulation of the newspaper leapt from 3,000 to 40,000. Dumas even found it necessary to set up a mass-production scheme whereby he would draft the outline of a plot and employ hack writers to fill out the chapters. Only in that way could he keep up with demand; his final output was around 270 novels.

This outpouring of fiction was accompanied by much discussion of artistic aims and the relationship between literature and the real world. The debate, which had begun in the 1830s, was a central preoccupation by the mid-1850s. Gustave Courbet, the painter whose work critics had derided as 'réaliste', defiantly entitled his 1855 exhibition 'Le Réalisme'; the following year Philippe Duranty founded the review *Le Réalisme,* and in 1857 Champfleury (pseudonym of Jules Husson or Fleury) published under the same title a volume of essays which applied many of Courbet's artistic theories to literature. The ideas are simple: Realist writers were to aim to represent the truth through close observation of contemporary reality; their subject was to be 'l'homme d'aujourd'hui dans la civilisation moderne';* their style was to be clear; and in contrast to the subjectivity of the Romantics, their presentation was to be impartial – in Champfleury's words, 'Le romancier ne juge pas, ne condamne pas, n'absout pas. Il expose des faits.'† The private letters of writers of the period, and the prefaces which they frequently appended to their novels, indicate how passionate were these attempts to produce and justify their literary theory.

In his preface to *Le Rouge et le Noir* (1831), Stendhal had used an arresting image to justify his depiction of 'la vérité, l'âpre vérité'.‡ He likened the novelist to a man walking down a rough road with a mirror on his back; sometimes the mirror will tilt upwards to reflect blue skies, but sometimes it will tilt down to reflect the mud and ruts of the track. The novelist, said Stendhal, is no more to blame for portraying the ugliness of life than the man is for allowing his mirror to reflect the dirt. Similar protestations against anticipated accusations of immorality preface many novels from the rest of this period, as writers grew increasingly interested in the social ferment around them and became concerned to record details of the real world, base as well as beautiful.

---

* 'the man of today in modern civilization'
† 'The novelist does not judge or condemn or absolve. He sets out facts.'
‡ 'the truth, the bitter truth'

Although Stendhal often repeated this idea that art must imitate reality, he also recognized that a degree of artifice was necessary to create an impression of being true to life. Unlike writers such as Balzac and Flaubert, he avoided using copious detail to convey an illusion of reality. He relied instead on the skilful choice of 'le petit fait vrai' – the telling detail which will capture the essence of a character or scene, often with a comic irony which was not always appreciated by contemporary readers. His narrators often intervene in the narrative to comment on the hero's behaviour. Although Stendhal's main protagonists – proud, solitary young men who die before the novels end – have many of the characteristics of the Romantic hero, they are at odds with a society which is portrayed with an irony and sharpness of focus missing from the mainstream of Romantic writing. *La Chartreuse de Parme* (1839), which tells of intrigues at a small Italian court between 1815 and 1830, wittily contrasts the imagination and dynamism of the central characters with the corrupt and stultifying court life; and in *Le Rouge et le Noir* the intelligent and impulsive young hero, Julien Sorel, shuns his humble rural origins and pursues his ambitions against a sharply drawn background of political and clerical rivalries and social hypocrisy. Stendhal's determination to give his novels the immediacy of the present is reflected in the use of the word 'chronicle', with its overtones of newspaper reporting on current affairs, in *Le Rouge et le Noir*'s subtitle, 'Chronique de 1830' (the year in which the novel was written). Although he drew a famous comparison between the intrusion of politics into the novel and the firing of a pistol-shot in the middle of a concert, Stendhal is constantly aware of a socio-political background to the events of his novels, and analyses it with wry wit.

Honoré de Balzac was more concerned with setting his novels against a minutely recorded background of telling details. In 1833 he had the idea of linking the characters he had already created and those yet to be invented into a vast pageant of French society, which became *La Comédie humaine*. In the 1842 *Avant-propos* to his collected work he acknowledged his debts to naturalists such as Buffon and Geoffroy Saint-Hilaire, and announced that he would apply techniques used in the study of zoology to the exploration of human society. Just as different species evolve in different environments, so humans are seen as deeply influenced by their surroundings, and locked in a struggle for the survival of the fittest. Balzac classified his stories into series (*Études de moeurs, Études philosophiques*) and subdivided the *Études de moeurs* into *Scènes de la vie privée, Scènes de la vie de province, Scènes de la vie parisienne, Scènes de la vie de campagne,* etc. Through his exuberant diversity of characters and situations Balzac paints a vivid and critical picture of French society in times of change. *Le Père Goriot* (1834) opens with a warning to the reader that he or she will be shocked to discover the hidden aspects of Parisian life which the novel will disclose, yet insists that 'All is true'. From the famous description of a seedy Parisian boarding-house whose dilapidated furniture, greasy surfaces and unpleasant smells anticipate the curious mixture of people who live there, the novel traces the initiation into Parisian society of Rastignac, an impoverished young provincial aristocrat. By moving his hero between the guest-house and the grand salons of Paris, Balzac puts him in contact with a cross-section of society including duchesses, bankers, servants, students, criminals and clergy, and reveals the calculated ruthlessness and dishonesty necessary to succeed in that world. There is a moral ambiguity in much of Balzac's writing: his most fascinating characters have a daring creative energy – like the arch-criminal, Vautrin, in *Le Père Goriot, Illusions perdues* (1843) and *La Dernière Incarnation de Vautrin* (1847), or Valérie Marneffe in *La Cousine Bette* (1846) – yet are deeply corrupt and dangerous. Money in all its manifestations – dowries, inheritances, debts, interest, bankers, misers and speculators – is central to his work, acting as a spur to ambition, a focus for corruption, or the cause of destitution. Like the lawyer, the money-lender has a special place in his novels because of his proximity to human misery.

By the 1840s George Sand had abandoned her earlier lyrical mode to write novels which reflected her fascination with the social and political questions of the day. In works such as *Le Compagnon du tour de France* (1841), *Le Meunier d'Angibault* (1845) and *Le Péché de M. Antoine* (1845) she introduces realistic description of industrial change as a background to her rather conventional plots; *La Ville noire* (1860) has claims to be the first French working-class novel, and uses first-hand evidence about the cutlery-makers of Thiers. Her letters, particularly those she exchanged with Gustave Flaubert, offer fascinating insights into her thoughts on literature and society; those expressing her shock and despair as the Commune crushed her long-held social optimism are especially poignant.

Flaubert himself was hailed as leader of the Realist movement, yet he scornfully disclaimed any association with it. As is generally the case with such labels, the finest writers resist classification. It is true that his novels do possess many of the characteristics associated with Realism: there are virtually no authorial interventions (Flaubert once wrote that the author should be like God in the universe, omnipresent, but nowhere visible); he chooses settings in the recent past for *Madame Bovary* (1857), *L'Éducation sentimentale* (1869) – which vividly evokes the atmosphere surrounding the 1848 revolution – and *Bouvard et Pécuchet* (1881); and his narrative is full of minute physical details of everyday life, such as the advertising hoardings, pavements crowded with umbrella-carrying pedestrians, boilers of bubbling asphalt and the smell of gas-lights in one evocation of a Parisian street. Yet, as his correspondence shows, Flaubert's main concern was with style. Working on *Madame Bovary*, he famously wrote of his ambition to write 'un livre sur rien'.* That novel, which tells the story of a young woman's inability to reconcile her dreams of passion and glamour – largely inspired by her reading of romantic literature – with the mediocrity of her existence as a country doctor's wife, has an essentially simple plot. But by subtle shifts in narrative perspective and meticulous attention to the ironies and inadequacies of language as well as of character, Flaubert transforms an almost banal plot into a masterpiece of French literature.

The brothers Edmond and Jules de Goncourt took the principles of Realism to extreme lengths. For them, the novelist was 'le raconteur du présent'† who must draw on close observation of reality and be unafraid to show the sordid side of life. One of their most striking works is *Germinie Lacerteux* (1864), a detailed account of the psychological and physical degeneration of a servant as she

---

* 'a book about nothing'
† 'the story-teller of the present'

devotedly cares for her elderly mistress. This closely observed case study is based on one of their own servants, who had lived with them and served them faithfully for many years while leading a life of increasing debauchery and debt; ironically, the observant brothers discovered the truth about her double life only after she died. For other novels they explored further afield and carefully researched their subjects, showing as much interest in analysing the hidden workings of the mind as in recording physical details. After Jules's death in 1870, Edmond continued to write in the same vein. *Madame Gervaisais* (1869) is a study of religious mania, set in Rome; *La Fille Élisa* (1877) tells the story of a prostitute imprisoned for murder; and *Les Frères Zemganno* (1879) combines an analysis of the deeper levels of brotherly love with an account of circus life.

After the decline of Romantic drama in the early 1840s, theatrical writing came to be dominated by a concern to portray contemporary society, either in lighthearted depictions of social stereotypes and mannerisms, or in serious, often didactic dramas analysing social and moral attitudes. The Romantics' portrayal of grand passions which could sweep aside the normal conventions of society gave way to more sober reflections on contemporary social issues. In *La Dame aux camélias* (dramatized in 1852 from his highly successful 1848 novel of the same name), Alexandre Dumas *fils* portrays the deep love between Marguerite Gautier, a courtesan (based on the well-known courtesan Marie Duplessis) and Armand Duval, a respectably middle-class young man. At the request of Armand's father Marguerite renounces her lover so that his sister's proposed marriage will not be jeopardized by scandal. Although the father finally relents after recognizing Marguerite's moral purity, the lovers' reconciliation at the end of the play comes too late and she dies of consumption. In its exploration of contemporary issues such as prostitution, family values, the plight of a woman on her own and the difficulty of finding a compromise between society and the individual, *La Dame aux camélias* marks a turning point in French theatre. Léonie d'Aunet (who was imprisoned for adultery with Victor Hugo and lost her children, friends and financial support as a result) was one of the rare women to write about such issues from her own experience. In her play *Jane Osborn* (1855) she movingly and defiantly portrays the problems facing an unmarried mother at that period. Dumas's own continuing preoccupation with questions of social reform is reflected in the titles of many of the well-constructed plays, such as *Le Demi-Monde* (1855), *La Question d'argent* (1857) and *Le Fils naturel* (1858), which followed his first theatrical success.

Like Dumas, Émile Augier sets his plays firmly within a contemporary, middle-class context, defending the bourgeois values of moral integrity, hard work, marital fidelity and filial respect while at the same time poking fun at the weaknesses of his characters and sharply criticizing social pretensions, vulgar display and political corruption. In *Le Gendre de M. Poirier* (1854), on which Augier collaborated with Jules Sandeau, the clash of values between the hereditary aristocracy and bourgeois *nouveaux riches* is wittily and entertainingly explored, although the play's happy ending is brought about at the expense of any clear resolution of the two classes' relative merits. Augier is particularly critical of financial greed, and in plays such as *Le Mariage d'Olympe*, *Ceinture dorée* (both 1855) and *Les Effrontés* (1861) he uses stock-market speculators, fraudulent social climbers and dishonest dealers to evoke materialistic excess, while continuing to uphold the bourgeois values of probity, thrift and domestic stability. Like most French playwrights of the time, Augier was influenced by Eugène Scribe, who was probably the most successful French dramatist of the first half of the nineteenth century, producing over 300 plays. The influence of his comedies and vaudevilles derived less from their subject-matter, which was often superficial, than from Scribe's gift for constructing a 'well-made play'. His sound craftsmanship enabled him to create ingenious plots out of trivial subjects while sustaining the audience's interest throughout the intricate action.

Eugène Labiche also tackles contemporary bourgeois foibles in his witty, good-natured comedies while astutely evoking the industrial and financial changes of the period. *Le Voyage de Monsieur Perrichon* (1860), for example, opens with a comic scene in a railway station as Monsieur Perrichon (a coach-builder) and his family anxiously prepare for their first rail journey, which will take them to the Alps to visit the fashionable Mer de Glace.

That Labiche should have chosen to begin his play in this way is a reflection of the upsurge of travel – and travel writing – in this period. In *Voyage d'une femme au Spitzberg* (1854) Léonie d'Aunet, who was probably the first European woman to cross Lapland, published an account of her part (at the age of 19) in the famous 1839 voyage of discovery to Spitzbergen. But the expansion in travel during this period was generally of a less arduous kind. The development of the railway system naturally helped to make travelling a real and relatively comfortable possibility for a wider, though still elite public, and travel reviews such as *Revue des voyages* and *Le Journal des voyages* helped to popularize the idea of travel beyond the frontiers of France. By 1864 a medical guide for travellers noted that travel was one of the most striking characteristics of nineteenth-century France, and one of its 'most intense and active passions'. The grandiose and didactic mode of earlier generations of travel writers such as Chardin, Volney and Chateaubriand gave way to a new wave of travel writing from authors who included Gautier, Nerval, Dumas and Arsène Houssaye. Their simpler, more immediate and often humorous tone is perhaps best exemplified by Gautier, whose travel writings include descriptions of Spain (*Tra los montes*, 1843; renamed *Voyage en Espagne*, 1845), England (*Caprices et zigzags*, 1845) and Russia (*Voyage en Russie*, 1867). There was particular interest in the Middle East, as Lamartine's *Voyage en Orient* (1835), Nerval's *Voyage en Orient* (1848–51), Fromentin's *Un Été dans le Sahara* (1859) and *Une Année dans le Sahel* (1859), and Flaubert's *Notes de voyage* all demonstrate; in his *Dictionnaire des idées reçues* Flaubert offers the tongue-in-cheek definition of an Orientalist as an 'Homme qui a beaucoup voyagé'.* Many writers of imaginative literature drew on the vogue for oriental exoticism. Works as widely spaced as Hugo's 1829 collection of poems *Les Orientales*, Flaubert's Carthaginian novel *Salammbô* (1862) and *La Tentation de saint Antoine* (1874), at which he worked on and off for nearly thirty years, attest to the abiding fascination of the Orient for French writers of this period.

---

* 'man who has travelled a lot'

Looking Back

One important response to the rapid changes in French society since the Revolution of 1789 was a renewal of interest in history. If the events of the present seemed confused and disturbing, it was felt they might begin to make sense when seen in relation to events of the past. Napoleon and later governments encouraged the expansion of historical and philological studies by creating chairs of history in every university, and every field of endeavour was touched by the new historical sense. Chateaubriand, looking back over the changes in French historiography in the preface to his *Études historiques* (1831), saw post-Revolutionary historical writing as falling into two main categories, which he called 'fataliste' and 'descriptive'. The so-called fatalist school, headed by François-Auguste Mignet, Adolphe Thiers and François Guizot, aimed to explain and to present general truths, rather than to offer colourful narrative. They produced political histories which focused on institutions and parties, and they stressed the need for rigour and authenticity, insisting on the 'vérité des faits eux-mêmes'.* Their aim was to concentrate on the central points, stripping away inessential detail to present an objective account of humanity's slow but inevitable progress towards the goal assigned by Providence. Thiers, in the preface to his *Histoire de la révolution française* (1823–7), went so far as to discount all previous attempts to write a history of the Revolutionary period on the grounds that the authors had been directly or indirectly involved in the events they described: their accounts were therefore to be dismissed as memoirs lacking the objectivity of true history.

On the other hand, 'descriptive' historians, such as Brugière de Barante, Jules Michelet, Edgar Quinet, Victor Cousin and Jacques Thierry, were concerned with making history come alive for the reader. These historians demanded a strong emotional involvement with the subject in order to achieve what Michelet called the '*résurrection de la vie intégrale*, non pas dans ses surfaces, mais dans ses organismes intérieurs et profonds'.† Rejecting the fatalistic approach,

---

* 'truth of the facts themselves'
† '*resurrection of life in its entirety*, not in its surface details, but in its deep, inner organisms'

they contended that moral judgements should be applied both to present social action and to past history. Whereas the 'fatalists' wrote almost exclusively about France, 'descriptive' historians' interests were wider-ranging. Influenced by Giambattista Vico, whose *Scienza nuova* (1752) was first translated into French by Michelet in 1827, they sought to include a broad sweep of background information in order to build up a composite picture which, in its complexity, would give a true and profound record of the life of the times. Vico's contention that all aspects of a culture must be used to throw light on a historical period was quickly seized on and became one of the foremost characteristics of historical writing in the mid-century, and these historians systematically and unashamedly borrowed techniques from the novel in order to achieve their aim of bringing the past to life.

Following on the immense popularity of Sir Walter Scott's novels (first translated into French in 1816), there were continual attempts throughout the 1820s and 1830s to formulate the purpose and problems of bringing together history and fiction. Many novelists argued that historical fiction could show the hidden movements of history by suggesting causes and tracing their outcome in a way that was closed to the historian, who was constrained by having to rely on already existing material. Alfred de Vigny commented in his 1827 preface to *Cinq-Mars* (1826) that in art, probability is more important than truth, and so the novelist can go beyond *le vrai* of the historian to arrive at a more profound or universal truth – *la vérité*. But on matters of detail they were divided: should a writer portray real historical characters, or would their appearance overwhelm the action? To what extent should an author strive for historical accuracy? Should one try to convey the language of a distant period, and how could this be done without making the work unintelligible?

Some authors were less concerned with the niceties of historical accuracy than with creating gripping plots full of passion and intrigue. In *Les Misérables* (1862), for example, Hugo intersperses a vast and complicated tale of drama and suspense with descriptions of historical events such as the Battle of Waterloo and the July Revolution, but the novel's interest lies far more in the fate of the characters than in the historical context. This tendency is particularly clear in the case of the Romantic dramatists, who used momentous and stirring events from the historical past to heighten their portrayal of the emotional anguish of their characters (see also page 126). Audiences were willing to overlook the liberties taken with historical authenticity if they were moved by the highly charged situation: tragic love, poignant disguise and unexpected recognitions, dilemmas of honour, acts of bravery and sacrifice. At the same time, the 'local colour' of historical costumes and sets provided visual impact, and in plays such as Hugo's *Marion de Lorme* (1829 – set in the reign of Louis XIII), *Hernani* (1830 – set under Charles V), *Lucrèce Borgia* and *Marie Tudor* (both 1833) the author indicates how the characters are to be dressed and how the stage is to be set. Alfred de Musset's historical plays, *André del Sarto* (1833) and *Lorenzaccio* (1834), were originally written to be read rather than performed, and are more reflective and personal than Hugo's dramas. But Musset has taken advantage of his freedom from the restrictions of staging to conjure up a picture of sixteenth-century Florence where both characters and action are firmly rooted in history.

Alexandre Dumas *père*, whose historical dramas, including *Henri III et sa cour* (1829) and *La Tour de Nesle* (1832), were hailed as triumphs for Romanticism, met with equal success when he turned to writing historical novels in the late 1830s. His immensely popular *Les Trois Mousquetaires* (1844) and its sequels *Vingt Ans après* (1845) and *Le Vicomte de Bragelonne* (1848–50) use the courts of Louis XIII and XIV as a backdrop for the dashing exploits of his invented characters. Many contemporary readers saw the historical novel as an easy and entertaining way of learning about the past – an attitude made fun of by Mérimée in asides to the reader in his *Chronique du règne de Charles IX* (1829), and by Flaubert who notes, tongue in cheek, in his *Dictionnaire des idées reçues* that whereas novel-reading corrupts the masses, historical novels are permissible because they teach history. (The historical novels produced by the long collaboration of Émile Erckmann and Alexandre Chatrian were popular as school prizes.) But a more common didactic role for the historical novel was as a vehicle for the author's own ideas. Vigny's prejudice in favour of the nobility colours *Cinq-Mars*; Hugo stated that he wanted *Notre-Dame de Paris* (1831) to stimulate public interest in medieval French architecture; and in *Sur Catherine de Médicis* (1842–3) Balzac uses the St Bartholomew's Day massacre to explore his views on recent events in France. Less directly, Flaubert's *Salammbô*, with its graphic and meticulously researched account of the mercenary revolt against the Carthaginians after the First Punic War, can be seen as an expression of the author's reactions to the 1848 Revolution.

For some writers the historical past was less a source of understanding recent events in France than a refuge from what they felt to be the ugliness of the modern world. In the case of Théophile Gautier, for example, the heavily researched period detail – Pompeii in *Arria Marcella* (1852), Ancient Egypt in *Le Roman de la momie* (1858), seventeenth-century France in *Le Capitaine Fracasse* (1863) – has more in keeping with his pursuit of an impersonal ideal of beauty than with any desire to make comparisons with recent French history. In his influential preface to *Mademoiselle de Maupin* (1835) Gautier had argued the case against utilitarian, moralizing or didactic literature: 'Il n'y a de vraiment beau que ce qui ne sert à rien.'* The pursuit of art for art's sake often coincided with the choice of subjects from the distant past, and from antiquity in particular, and it seems likely that that choice was often a *fugue* from the present. In his collection of poems *Émaux et camées* (1852), many of which evoke images from classical antiquity, Gautier describes how he has shut himself away from the political storms outside to concentrate on his finely chiselled poetry. Gautier's literary theories influenced the Parnassian group of poets, who aimed to write impassive, impeccably formed poetry often evoking immobilized moments from the distant past. The leader of the Parnassians was Leconte de Lisle, who believed that the morally and socially harmonious society of which he dreamed was prefigured in Ancient Greece, and his *Poèmes antiques* (1852) reflect his idea that poetry should return to the 'sources éternellement pures'† of antiquity in order to recover its past dignity. Rejecting all links between poetry and the contemporary world of politics and social mediocrity, he hoped that by studying recent historical and philological research

---

* 'Only that which has no function is truly beautiful.'
† 'eternally pure sources'

he could become 'une sorte de contemporain de chaque époque'*
and so evoke it accurately and objectively.

The preoccupation with history, so characteristic of this period,
clearly manifested itself in writings about the past, but paradoxically
it also influenced the way in which many writers wrote about the
present. If examining the historical past was seen as a way of
explaining or understanding the present, so the present came to be
seen as history in the making, and had to be recorded for posterity.
Balzac described French society as a historian supplying him with
information which he would record like a secretary. He intended his
Comédie humaine (see pages 130–1) to be the great social record of
nineteenth-century France, and regretted that the civilizations of
antiquity had not left behind a similar account of their times. His
novels contain frequent references to aspects of French life which are
about to vanish for ever – the opening pages of *Illusions perdues*
(1837–43), for example, give a detailed description of the workings
and terminology of an obsolescent printing press. Time and again
novelists of this period describe their works, set in the immediate
present or immediate past, as contemporary history. Émile Zola
asserted that *L'Assommoir* (1877), his working-class novel depicting a
laundress's decline into alcoholism and destitution, was a work of
great historical and social interest, and his Rougon-Macquart series of
novels was to depict 'l'Histoire naturelle et sociale d'une famille sous
le second Empire'† (see also pages 149 – 50). The work of Edmond and
Jules de Goncourt (see also pages 132–3) includes social histories of
France during the Revolution and the Directory, and important
writings on art history, such as their *L'Art du dix-huitième siècle*
(1859–75). That historical perspective finds an echo in their belief that
their closely documented novels of contemporary life depicted
'history which might have happened'. They considered their novels
to reveal 'l'Histoire morale contemporaine';‡ and their great *Journal*,
too, is a consciously historical record. Recognizing the interest to
posterity of the circles in which they moved, they transcribe their
conversations and record events as they happened, providing a mine

---

* 'a sort of contemporary of each period'
† 'the natural and social history of one family under the Second Empire'
‡ 'contemporary moral history'

of fascinating information about writers and artists of the day. With a similarly acute awareness of having lived through a period of political, literary and artistic change, Maxime Du Camp records his experiences for posterity both in *Souvenirs de l'année 1848* (1876) and in *Souvenirs littéraires* (1881), where he looks back over his long involvement with Flaubert and other major literary figures of the day.

Looking Beyond

The period 1820–80 was one of rapidly expanding knowledge. Ampère's important work on electromagnetism dates from the 1820s, as does much of the exploration of evolutionary theories by biologists such as Lamarck, Cuvier and Geoffroy Saint-Hilaire. Discoveries by chemists like Gay-Lussac and Berthelot pushed forward the boundaries of their subject, and Niepce and Daguerre pioneered photography. Photographic techniques developed so swiftly that by the early years of the Second Empire Parisians were flocking to Nadar's studio to have their portraits taken; a vivid and extensive photograpic record exists of contemporary scenes and personalities from the 1850s on. By 1858 Nadar was combining his enthusiasms for photography and flight by experimenting with aerial photographs taken from a balloon, and during the siege of Paris he used hot-air balloons to send sackfuls of letters out of the capital – the world's first airmail. Claude Bernard's lucid explanation of the rules of experimental medicine in his *Introduction à la médecine expérimentale* (1865) caught the public imagination, and Pasteur's work on fermentation, antisepsis and bacterial action transformed medical practice. This scientific revolution challenged many fundamental assumptions and encouraged widespread confidence in the potential of science and technology to push beyond the limits of the known and improve the human condition. Although Flaubert spoke for many when he warned against excessive faith in scientific progress in his depiction of the preposterous chemist, Homais, in *Madame Bovary,* much of the literature of this period is strongly marked by an interest in scientific developments and method – the novels of Balzac and Zola are obvious examples, as are Hippolyte Taine's wide-ranging critical studies, in which he argued that literature should be a 'collection of experiments' which would expose the underlying physical and psychological reasons for human behaviour.

The restless dissatisfaction with the status quo which characterizes the political turmoil of this period, and from which the drive to expand the known universe through scientific investigation perhaps also stems, manifested itself in other ways. A number of humanitarian thinkers sought the transformation of society through religion. Lamennais argued that society's salvation could come only in a liberal democracy subordinated to the supreme authority of Catholicism, and in his *Paroles d'un croyant* (1834) he expressed these utopian ideas in such a sweeping, messianic style that the typesetters were said to have been moved to tears as they prepared the work for the press. Traditional religion was felt by many to be wanting, and new religious sects, from Swedenborgians to Étienne Cabet's utopian 'Icarians', sprang up. Some thinkers, such as the positivist philosopher Auguste Comte, emphasized the social role of their new religion, while others like Victor Cousin stressed the need for guiding metaphysical concepts. Cousin, for example, advocated a 'natural religion' based on reverence of that which is *vrai, beau* and *bien*.*

In a climate of such experimental religious ferment, it is hardly surprising that a visionary, mystical current should run through much of the literature of this period. In some authors such as Balzac, it co-exists with a more sober determination to describe the observable world of contemporary reality. Impressed by the mystical doctrines of Swedenborg, Balzac claimed in his mysterious novel *Séraphita* (1835) that 'Nous sommes nés pour tendre au ciel.'† Our lives are driven by mysterious forces, he argues, and the role of his miraculous central character, who is both male and female, is to reveal the path to heaven so that we may penetrate beyond the realms of the known and aspire to hidden, mystic truths. Even in a novel set as firmly in contemporary French society as is *La Peau de chagrin* (1831), Balzac explores the operation of irrational, super-

---

* true, beautiful and good   † 'We were born to strive towards heaven.'

natural forces, while in *Louis Lambert* (1832–5), which purports to be the biography of a fellow student at the College de Vendôme, he probes into aspects of illuminism and the occult.

The fantastic, with its freedom from the restrictions of everyday life, enabled writers to give free rein to their imagination. At the same time it served as a warning to readers that things might not be as safe and predictable as they thought. Exploring the regions of the mind that are usually kept secret, and exploiting the powers of the imagination to their fullest, writers drew inspiration from dreams, hallucinations and even madness in their quest to challenge the boundaries of experience.

Charles Nodier was one of the first writers of the period to exploit the irrational as a literary source, realizing that 'la voie du fantastique pris au sérieux serait tout à fait nouvelle'.* In his short story 'Smarra ou les démons de la nuit' (1821), inspired by Apuleius's *Golden Ass,* he used the free association of dreams to explore the intense and unfamiliar visions of a mind liberated from the constraints of reason. In essays such as 'Du fantastique en littérature' (1830) and 'De quelques phénomènes du sommeil' (1831 – both published in *La Revue de Paris*) he elaborated his idea that literature may be expanded and enriched by tapping the realms of dream and fantasy.

The poet Nerval combined dream and hallucination with images from the real world; he described his sonnets as a kind of supernatural reverie, and his work shows the influence of his wide reading in esoteric doctrines, theosophy, illuminism, mesmerism and other mystical and occult writings. His aptly named collection of prose and poetry, *Le Rêve et la vie* (1855), includes 'Aurélia', an account of hallucination and delirium where the writer records various stages of his mental derangement in language of great clarity and beauty. In one passage, in what he calls an 'épanchement du songe dans la vie réelle',† he describes the sensation of being drawn upwards by a distant star towards a realm of infinite wonder and mystery, then suddenly finding himself back in a Paris street surrounded by a solicitous night patrol. Nodier and Nerval's desire to push beyond the limits of everyday reality and explore the

---

* 'the fantastic, taken seriously, would be completely new'
† 'outpouring of dream into real life'

recesses of the human psyche points forward to the work of Lautréamont (pseudonym of Isidore Ducasse), whose lyrical prose fragments, *Les Chants de Maldoror* (1868), contain nightmarish, hallucinatory and often horrifying imagery; Lautréamont was to be claimed by the Surrealists as one of their precursors.

The urge to reach out beyond the boundaries of the known is expressed differently but no less intensely by the poet Charles Baudelaire. In 'Le Voyage', the last poem in his collection *Les Fleurs du mal* (1857), Baudelaire's traveller voices his disappointment that, despite the wonders he has seen on his travels, he can never truly escape from the world, which he describes as 'monotone et petit'.* The poem ends with him eager to travel on into death in the hope that in that realm of the unknown he may at last find 'du *nouveau*'.† Throughout *Les Fleurs du mal* Baudelaire expresses a longing to push beyond the limits of human experience and reach out for some elusive absolute. Yet while he sees this impulse as evidence of humanity's highest dignity and an essential source of creativity, he also recognizes the terrifying obstacles that hold individuals back. The tension between creative yearning and the destructive forces of lethargy, apathy and mediocrity lie at the core of the collection. Baudelaire was convinced that the creative artist could distil beauty from the most unpromising sources, once commenting that his poetry could transform mud into gold. But certain of his poems shocked the establishment, and only a few months after the unsuccessful prosecution of *Madame Bovary* for indecency, a number of the poems in *Les Fleurs du mal* were banned as blasphemous and obscene. Baudelaire's pursuit of the new and his desire to avoid the commonplace led him to explore new techniques as well as new subject-matter, and he experimented with prose poems, abandoning verse form in favour of increased suppleness and tonal variation in his beautiful *Petits Poèmes en prose* (1869). His suggestive and personal use of symbols, his view of the external world as the expression of a spiritual essence and his concept of synaesthesia (the ability of one sense impression to convey another, vividly evoked in his sonnet 'Correspondances') all left a profound influence on later nineteenth-century poetry.

---

* 'monotonous and small'   † 'something *new*'

Baudelaire was considered by the adolescent poet Arthur Rimbaud to be the king of poets. But Rimbaud's own writing is much stranger, more energetic and unconstrained than Baudelaire's, and is characterized by a spirit of revolt against authority in any form, whether God, Napoleon III, his mother, the local librarian, or poetic convention itself. In one of his most celebrated poems, 'Le Bateau ivre' of 1871, he imagines himself as a boat drifting wildly down rivers and across oceans, and, in haunting and violent imagery which defies logical analysis, conveys both his need for total freedom and his vulnerability. In Rimbaud's view, the poet must be an instrument of change, and in two famous letters to friends (the 'lettres du Voyant') he expresses his conviction that the poet must submit himself to every kind of experience, however vile, and through a 'long, immense et raisonné dérèglement de tous les sens',* dissolve the distinctions between the inner and outer world. Thus he hopes to achieve a visionary state which will lead to the discovery of universal truths. *Une Saison en enfer* (1873) charts the course of these experiments. New ideas demanded new forms of expression, he believed; *Une Saison en enfer* and *Les Illuminations* (published 1886) are written in often obscure but compellingly vivid prose in which imagination and reality are strangely mixed as the poet strives to capture his tumultuous visions. Although the richly allusive vigour of Rimbaud's poetry has provided inspiration for many twentieth-century writers, his imaginative and rebellious writing is perhaps the ultimate expression of the restless, questing turbulence of this period of revolutionary change.

---

* 'long, immense and rational disturbance of all the senses'

Further Reading

D.G. Charlton (ed.), *The French Romantics*, 2 vols (Cambridge: Cambridge University Press, 1984).

Alison Fairlie, *Imagination and Language. Collected Essays on Constant, Baudelaire, Nerval and Flaubert*, ed. Malcolm Bowie (Cambridge: Cambridge University Press, 1981).

F.W.J. Hemmings (ed.), *The Age of Realism* (Harmondsworth: Penguin, 1974).

Linda Nochlin, *Realism* (Harmondsworth: Penguin, 1971).

Claude Pichois, *Le Romantisme. Vol. II: 1843–1869* (Paris: Arthaud, 1979).

Brian Rigby (ed.), *French Literature, Thought and Culture in the Nineteenth Century: A Material World. Essays in Honour of D.G. Charlton*, Warwick Studies in the European Humanities (Basingstoke and London: Macmillan, 1993).

CHAPTER 7

The Late Nineteenth and Early Twentieth Centuries (1880–1940)

TOBY GARFITT

By 1880 the Third Republic had got over its early jitters. The conservative, monarchist president, Marshal MacMahon, had been replaced in the previous year by the moderate Republican Jules Grévy. The heritage of the French Revolution was affirmed by the readoption of the Marseillaise as the national anthem and of 14 July, Bastille Day, as the national festival. The principle of compulsory, free, non-religious primary education for all was quickly established. A decade of political scandals in the 1890s, of which the most important was the Dreyfus affair (essentially a tussle between those who believed that it was quite wrong to make one probably innocent Jewish officer a scapegoat in a case of espionage, and those who believed equally fervently that the honour of the army must not be challenged at any cost), gave way to a more settled period of domination by the Radical Party, when the newly acquired colonial empire was consolidated. The Paris of this 'Belle Époque' seemed to be the capital of the civilized world. The nightmare of the First World War brought about neither a change of constitution (the Third Republic survived until 1940) nor a diminution of the role of Paris, but the stability had been fatally undermined. A decade of frenzied creativity was followed by one of serious questioning in the face of economic problems (the Wall Street crash), political threat (the rise of fascism in Italy, Germany and Spain) and doubts about the post-war order of the world.

Naturalism and After: 1880–1910

The 1880s were dominated by the novel. The critic Sainte-Beuve's prediction of 'industrial literature' (in an article in 1839) came true. Advances in paper-making and printing technology (see also page 128), improved communications, and the equation of education with progress all favoured the production of huge amounts of reading matter. Much of this was in the form of *romans-feuilletons* serialized in newspapers before being published in book form, continuing the tradition of Sue's *Mystères de Paris* and Ponson du Terrail's *Rocambole* series. Among the most prominent of these *feuilletonistes* were Montépin, who wrote 140 novels with titles like *Les Deux Orphelines* (1874), Mérouvel, whose *Chaste et flétrie* (1889) was often reprinted, and Féval, with over 200 novels to his name. Several of them managed to combine popular appeal and a measure of genuine literary value. If Ohnet's *Serge Panine* (1881) and *Le Maître de forges* (1882: a novel, soon turned into an equally successful play, featuring an industrialist who turns out to be surprisingly sensitive), which outsold even Zola's most successful works, were sneered at by some critics, Daudet was praised for his light-hearted mockery of *méridional* boastfulness in *Les Aventures prodigieuses de Tartarin de Tarascon* (1872) and its sequels. Verne's scientific adventure stories, which (with their striking red-and-gold covers) helped to form the literary taste of generations of children, are increasingly being recognized as far more than merely children's tales.

In addition, two books published in 1878 had the distinction of being read by almost every French schoolchild in the following half-century: *Sans famille*, Malot's novel about a foundling boy, which was rapidly adopted as a reading book in the new primary schools, and *Le Tour de France par deux enfants*, by 'G. Bruno' (actually Madame

Fouillée, the wife of a prominent philosopher), commissioned as a textbook but as exciting as any adventure novel.

Zola was a professional journalist who exploited the link between the *feuilleton* and the book to achieve huge sales. He used the first as publicity for the second, insisting that the book should appear as soon as possible after the serialized version. After the colossal success of *L'Assommoir* (1877), with its evocation of working-class life in Paris (see page 140), Zola never looked back. *Nana* (1880), the sequel to *L'Assommoir*, which charts the career of Gervaise's daughter as a prostitute who eventually vows to ruin 'les classes d'en haut',* sold nearly 200,000 copies before Zola's death in 1902, and even that record was beaten by *La Débâcle* (1892), a novel about the Franco-Prussian War. He was the first writer to formulate an aesthetic based specifically on the novel. Realism had had as much to do with the visual arts as with literature (see page 129), but the naturalism which Zola promoted from as early as 1866 was essentially concerned with the novel. Rather than rejecting previous literary movements, Zola claimed that they were precursors of Naturalism: 'le romantisme apparaît comme le début logique de la grande évolution naturaliste'† ('Lettre à la jeunesse', in *Le Roman expérimental*, 1880). Naturalism was to be simply the application to the novel of the contemporary disciplines of scientific observation. The world should be described in detail, exactly as it was, and human characters studied in terms of their conditioning by heredity and the environment, even if that made them seem like animals (as in *Thérèse Raquin*, 1867). Zola appealed to various recent scientific works, and also to the evolutionary theory propounded by Taine in relation to literature. Many of his ideas had in fact already been exploited by the Goncourt brothers, who had begun as historians of eighteenth-century art and society and had then turned to documenting their own times in their *Journal* and in novels (see also pages 132–3). Their preface to *Germinie Lacerteux* (1864) claimed that the novel was the equivalent of 'l'Histoire morale contemporaine'.‡

---

* 'the upper classes'
† 'Romanticism can be seen as the logical beginning of the great move towards naturalism.'
‡ 'the history of contemporary manners'

Zola's mixture of popular science, sex, violence and working-class subjects proved irresistible, even if the idea of the novel as a scientific experiment was questionable. His imagination was far too fertile to be confined by the framework he had chosen, in any case, and his journalistic fervour in the service of a simple socialist message was hardly that of a detached observer. It is perhaps best to see his claim that the novelist is a kind of experimental scientist as an example of his remarkable images, like that of the pit in *Germinal* (1885) as a devouring creature. Indeed, his monumental Rougon-Macquart series of twenty novels, subtitled 'Histoire naturelle et sociale d'une famille sous le Second Empire',* is based on an image: the rise and fall of the family represents the rise and fall of the regime.

Zola's Naturalism, for all its pretensions to modern scientific detachment, was personal to him, and he had no real disciples. His subject-matter and documentary approach were widely copied, but few matched his visionary power or the vitality of his language, based to some extent on real speech patterns, or the breadth of his coverage of society, from the new urban underclass to the world of politics and high finance (in *La Curée*, 1872) and that of the Impressionist painters (in *L'Oeuvre*, 1886).

A group of writers whom Zola had encouraged brought out a volume of short stories in his honour, *Les Soirées de Médan* (1880), but within a few years most of them had moved away from his brand of Naturalism. Maupassant's 'Boule de suif' first appeared in that collection. Maupassant had earlier come under the influence of Flaubert, and Naturalism was only a convenient stage in his writing career. His novels, including *Bel-Ami* (1885) and *Pierre et Jean* (1888), convey a cruel sense of the inevitable disillusionment of human existence, quite different from the underlying optimism of Zola with his myth of regeneration, while his hundreds of skilful short stories often reveal a tragic or disturbingly bizarre twist to the most ordinary situation. Huysmans, another member of the Médan group, pushed Naturalism to its extreme in the exotic inventories of Des Esseintes's house in *A rebours* (1884), a novel in which description is at the service of a new aesthetic of decadence. Naturalism was being explicitly rejected by erstwhile admirers of Zola, and in 1887 several

---

* 'the natural and social history of a family under the Second Empire'

of them signed a manifesto repudiating the coarseness of his portrayal of the peasantry in *La Terre*. Maupassant's preface to *Pierre et Jean* contains the claim that 'les Réalistes de talent devraient s'appeler plutôt des Illusionnistes':* the idea of an objective description is simply untenable. In the opening pages of Huysmans's *Là-bas* (1891) Durtal criticizes the Naturalist novel for its repetitive inventories and its utter sterility.

What was the way forward? Looking for what he calls a 'naturalisme spiritualiste',† Durtal mentions the name of Dosto-evsky, whose works (along with those of Tolstoy) had just been translated into French, but it was to be another twenty years before Dostoevsky's influence became important. The anti-naturalist reaction was initially to take the form either of a rediscovery of Western spirituality or of a renewal of the French psychological novel (*roman d'analyse*) by an appeal to modern psychology. Huysmans himself followed the former path, ending up by writing novels which celebrate medieval Christian art (*En route*, 1895; *La Cathédrale*, 1898), as did Bloy, with his powerful indictments of contemporary secularism (*Le Désespéré*, 1887; *La Femme pauvre*, 1897) which prefigure Bernanos. Bourget's *Le Disciple* (1889) combines the study of a dilemma of conscience with an attack on the philosophical tradition of positivism that underlay Realism and Naturalism. *L'Ève future* (1886) by Villiers de l'Isle-Adam, who had already made a name for himself with his *Contes cruels* (1883), united science fiction and philosophical idealism in the story of an 'andréide' (robot) invented by the scientist Edison which becomes inhabited by a human mind. Novels that were more technically adventurous attracted little attention at the time, although they can now be seen to have foreshadowed later developments: Dujardin's *Les Lauriers sont coupés* (1887), an attempt to capture the immediacy of experience by using a primitive form of interior monologue; Jarry's linguistically explosive *Le Surmâle* (1902); and the strange visions of Roussel (*Impressions d'Afrique*, 1910; *Locus solus*, 1913) who was later hailed as a 'magnétiseur' by the Surrealists. Two other works that made scarcely more of an impression also proved to be prophetic in their own way: Valéry's *Une Soirée avec M. Teste* (1894) and Gide's

---

* 'Realists of any talent should rather call themselves Illusionists'
† 'a spiritual form of naturalism'

Paludes (1895) are meditations on what the genre of the novel might become rather than novels themselves (Gide called his a *sotie* or burlesque).

These experimental works did not bear fruit until after the war. In the meantime, the post-Naturalist vacuum was filled by fresh types of adventure novel: Loti's evocations of distant and often hostile places (the Turkish *Aziyadé*, 1879; *Pêcheur d'Islande*, 1886; *Madame Chrysanthème*, 1887), amongst which should be counted the strange land of childhood, an important theme in this period (*Le Roman d'un enfant*, 1890: compare Renard's *Poil de Carotte*, 1894); the Moroccan tales of the Tharaud brothers and the science fiction of the Rosny brothers; the historical romances of Le Roy (*Jacquou le croquant*, 1898); and the new genre of the detective novel, with Leblanc's Arsène Lupin (*Arsène Lupin, gentleman-cambrioleur*, 1907) and Leroux's Rouletabille (*Le Mystère de la chambre jaune*, 1908) breaking out of the mould of Gaboriau's Inspector Lecoq and Conan Doyle's Sherlock Holmes in their almost poetic celebration of mystery and mystification. Allain and Souvestre's *Fantômas*, a rambling epic published over many years (with a film version as well from 1913) and featuring the exploits of an evil master-criminal, was extremely popular, being later described by Cendrars as 'l'Iliade de notre époque':* a whole generation of writers, including the Surrealists and Sartre, were influenced by it.

Women's writing was very important in this period, when the rise in literacy together with the lack of opportunities for employment outside the home produced a situation where women were not only the biggest consumers of novels but possibly the biggest producers too. Zénaïde Fleuriot's eighty-three novels, serialized in the popular magazine *La Veillée des chaumières* from 1877, were frequently reprinted and had a formative influence on generations of future writers such as Mauriac. Maryan, who wrote even more, featured women who have to face up to the problems of life and find their own solutions: titles like *L'Erreur d'Isabelle* (1884) are ripe for rediscovery, more so than the escapist novels of the brother-and-sister team writing as Delly, or the satirical society portraits of Gyp. Rachilde, the wife of the editor of *Le Mercure de France*, had a *succès*

---

* 'the Iliad of our day'

de scandale with her portrait of a bisexual couple in *Monsieur Vénus* (1884); Myriam Harry won the first Prix Femina (awarded by a panel of women, but not necessarily to a female author) in 1904 with *La Conquête de Jérusalem*; and in 1910 former farmworker and dressmaker Marguerite Audoux also won the Femina for her autobiographical novel *Marie-Claire*, which sold 75,000 copies in a few weeks. In 1909 alone there were no fewer than three studies published on contemporary women's writing.

Symbolism: Poetry and Drama of the *Fin de Siècle*

The year 1900 marks a natural break in the French poetic tradition, following the deaths of Verlaine in 1896 and Mallarmé in 1898. Until then the two most important tendencies had been Parnassianism (see also pages 139–40) and Symbolism. The first series of *Le Parnasse contemporain* in 1866 had been followed by two more, in 1871 and 1876, which were marked by a much greater conservatism in political outlook and poetic form. Dierx, Mendès, Coppée, Sully Prudhomme and Heredia (*Les Trophées*, 1893) produced beautiful, highly crafted, evocative poetry which had considerable success: the last three all became members of the Académie française, as did the father of Parnassianism, Leconte de Lisle; and in 1901 Sully Prudhomme, who had turned to writing longer, more philosophical poems, was the first recipient of the Nobel Prize for Literature. This all reinforced the Romantic myth of the poet who could aspire to a role in society, and publishers continued to include large numbers of poetry titles in their catalogues, although often insisting that the author should bear the production costs. Rimbaud's *Une Saison en enfer* (1873) was one example of a text thus published *à compte d'auteur* (see page 145). Even after the turn of the century it was not uncommon for a young author, whether primarily a poet or not, to begin with a volume of verse: Mauriac, for instance, first came to the attention of the literary world with *Les Mains jointes* in 1910.

Symbolism was of more lasting significance than Parnassianism, but it had difficulty becoming established. The literary salons were not open to the younger rebels, who started their own groups, clubs and reviews. Verlaine's *Les Poètes maudits* (1884) drew attention to Corbière, whose *Les Amours jaunes* had appeared in 1873; to Rimbaud, whose poetry, also written over ten years before, had remained largely unpublished; and to Mallarmé. Since the 1860s Mallarmé had been working on purifying poetic language in order to 'peindre non la chose, mais l'effet qu'elle produit'.* His sonnets, the longer sequences of *Hérodiade* and *L'Après-midi d'un faune*, the prose poems and other meditations in prose on questions of language, meaning and the absolute, were scarcely understood in his lifetime, but he was venerated as a master by those who came to his flat in the rue de Rome every Tuesday from 1885 onwards to hear his remarkable conversation-lectures on similar themes. By 1886 the brief phase of decadence, inspired by revolt against conventional values, encouraged by Verlaine's poem 'Langueur' (first published in 1883) and Huysmans's novel *À rebours* (1884), and illustrated by Laforgue's *Les Complaintes* (1885), was giving way to Symbolism, as many young poets evolved a more coherent doctrine and practice.

For all their internal disagreements, the Symbolists were united in emphasizing a critical preoccupation with language as such, both in the practice of poetry and in theoretical discussion of it. The influence of Wagner, via Dujardin's *Revue wagnérienne* and Mallarmé, consolidated the shift from the Parnassian association of poetry with the visual arts to a new one with music, and at the same time there was an openness to the pessimistic idealism of Schopenhauer. On the technical front, several poets almost simultaneously discovered the possibilities of *vers libre*, abandoning the regularity of traditional metre in favour of more flexible, subjective units. There was undoubtedly a sense of common purpose among those who called themselves Symbolists in 1886, such as Kahn, Ghil, Moréas, Vielé-Griffin and Régnier, even though their paths diverged soon afterwards. Several reviews were founded to publish Symbolist verse, among the more important being *La Plume* and *Le Mercure de France*, which became the leading literary review in France by the

---

* 'paint not the thing itself, but the effect it produces'

turn of the century and also functioned as a publishing house. There was a concurrent movement in Belgium (see also page 206): Verhaeren, Mockel, Rodenbach and Maeterlinck rank with the best of the French Symbolists, while showing less of a tendency to cut themselves off from the real world.

Women also had a high profile in the field of poetry at the beginning of the century. With the decline of Symbolism, several passionate and lyrical voices made themselves heard, among them Lucie Delarue-Mardrus with *Occident* (1900), Anna de Noailles with *Le Coeur innombrable* (1901) and Renée Vivien with the lesbian poems of *Cendres et poussières* (1902). Among their male counterparts, enthusiasm for living and for the possibilities of the human spirit dominated the experiments of the Groupe de l'Abbaye with Vildrac and Duhamel, while Apollinaire, Salmon, Jacob and others were beginning to celebrate the power of the imagination in their poetry.

Symbolism also made a major contribution to the theatre. The year 1870 can be seen in retrospect to have marked a turning point, with the first Paris production of the short play *La Révolte* by Villiers de l'Isle-Adam. While preserving the format of domestic drama made popular by playwrights like Dumas *fils* (see page 133), Villiers gave particular emphasis to the exposition of an idealistic philosophy which undermined the familiar bourgeois ideology of the genre. Gourmont's novel *Sixtine* (1890) included a description of a performance of *La Révolte* which made it seem a kind of manifesto for the new Symbolist generation, and in 1894 Villiers's *Axël*, a long allegorical play influenced by Wagner and full of ideas about the conflict between material possessions and spiritual freedom, was warmly received. Meanwhile Fort's Théâtre d'Art (1890–2) was experimenting with more revolutionary concepts of theatre, present-ing scenic performances of poems as well as the Symbolist dramas of Maeterlinck (*La Princesse Maleine*, 1889; *Pelléas et Mélisande*, 1892). Lugné-Poë's Théâtre de l'Oeuvre succeeded the Théâtre d'Art in 1893 and was closely identified with Symbolist drama for several years.

Symbolism in the theatre was partly an extension of the poetic ideas of Baudelaire (see page 144) and Mallarmé, and partly a reaction against existing forms which continued to enjoy enormous success, whether the well-made comedies and historical plays of Sardou (*Madame Sans-Gêne*, 1893), the light satires of Pailleron and the vaudeville of Feydeau (*La Dame de chez Maxim*, 1899), or the newer, naturalistic dramas of Becque (*Les Corbeaux*, 1882) and others, as presented by Antoine at his Théâtre Libre (1887–96). The materiality and directness of representation of traditional theatre, indeed the very use of actors to portray characters, seemed to be incompatible with the Symbolist aesthetic. That might have led to a total rejection of theatre, but in fact it inspired a profound rethinking of the genre which was to be continued in the discourse of theatrical modernism in the twentieth century. Maeterlinck can be seen to have been at least as important a precursor of Artaud, Beckett and Ionesco as was Jarry, whose iconoclastic *Ubu roi*, with its grotesque, puppet-like characters and its distortions of language, was first staged in 1896.

By 1900, however, there seemed to be few French playwrights of the stature of Ibsen and Strindberg. Rostand achieved two great successes with the heroic verse comedy *Cyrano de Bergerac* (1897) and the historical drama *L'Aiglon* (1900), appealing to the Romantic tradition and also to the contemporary need for emblematic national figures. Roussel, better known as an experimental novelist, challenged the very limits of theatre with the 7,000 lines and over 400 characters of *La Seine* in about 1900, but the play was never performed, and indeed was only published in 1994. Claudel, who had been writing plays in a radically new kind of poetic language inspired by Rimbaud and Wagner since the 1880s, only came to prominence in 1914 with *L'Otage* and *L'Échange* (he was in fact first hailed as a poet: his *Cinq Grandes Odes* (1910) developed the *vers libre* of the Symbolists into a *verset* of biblical inspiration, and affirmed the role of the poet in helping to create the world). His earlier works, including *Tête d'or* and *Partage de midi*, were not fully appreciated until the 1940s and 1950s. The fate of Claudel's plays illustrates an important shift that was taking place: it was to be the theorists and directors rather than the playwrights who were now initiating the most significant changes in the theatre. Copeau's Théâtre du Vieux-Colombier, founded in 1913, showed the way ahead. It was not a question of extravagant staging: rather, there was a return to a bare theatrical space, together with new emphases on the aesthetic coherence of the whole spectacle and on the craft of the actor (including gymnastic training). There was only time for one season before the outbreak of war, but Copeau's seventeen productions, which included *L'Échange*, were decisive for the development of post-war theatre.

War and Renewal: 1910–30

The loss of Alsace and part of Lorraine to Germany in 1871 had never been fully accepted by the French, and the acquisition of a colonial empire in Africa and Indo-China in the 1880s had not made up for it. The novels of Barrès, in particular *Les Déracinés* (1897), the first volume of a trilogy entitled *Le Roman de l'énergie nationale*, appealed to nationalist feeling and attacked the Germanic idealism that had penetrated both the French educational system and the doctrines of Symbolism. Then the two volumes of *Les Bastions de l'est, Au service de l'Allemagne* (1905) and *Colette Baudoche* (1909), specifically encouraged the idea that Alsace and Lorraine were French and should be won back. Bazin's *Les Oberlé* (1901) did the same, in a less combative manner. Political passions had already entered the novel in the wake of the Dreyfus affair, with Barrès defending the army and the previously sceptical Anatole France taking up the cause of Dreyfus (*M. Bergeret à Paris*, 1901) for a while before reverting to scepticism (*Les Dieux ont soif*, 1912). There was also a new current of socially aware literature, following on from Zola and the ex-Communard Vallès (*L'Insurgé*, 1886), of which the most important representative was Charles-Louis Philippe (*Bubu de Montparnasse*, 1901). Péguy, whose *Cahiers de la quinzaine* published the works of many major writers between 1900 and 1914, was an ardent Dreyfusard socialist who was increasingly drawn towards nationalism and a mystical Catholicism (the poem 'Le Mystère de la charité de Jeanne d'Arc' appeared in 1910). Péguy's essay 'Notre Patrie' evokes the threat of imminent war with Germany after the

Tangier episode in 1905. By 1912 there was a strong feeling, at least among the young intellectuals questioned in Agathon's survey *Les Jeunes Gens d'aujourd'hui*, that war would be a good thing, not only to regain the lost provinces, but because it was in itself virile and purifying. Psichari's novel *L'Appel des armes* (1913) portrayed the army as a spiritual brotherhood.

That same year, 1913, saw the publication of several novels that were far more original in their conception and technique: the genre was at last beginning to be renewed by a more truly literary energy. One important force in this renewal was the literary review *La Nouvelle Revue française* (*NRF*), founded by Gide, Schlumberger, Copeau and other ex-Symbolists in 1909. The *NRF* offered not a narrow doctrine but a commitment to literary values which enabled it to recruit the best emerging talent. One early recruit was Roger Martin du Gard, whose *Jean Barois*, first serialized in the *NRF*, was not merely a retrospective assessment of the Dreyfus affair but an attempt to integrate both theatrical writing and historical documents into a work of narrative fiction. Alain-Fournier's *Le Grand Meaulnes* captured the spirit of adolescence in a haunting novel of mystery and desire.

Proust's *Du côté de chez Swann*, originally rejected by the *NRF* on Gide's advice because it seemed to be merely a chronicle of upper-class society life, was the first volume of a work, *A la recherche du temps perdu*, which has probably had a greater impact on the novel in the twentieth century than any other. In it Proust concentrated on conveying shifting, subjective impressions in a complex and suggestive language, abandoning traditional concepts of character, subject, time and truth. *A la recherche* goes beyond *Jean Barois* in its totalizing ambitions, making the novel like Wagnerian opera or the drama advocated by certain Symbolists. Recurrent themes and images provide the texture of the work, which kept growing as Proust was writing it, so that the original two parts became separated by a long central section, and each of these was subdivided in turn.

Although Proust continued to write during the war, literary life was not in general able to function as before. A whole generation of writers was killed in the conflict, which claimed over a million

French lives, some of the greatest in the first few months: Péguy, Alain-Fournier, Psichari. Most others were actively involved. In the first two years there was much patriotic literature, most of it best forgotten, but then came a series of fictionalized personal testimonies which revealed the awfulness of the trenches, denounced militarism whether explicitly or implicitly, and achieved unprecedented sales. Barbusse's *Le Feu*, an uneven but powerful portrayal of the day-to-day life of a squad of soldiers on the Northern Front, sold a quarter of a million copies in two years, when 10,000 would have been a success by pre-war standards. Bertrand's *L'Appel du sol* offered a more patriotic interpretation of similar experiences, while the pacifism of Werth's *Clavel soldat* emerged naturally from his sympathetic descriptions of ordinary men caught up in the horrors of war. *Les Croix de bois*, by Dorgelès, did not appear until 1919, reflecting the reluctance of many to speak about the war while it was still going on. Dorgelès is more restrained than Barbusse and Bertrand, preferring to offer documentation and leave it to the reader to make judgements. Duhamel's *Vie des martyrs* and *Civilisation* are collections of short sketches which emphasize the sufferings and humanity of soldiers and medical staff behind the lines. The most memorable poetry to come out of the war was rather different. There was little protest poetry. Apollinaire's experience of the Front provided him less with ideas than with a rich source of images and an emotional stimulus which found expression in *Calligrammes* (1918), where the typographical exuberance of the picture poems is married with more traditional elements in a constant oscillation between what he called 'ordre' and 'aventure'.

After the war there was an explosion of literature and indeed of culture. There were those who reflected on the traumatic experience of modern mechanized warfare and tried to draw lessons about the viability or otherwise of European civilization. Alain's *Mars ou la guerre jugée* (1921), a series of essays analysing militarism, and Valéry's essay 'La Crise de l'esprit' (1919) were among the most significant, raising wider issues than Rolland's earlier, important *Au-dessus de la mêlée* (1915), which had been a call not to remain aloof but rather to be committed to working for peace and reconciliation while supporting one's own country. There were many others who were indelibly marked by the war – few had not lost relatives and friends – even if they did not make it the explicit subject of their work. The cult of youth, the seeds of which were evident before the war, was given impetus by the fact that so many young people lost their fathers. Radiguet, hailed as the new Rimbaud, died at 20 after writing two glittering novels of psychological analysis (*Le Diable au corps*, 1923, and *Le Bal du comte d'Orgel*, 1924): he and the hero of Cocteau's *Thomas l'imposteur* (1923), representing the myth of the liberated, irrational and magically successful adolescent (in a wartime setting), were among the numerous heirs of Gide's Lafcadio, the original perpetrator of the *acte gratuit** in *Les Caves du Vatican* (1914).

An alternative response to the destruction of the old world and the arrival of the machine age was to celebrate the mystery of the land. This new form of regionalism, indebted to some extent to Barrès, proved popular, and major literary prizes were won by the black West Indian writer Maran (see pages 217–18) for a novel about African family life (*Batouala*, 1921), Pérochon (*Nêne*, 1920), Châteaubriant (*La Brière*, 1923) (both about the west of France) and Genevoix (*Raboliot*, 1925, set in central France), while Pourrat's four-volume *Gaspard des montagnes* (1922–31) tapped the rich vein of legend from the Auvergne. The Swiss writer Ramuz (see also page 206) went beyond regionalism to achieve a mystical quality which later affected language itself: *La Vie de Samuel Belet* (1913) was followed in 1926 by *La Grande Peur dans la montagne*, which represents the struggle of the individual and the community against the almost supernatural forces of nature. Bosco and Giono wrote about Provence in a similar manner in the 1930s.

This was the period in which the avant-garde made the biggest impression. Marinetti's Futurist Manifesto of 1909 had been one indication of the pre-war ferment in artistic and literary circles. Cendrars's object-poem 'La Prose du Transsibérien' appeared in 1913, as did Apollinaire's *Alcools*, with its evocation of a world falling apart and its exploitation of modernist themes and techniques, especially in 'Zone'. It was the return of Apollinaire from the Front in 1916 and

---

* unmotivated act

his contacts with Reverdy, Albert-Birot, Soupault and Breton that prepared the way for the French version of the Dada movement, precipitated by the arrival of the Romanian poet Tzara in 1919. The anarchistic tendencies of Dada soon gave way to the more ambitious aims of Surrealism under the leadership of Breton: to change the world by changing the way we see it. The Surrealist manifestos and reviews, the experimental and lyrical poetry of Breton, Desnos and Eluard, and the novels of Breton and Aragon paradoxically formed a more coherent set of texts, with their repudiation of rational control and their emphasis on the unconscious, than those of previous modernist groups. The Surrealists also placed themselves in a definite if radical literary tradition, claiming to be the ultimate heirs of Baudelaire and drawing attention to Nerval, Lautréamont and Rimbaud as precursors (see pages 143–5).

In the theatre the unconventional visual creations of Cocteau (*Les Mariés de la Tour Eiffel*, 1921; *Orphée*, 1925) were independent of Surrealism, drawing their inspiration rather from the Russian ballet and from Apollinaire's *Les Mamelles de Tirésias* (1917). In 1926 Artaud's Théâtre Alfred Jarry paid homage to a great predecessor, and already the buffoonery of Crommelynck (*Le Cocu magnifique*, 1920) and his use of masks had recalled Jarry's style. But in fact it was neither these nor Surrealism that revitalized the theatre in the 1920s, but rather a group of four directors (the 'Cartel'), Dullin, Jouvet, Pitoëff and Baty, who broadly followed Copeau's aesthetic programme (rejection of realism in favour of a poetic theatre rooted in contemporary experience), while each developing his own distinctive style. Lenormand's psychological dramas, for instance, were mostly created by Pitoëff or Baty, while Jouvet's name is inseparable from that of Giraudoux, whose plays he staged from 1928 onwards. At the same time popular 'boulevard' theatre remained as healthy as ever, typified by the actor-director Sacha Guitry: Paris had a wide range of successful companies and was the theatrical capital of Europe.

The literary giants immediately after the war were Proust, Gide and Valéry. The Prix Goncourt for 1919 was awarded, for once, to a novel of outstanding literary merit, Proust's *A l'ombre des jeunes filles en fleurs* (the second volume of *A la recherche*). The previous few prizewinners had been mainly works of *témoignage* (those of Barbusse, Bertrand and Duhamel), and the publishers of Dorgelès's *Les Croix de bois* were naturally indignant that the 1919 prize had not gone to this equally important novel: they produced it with a publicity wrapper announcing 'Prix Goncourt 1919', and in tiny letters underneath, '4 voix sur 10',* and were successfully sued by Proust's publishers. Before the war little attention had been paid to literary prizes, and Pergaud's *De Goupil à Margot*, which won the Prix Goncourt in 1910, surprised his publishers by selling far more copies than expected. (Pergaud is better remembered today for *La Guerre des boutons*, a novel about village schoolboy gangs, which was made into a popular film in the 1960s.) The war novels changed all that, and his prize gave Proust a wide audience. Even so, his long and highly intellectual novel, appearing in isolated volumes, sold far fewer copies than many others of the period, some of which were heavily publicized.

In this new commercial era, the adventure novels of Benoit (*L'Atlantide*, 1919, with its echoes of Rider Haggard) were launched by Albin Michel with a huge campaign, matched by Grasset's publicity for Hémon's novel about Canada, *Maria Chapdelaine* (1921). Grasset's promotion of Radiguet in terms of a personal image rather than for the literary merit of his works was widely condemned but paid off handsomely, and the scandalous portrayal of a liberated woman in Margueritte's *La Garçonne* (1923) proved equally lucrative for Flammarion. Indeed, just as the theatre at this period was dominated by directors rather than playwrights, other forms of literature were dominated by publishers. A successful author would be retained by one particular publishing house, paid a monthly salary as an advance against royalties, and given a contract which gave the publisher rights over future books. Grasset, having begun with few literary contacts of his own, was particularly pushy, whereas the firm of Gallimard, which grew out of the *NRF*, inherited a large stable of writers and had little difficulty attracting more. Proust, Gide and Valéry were all published by Gallimard, as were Apollinaire, Aragon, Breton, Cocteau, Éluard and Martin du Gard. Grasset boasted Mauriac, Maurois and Montherlant, and when he enticed Morand away from Gallimard he launched a new collection entitled 'Les 4 M'.

---

* '4 votes out of 10'

Gide had been planning for years to write a new kind of novel. *Paludes* had been a rejection of the Symbolist literary salons, while *L'Immoraliste* (1902) and *La Porte étroite* (1909) marked a return to the analytical tradition of Constant's *Adolphe* (see page 117) informed by a pervasive irony, a strong sensuality and a preoccupation with style. *Les Faux-monnayeurs* (1925), developing ideas contained in *Les Caves du Vatican* (1914), is an invitation to reinterpret experience on different levels, and at the same time to be aware of the artistic process at work. Gide's repudiation of realism in this 'oeuvre déconcentrée'* is comparable to Proust's. The text is constantly turning its back on us as readers and reflecting on itself, and its deliberate open-endedness is only one among many features that demand to be considered in terms of aesthetic theory rather than conventional narrative. At the same time, its kaleidoscopic treatment of character owes something to Dostoevsky, whom Gide was largely responsible for popularizing in France through the lectures he gave to mark his centenary in 1921. *Si le grain ne meurt* (1926) is technically less interesting, but it was a landmark both in the genre of autobiography and in the literary portrayal of homosexuality, partly as a result of Gide's refusal to heed Proust's advice not to say 'je'. In the end his most satisfying achievement may be his *Journal*, out of which all his other works can be seen to have grown.

Valéry had also been thinking towards the novel in the 1890s, and a later comment of his, that he would never write a sentence of the type 'La marquise sortit à cinq heures',† was enthusiastically taken up by the Surrealists. After some early essays and poems he published nothing for twenty years, concentrating on keeping his wide-ranging *Cahiers*, which only became known after his death and have increased his reputation even further. In his lifetime he was most admired for the long intellectual poem *La Jeune Parque* (1917) which deals, like Mallarmé's *Hérodiade* and Proust's *A la recherche*, with the drama of human consciousness; for the dense, shorter poems of *Charmes* (1922), including 'Le Cimetière marin'; and for the Platonic dialogues *L'Âme et la danse* and *Eupalinos* (both 1923).

While no other writer could match these three, there have been few decades to rival the 1920s for the level of high-quality literary

---

* 'decentralized work'   † 'Her ladyship went out at five o'clock.'

activity. Giraudoux, in *Suzanne et le Pacifique* (1921), a parody of the desert-island novel, celebrated language at the expense of reality. Montherlant was somewhat similar to Gide in his combination of youthful fervour and aesthetic concern. His essays and novels (he did not begin writing plays until the 1940s) emphasized gesture and commitment for their own sake, in such areas as war and sport, rather than values: one collection was entitled *Service inutile* (1935). Both Cendrars (*Moravagine*, 1926) and Morand, whose *New-York* sold over 150,000 copies in 1930, reflected the excitement of the post-war world in their cinematic evocations of travel, and Michaux and Kessel also appealed to that sense of adventure. Mauriac, like the others, displayed a cult of youth, but contrasted the laxity of Paris with the strict moral codes of provincial France (*Destins*, 1928). His novels about individuals caught between the irreconcilable claims of family, personal fulfilment and religion, such as *Thérèse Desqueyroux* (1927), were inspired by his reading of Racine and Pascal, and he considered much of the modern output of so-called novels to be unworthy of the name (*Le Roman*, 1928).

Colette, who had already written the *Claudine* series of schoolgirl novels before the war under her husband's name, gave a new twist to the analysis of sexual and social relationships in *Chéri* (1920) and *Le Blé en herbe* (1923), where the male characters are denied any heroic stature and the female characters are more resourceful and generally more interesting. Colette was by far the dominant woman writer of the 1920s, although Jeanne Galzy's *Les Allongés* (1923), about the experience of illness, was very popular, and in this decade obsessed with women a novelist like Raymonde Machard could achieve sales of over 200,000 copies for bodice-rippers like *La Possession* (1927). It was also at this period that Marguerite Yourcenar began to write, but it was another thirty years before she achieved fame (see page 182).

The brevity of many of these novels stands in sharp contrast to the sagas of the *roman-fleuve* or *roman-cycle*. Already before the war Rolland had completed the ten volumes of *Jean-Christophe*, the story of a modern genius in a world of mediocrity. Now came Duhamel's *Vie et aventures de Salavin*, to be followed in the 1930s by his *Chronique des Pasquier*; and in 1922 Martin du Gard began publishing *Les*

Thibault, which was only finished in 1940. These attempts to understand the evolution of individuals and families against the changing background of modern French history announce the more serious mood of the 1930s. The apogee of the *roman-cycle* was to be reached with *Les Hommes de bonne volonté* by Romains, who turned to the novel after a successful career as a poet and comic playwright (*Knock*, 1923). In these twenty-seven volumes, only loosely connected to each other, he surveyed and reflected on a quarter of a century of French public and private life, including the experience of the war (*Verdun*, 1938).

A more reflective and expansive current of poetry also began to emerge alongside that of Surrealism. Ségalen, who died in 1919 but whose poetry was only just becoming known (*Stèles*, 1914), Saint-John Perse (*Anabase*, 1924) and Supervielle (*Gravitations*, 1925) echoed the pre-war work of the Symbolist poet Milosz in their evocations of a spiritual quest, and allied it with a certain exoticism, while Jouve (*Les Mystérieuses Noces*, 1925) was more overtly Christian but also more Freudian. Marie Noël wrote spiritual poems of great simplicity (*Les Chansons et les heures*, 1920). All these were outstripped in popularity by the sentimental verse of Géraldy (*Toi et moi*, 1921).

The Human Condition: 1930–40

Many literary historians agree that 1930 was an important turning point. Taking up Thibaudet's idea of a 'période de vie facile'* from 1918 to 1930, characterized by expansion, Magny uses the image of the diastole or dilation of the heart, to be followed by a period of systole or contraction featuring *repliement, inquiétude, angoisse* and *déréliction*.† Picon speaks of the emergence of 'une génération éthique',‡ trying to analyse the problems of the human condition at individual and national level and to find a way ahead, and as much at home in the essay as in the novel. The work of Saint-Exupéry is emblematic of this shift. His early novels, echoing the theme of

---

* 'an age of happy irresponsibility'
† withdrawal, worry, anxiety and abandonment   ‡ 'an ethical generation'

aviation already found in Kessel's *L'Équipage* (1923), combine the thrill of adventure with the exaltation of teamwork (*Vol de nuit*, 1931), which already suggests a more serious concern. Then his short stories (*Terre des hommes*, 1939; *Le Petit Prince*, 1943) and essays (*Citadelle*, 1948) explore the importance of solidarity and a humanistic spirituality.

For many, the new concerns were of a political order. There were already signs of the emergence of a new working-class literature in the 1920s, with Aymé, Guilloux, Poulaille and Dabit, whose *Hôtel du Nord* was the first winner of the new Prix du Roman Populiste in 1929. In 1937 the Prix Goncourt was awarded to a Belgian populist writer, Plisnier. The Communist novel also made its appearance. Communism, which had been more of an adventure than a serious option for many in the 1920s, now presented itself as the only viable defence against the rise of fascism. Aragon broke off his uneasy relationship with the Surrealist group and became a militant Communist. The doctrine of socialist realism governed his series of modern historical novels *Le Monde réel* (beginning with *Les Cloches de Bâle*, 1934), as it did those of Nizan (*Le Cheval de Troie*, 1935). Organizations such as the Association des écrivains et artistes révolutionnaires (AEAR) and the Comité de vigilance des intellectuels antifascistes (CVIA) brought together militants and fellow-travellers. Intellectual detachment was difficult to justify. The critical attitude of Alain to authoritarianism led him to play an active role in the CVIA. Rolland, having opposed Barbusse's arguments in favour of Communism, finally aligned himself with Moscow. Gide adopted a pro-Soviet stance, and was then vilified for the U-turn he performed in his *Retour de l'URSS* (1936). Benda's plea for intellectuals not to dirty their hands in the political arena (*La Trahison des clercs*, 1927) found few echoes after 1930, although Grenier, whose lyrical-metaphysical essays *Les Îles* made such a profound impression on his pupil Camus in 1933, launched a rare attack on blind commitment to political or religious systems in his *Essai sur l'esprit d'orthodoxie* (1938).

Literature that is ideologically committed runs the risk of losing much of its aesthetic validity. Malraux managed to avoid falling into that trap. Having begun in the 1920s as an adventurer, like Saint-Exupéry, he turned to urgent questions of history and revolution (inspired by his experiences in the Far East), but used them as themes rather than to make a particular political point. *La Condition humaine* (1933), for all its evocations of the revolutionary struggle in Shanghai, is essentially about the search for meaning in the face of death, and if *L'Espoir* (1937), written in the thick of the Spanish Civil War, advocated the acceptance of Communist discipline in the short term, it is as much to do with fraternity and the conquest of destiny. Malraux's later works were to be wide-ranging reflections on the history of art and culture. Guilloux rose above his earlier populism, and in *Le Sang noir* (1935) used the events of a single day in a Breton provincial town in 1917 to raise similar questions about human values. Giono's kind of commitment was different: he also explored fraternity and destiny, but in his case by creating powerful poetic myths based on rural communities (*Que ma joie demeure*, 1935). His pacifism appeared reactionary to some, even though pacifism was traditionally a left-wing phenomenon. There were also those who deliberately adopted extreme right-wing values: Drieu la Rochelle's aspiration to strength led him to reject what he saw as the decadence of democracy and to idealize his experience of war in *La Comédie de Charleroi* (1934) and *Gilles* (1939), while Brasillach in *Les Sept Couleurs* (1939) did for the history of the European right what Aragon, Nizan and Malraux had done for the left.

Céline's *Voyage au bout de la nuit* (1932), ostensibly the story of one man's experience of war, colonialism, the New World and the working-class suburbs of Paris, and initially greeted as a left-wing novel, was in fact an attempt to reinvent novelistic language on the basis of emotion rather than reason. In their linguistic exuberance, his *Voyage* and *Mort à crédit* (1936) can be compared to the works of Rabelais and Proust, although the overt anti-semitism of other writings has adversely affected Céline's literary reputation. Bernanos also refused to describe the world in traditional categories and language. In *Sous le soleil de Satan* (1926) he had boldly inscribed the supernatural at the heart of daily existence, and in the diptych of *Journal d'un curé de campagne* (1936) and *Monsieur Ouine* (1946) he developed a new Catholic realism which made use of dream and the fantastic. Green, in *L'Autre Sommeil* (1931) and *Minuit* (1936), also showed characters profoundly dissatisfied with ordinary existence and posed searching metaphysical questions, but did not explicitly confront the two major themes of Christian redemption and homosexuality until the 1950s. Mauriac, on the other hand, offered more hope of a resolution of the conflict between flesh and spirit, in novels which expand the scope from the individual to the family (*Le Noeud de vipères*, 1932; *Les Anges noirs*, 1936). Many of these novelists also wrote important essays of political and social analysis, among them Nizan, Malraux, Drieu, Brasillach and Bernanos, whose *Les Grands Cimetières sous la lune* (1937), a *grand reportage* on the atrocities of the Spanish Civil War, marked his decisive break with the right-wing Action Française movement.

In this period of rather masculine concerns (women are all but absent from the works of Malraux and Saint-Exupéry), two women of Russian birth made a significant impact on French literature at different ends of the spectrum. Elsa Triolet, the wife of Aragon and the inspiration for much of his writing (especially his later poetry), and later to win the Prix Goncourt herself, published her first novel *Bonsoir Thérèse* in 1938. In it escapism, rather than political commitment, is offered as a response to the dehumanization of the modern world. Nathalie Parain, a professional artist, helped to create the modern illustrated children's book for the collection Les Albums du Père Castor in 1931. (Brunhoff's first *Babar* book in the same year used a similar approach, whereas the style of the *Tintin* adventures, which first appeared in a magazine in 1929, owed more to the tradition of the picture story as pioneered in *Les Pieds nickelés* as early as 1908.)

Not all the prose fiction of this decade was weighed down by historical or metaphysical questions. Queneau's *Le Chiendent* (1933), influenced by his Surrealist phase, portrayed a crisis of language more than of civilization. Ernst's captionless collage novels, such as *Une semaine de bonté* (1934), prefigured the later work of Robbe-Grillet in their parodic playing with visual images and the codes of melodrama. Breton's *L'Amour fou* (1937) continued the visionary reinterpretation of everyday life that had characterized *Nadja* (1928) with its manifesto-like conclusion ('La beauté sera CONVULSIVE ou ne sera pas'*). Gracq's *Au château d'Argol* (1938) is a poetic, personal novel, the heir not only of Surrealism but of an older mythical tradition. The Provençal novels of Bosco, including *L'Âne culotte* (1937), are less regionalist than telluric, reminiscent of those of Ramuz, and drawing on occultism like those of Breton and Gracq. Jouhandeau also hinted at the supernatural, while concentrating on satirical portraits of provincial society (*Monsieur Godeau marié*, 1933), and Montherlant played rather cynically with the contradiction between Christian idealism and hedonism in *Les Jeunes Filles* (1936) and its sequels. In contrast, Cohen's *Solal* series (1930–68) offered a gently hopeful view of life.

The lion's share of the major literary prizes in the 1920s and 1930s went to the four publishing houses of Gallimard, Grasset, Albin Michel and Denoël (a latecomer to the scene, in 1928). There was cut-throat competition between them, with the economic situation biting from 1929 onwards. Diversification was one solution: Gallimard launched *La Revue musicale* as early as 1920. Another was the development of prestigious collections (Grasset's Cahiers Verts from 1921, Gallimard's Bibliothèque des Idées in 1927, and Bibliothèque de la Pléiade, taken over from its founder in 1933) or of new types of literature such as the detective novel. The year 1931 saw the arrival of Simenon's Inspector Maigret, with the publisher Fayard bringing out one volume a month. It was a former employee of Grasset who pioneered the trail-blazing Le Masque collection of detective stories in 1925, and Gallimard's *Détective* magazine, launched in 1928, regularly sold a third of a million copies, far more than the nevertheless successful literary reviews founded in the same period (*Les Nouvelles littéraires, Candide, Gringoire, Je suis partout*). The *NRF*, however, also under the Gallimard umbrella, continued to be the most dynamic focus for creative writers of a wide variety of literary and political persuasions.

In the field of poetry the 1930s appeared to be less innovative than the 1920s, although many of the Surrealist poets continued to write (Éluard, *Les Yeux fertiles*, 1936). Michaux, Ponge, Artaud, Queneau, Tardieu, Char and Follain had all begun to produce poetry, but were

---

* 'Beauty will be CONVULSIVE or nothing.'

not appreciated until much later. Daumal, excluded (like so many others) from the Surrealist group by Breton along with his companions in the Grand Jeu movement, pursued his spiritual quest in *Le Contre-ciel* (1935). La Tour du Pin's *La Quête de joie* (1933) offered a mystical blend of sensuality and spiritual aspiration. Audiberti began as a poet with *L'Empire et la trappe* (1930) before turning to novels and then to the theatre.

In the theatre the age of the great directors continued, with the most striking phenomenon of the decade being the partnership between Jouvet and Giraudoux. The success of *Siegfried* in 1928 heralded the arrival of an author worthy of a stage which fifteen years of reform had purged of much of its low-brow commercialism. While sometimes touching on topical issues such as international relations (*La Guerre de Troie n'aura pas lieu*, 1935), Giraudoux and Jouvet worked mainly on the level of myth and always managed to achieve a poetic lightness of touch, turning the dramatic spectacle into a 'féerie'.* Jouvet also staged Cocteau's *La Machine infernale* in 1934, a more mature play than *Orphée*, raising questions about the human condition in terms of free will and the power of language. Dullin directed the plays of Salacrou, who conveyed not just the restlessness of his generation but a real sense of the absurdity of existence, before the concept became fashionable (*Une Femme libre*, 1934). Pitoëff was responsible for launching Anouilh in 1937 with *Voyageur sans bagage*, although from 1940 it was Barsacq who directed this author's best-known plays, with their existential themes and highly theatrical presentation.

In the early 1930s Artaud showed himself to be ahead of his time in a series of essays which was published in 1938 as *Le Théâtre et son double*. He attacked the principles of the Cartel, whose members had respected the dramatic text and had looked back to the Greek tradition. Drawing inspiration from Oriental theatre and dance, Artaud advocated a 'théâtre de la cruauté'† in which the audience would be made painfully aware of primitive spiritual forces through the use of bright lights, loud sounds and ritualized gestures.

---

* 'fairytale experience'   † 'theatre of cruelty'

As the 1930s drew to a close, all literary genres were marked by a retreat from gratuitous experimentation, and a twin emphasis on *témoignage* and lucidity. The work of Camus and Sartre, which covers several genres (theatre, novel, essay – see pages 174–83), exemplified this new trend.

Further Reading

David Baguley, *Naturalist Fiction, the Entropic Vision* (Cambridge: Cambridge University Press, 1989).

Germaine Brée and Edouard Morot-Sir, *Littérature française. Vol. 9: Du Surréalisme à l'empire de la critique* (Paris: Arthaud, 1984).

Georges-Emmanuel Clancier, *Panorama de la poésie française de Rimbaud au Surréalisme*, 3rd edn (Paris: Seghers, 1970).

Dorothy Knowles, *French Drama of the Interwar Years* (London: Harrap, 1967).

Raymond Pouilliart and Michel Décaudin, *Littérature française. Vol. 8: De Zola à Guillaume Apollinaire* (Paris: Arthaud, 1984).

Eliane Tonnet-Lacroix, *La Littérature française de l'entre-deux-guerres* (Paris: Nathan, 1993).

CHAPTER 8

French Literature since 1940

COLIN DAVIS

France was invaded by Germany in 1940 and occupied until 1944, with the unoccupied part of France governed by the collaborationist Vichy regime headed by Marshal Pétain. The liberation was followed by a period of often brutal *épuration* (purges), during which scores were settled between self-declared Resisters and alleged collaborators. General de Gaulle, leader of the Free French movement, became the first president of the Fourth Republic, and women were finally given the vote in 1945. De Gaulle resigned from office in 1946, but returned to power in 1958 to preside over the founding of the Fifth Republic.

After the war France became involved in a series of violent struggles as its colonies sought independence. In particular the Algerian War, beginning in 1954, divided the nation and led to allegations of war crimes against the French army; the independence of Algeria was finally proclaimed in 1962 (see also page 219).

In 1957 the Treaty of Rome led to the founding of the Common Market (out of which the European Union evolved) with its six original members: France, Germany, Italy, Belgium, the Netherlands and Luxemburg. In the sixties, social and political unrest culminated in the student agitation and general strike of May 1968. Although de Gaulle remained as president during this period, he resigned in 1969 and died in 1970. The events of May 1968 contributed to a general change in the political and intellectual landscape: the influence of

Marxism declined, as artists and thinkers sought liberation from constraining systems of thought.

Moral Dilemmas (1940–70)

Aujourd'hui maman est morte. Ou peut-être hier, je ne sais pas. J'ai reçu un télégramme de l'asile: 'Mère décédée. Enterrement demain. Sentiments distingués.' Cela ne veut rien dire. C'était peut-être hier.*

This is the first paragraph of Albert Camus's *L'Étranger*, published in 1942, and so appearing right at the beginning of the period to be discussed in this chapter. The novel describes an apparently disconnected series of events in the life of its protagonist, Meursault, a white Frenchman living in Algeria: his mother dies, he starts an affair, he kills an Arab on a beach; at the end of the novel he is in prison, awaiting execution for murder. Many of the important features of modern literature are already present in the opening lines of the text. The first word, 'Aujourd'hui', seems to offer precise information, but nevertheless refers to a moment in time which remains unidentifiable. This is followed by a potentially ambiguous construction, 'maman est morte': does this mean that she is now dead (implying that she may have died some time ago), or that she actually died on the day in question? The next sentence seems to resolve this question in favour of the latter construction; but in fact this resolution is of little help to the reader, since we do not know what the deictics 'today' or 'yesterday' refer to, and anyway the word 'peut-être' indicates the narrator's own continuing uncertainties. Any emotion which might be bound up with the death of the mother is absent from the text, either suppressed by the narrator or inexpressible except in the most formulaic clichés: 'Sentiments distingués.' The narrator warns us that 'Cela ne veut rien dire', but again it is not clear what this phrase refers to: the death of

---

* 'Today mother died [is dead]. Or perhaps yesterday, I don't know. I received a telegram from the home: "Mother deceased. Burial tomorrow. Deepest sympathies." That doesn't mean anything. Perhaps it was yesterday.'

the mother? The telegram? Or the whole of the text that we are currently reading?

The ambiguities that we can see here, the calculated disorientations of the reader, the implied reflection on the limitations of language, and the threat of a descent into nonsense, remain the central issues of French literature from the 1940s to the present day. In the course of *L'Étranger* another crucial problem emerges: the question of values. Meursault, the narrator, commits the apparently senseless murder of an Arab. At his trial, the criteria on which his guilt or innocence are judged are ruthlessly ironized. The prosecution illustrates his moral degeneracy by the fact that he drank coffee and smoked a cigarette over his mother's coffin, that he failed to cry at her funeral, and that on the following day he went to see a comedy film and took a new lover. Moreover, the public execution that awaits him at the end of the novel is no less barbaric than his own meaningless act. In his own narrative, then, Meursault implies that he is the innocent victim of a society which brutally suppresses the misfit whom it cannot understand and who acts according to different principles. But Meursault is not the paragon of sincerity and victim of injustice that he tends to make of himself in his own account. We need to be aware here, as in all narrative of the century, that the text may be misleading us. Meursault is, after all, a murderer. He kills without conscience, without apparent motive (the fact that the Arab was threatening him with a knife is barely sufficient, since Meursault was holding a revolver at the time), and without remorse (though he does regret the inconveniences which arise from being imprisoned). And perhaps he knows more about the crime than he is letting on: why did he return to the spot where he had previously encountered the Arab? Is it significant that it is precisely an Arab who is murdered? Could Meursault be acting on some racist impulse (Meursault, like Camus, came from a family of European origins living in Algeria)?

In Camus's sparse parable of what became known as the absurd, there are more questions than answers. The reader is likely to be confused by the knowledge that Meursault is guilty and by the implication in the text that he is somehow innocent, unjustly judged by an uncomprehending society. But if the values of society are arbitrary and hollow, what is there to replace them? The novel undermines the system of justice and established values, but leaves us with the dizzying perspective of having no criteria on which to condemn Meursault's mindless criminality.

The moral ambiguities and confusions with which *L'Étranger* confronts the reader are the thematic counterpart of the textual ambiguities illustrated in its opening lines. The rest of this chapter will discuss how, with differing emphasis, much of the important writing of recent years explores these same issues.

The experience of the French defeat by the Germans in 1940 and the following years of Occupation served as a turning point for many writers of the period. They gave focus to ethical dilemmas explored in the 1930s by writers such as Malraux and Mauriac (see pages 164 and 167), obliging their successors to take position in a world of muddled morality. In this respect the evolution of Jean-Paul Sartre, whom some regard as the most important French intellectual of the twentieth century, is instructive. (See also pages 228–33.) His pre-war novel *La Nausée* (1938) is a study of existence, futility and the senselessness of life, and of the ways literature confers inauthentic meaning on the flux and chaos of lived experience. The notion that art should be committed to some political or ideological cause is ridiculed as a comforting lie told to give ourselves an illusory sense of purpose. Yet by the mid-1940s Sartre was the best-known champion of 'la littérature engagée' (see below), advocating it in theory in his essay 'Qu'est-ce que la littérature?' (in *Situations II*, 1948), putting it into practice in his novels and plays, and providing a forum for further discussion in *Les Temps modernes*, the influential journal founded with Simone de Beauvoir in 1945.

Sartre carefully distinguished between committed literature and polemical or didactic literature. As outlined in 'Qu'est-ce que la littérature?', committed literature is not a form of propaganda which attempts to bludgeon its reader into sharing the author's opinion. In fact, committed literature is a slightly misleading translation of *la littérature engagée*: literature should be (and always is, in Sartre's view) *engagée* in the sense of involved, bound up in, rather than following an unswerving commitment to a particular view or course of action. This does not mean that the text can never express an authorial view. In Sartre's *Le Sursis* (1945), the second of the unfinished cycle of novels entitled *Les Chemins de la liberté* (1945–9), the Munich Treaty of 1938 (which effectively allowed Hitler to invade Czechoslovakia) is presented as an ignominious betrayal by French and British politicians, in counterpoint to and hence implicitly compared to an act of rape.

But such passages of undisguised outrage are the exception rather than the rule in the best committed literature of the period. Ambiguity is in fact its more characteristic feature. The central themes of choice, action and responsibility would be shorn of their power and relevance if they were depicted as easy solutions to urgent historical problems. The supporters of the Resistance in Simone de Beauvoir's wartime novel *Le Sang des autres* (1945) are aware that their actions will lead to the deaths of innocent French citizens through Nazi reprisals. They decide that such a price is worth paying, but the reader is not coerced into accepting their decision. The difficulty of choice dramatized in such texts results in an openness to interpretation, as actions are always ambiguous, their meaning never fully commanded by any character or author. Thus, two texts which apparently bear a message of resistance, Vercors's short novel *Le Silence de la mer* (1942) and Anouilh's play *Antigone* (1944), have been seen at least by some readers and audiences as coming dangerously close to collaboration. In *Le Silence de la mer* a Frenchman and his niece refuse to communicate with a German officer billeted in their house. But the officer is depicted as patient, civilized and humane; the silence of his unwilling hosts may seem petty, spiteful and futile rather than a genuine act of resistance. In Anouilh's version of the Antigone story, the Greek princess who defies tyrannical laws in order to bury one of her brothers may well have appeared to its original French audiences as a symbol of resistance; nowadays many readers and spectators find her actions childish (she insists on having her own way), senseless (she does not believe in the religious ritual she is enacting) and suicidal. On the other hand, Créon, the tyrannical king, may appear to be a more reasonable character, accepting the necessity for compromise if real changes are to be effected. The fact that such interpretations may go against authorial intention or original reception of the works does not necessarily invalidate them. They are possible because the texts in question dramatize the precariousness of action and meaning, showing that responsibility is borne by the individual (and ultimately by the reader) rather than guaranteed by some external, absolute and fixed system of values.

This is most clear in Sartre's own literary works. Sartre has the reputation of someone for whom literature serves as a vehicle for the expression of philosophical doctrine. This is, however, a fundamental misunderstanding of the tentative, ambiguous and exploratory nature of his literary writing. For Sartre, actions and choices are inserted in a context which may change or annul their meaning; characters may fail to grasp their own motives and the consequences of their actions, thereby transforming the authenticity which they aimed to achieve into the worst kind of bad faith. In *Les Mouches* (1943) Oreste returns to Argos, where he was born, and realizes that his existence up to that point had been futile. He decides to commit an irrevocable act: he assassinates the king and queen, Égisthe and Clytemnestre (who is also his own mother), thus removing tyrants from power and giving the people of Argos the chance to rid themselves of the guilt, superstition and blind obedience in which they had been imprisoned. Oreste's apparently exemplary act of existentialist self-creation has evident resonances of resistance to the German Occupation during the war. But on examination, Oreste's heroism may be more fraught than it appears. He may be motivated as much by revenge (Égisthe and Clytemnestre had murdered his father) or by a desperate need for a sense of belonging as by purely political considerations; by leaving Argos at the end of the play he avoids the dangers of replacing Égisthe's rule with his own, but also risks making his act futile, as the people of Argos may well ignore his lesson in freedom and revert to their old ways. Oreste's self-liberation may turn out to be as senseless as it is violent.

Sartre's novels and plays explore the obstacles in the path to freedom: the influence of others, self-delusion, the role of family, social background and historical context. In *Huis clos* (1944) three characters are trapped in a bourgeois hell, unable to affirm themselves without the collusion of their antagonistic companions. In *Les Mains sales* (1948) Hugo wants to commit a political assassination; but after the event he still cannot understand his own motives, and anyway by a quirk of history the party which ordered the assassination has now adopted the views of his victim; the play ends with Hugo going to a meaningless death. In *Les Séquestrés d'Altona* (1960), Sartre's last original play, the prospects of freedom have been all but extinguished, as the central figure, Frantz, appears as the hideous product of family, society and history. Like Hugo, he eventually escapes into death because he cannot face up to the world as it is.

Committed literature is committed in as far as it faces up to questions which, in the France of the 1940s and 1950s, had an immediate relevance and urgency: the admissibility of violence in political struggle, torture, revolution, the relationship between means and ends in the pursuit of effective resistance to tyranny. As the French were drawn into the Algerian War of Independence in the mid-1950s and were accused of committing some of the same atrocities as the Germans in the 1940s, such themes were still of pressing importance. Frantz, in *Les Séquestrés d'Altona*, had permitted the torture of Russian partisans during the Second World War; produced at the time of the Algerian War, Sartre's play implicitly draws a comparison between the French and the Nazis (the similarity between 'Frantz' and 'France' is no coincidence). The point is not so much to convey a philosophical or political message as to draw the audience into the process of choice, judgement and responsibility. Ultimately, the audience is both judge and accused, led to condemn but also to acknowledge complicity, as the play ends with a tape-recorded speech indicting human barbarity in the twentieth century. In Sartre's version of it, then, committed literature depends for its effects on the engagement of the reader or spectator in the text; and if we are engaged we are also compromised, as we are confronted with our desire to avoid choice and evade responsibility.

Along with Sartre, the most important literary figure of the immediate post-war years was Camus. (See also page 232.) Camus's personal and intellectual relations with Sartre were at first close, then embittered by their public and much-publicized rift in the 1950s. Camus on the whole remains more moderate than Sartre, less willing to envisage radical political and ethical solutions; but his work is very much rooted in the same need to explore the limits and consequences of human action in a historical context where no values can be taken for granted. He provided in *L'Étranger* the hero and in *Le Mythe de Sisyphe* (both 1942) the most potent symbol of the absurd: Sisyphus rolls his rock up a hill and then watches it roll back down again. Camus's conception of the absurd derives from the tension between the human desire for order and meaning on the one hand and the resistance of the world to that desire on the other; the world eludes the purpose and significance which we inevitably and instinctively try to impose on it. This tension gives rise to the fundamental problem of values which haunts Camus's principal fictional works: if terms such as right and wrong, good and evil, have no real meaning, how is it possible to affirm any set of values over any other? Meursault in *L'Étranger* kills the Arab partly because he can see no reason not to: he is oblivious of any moral, religious or social imperative which might make such an action wrong. The protagonist of Camus's play *Caligula* (1945) discovers that death annuls all human values, so that no act is inherently any better or worse than any other. But this levelling of values is intolerable: Meursault must be executed for the murder he commits; Caligula is murdered by his subjects, who refuse to accept the violent consequences of his insight. Camus's work, then, is propelled by a rejection of established values, and by the awareness that a simple abandonment of those values results in barbarism.

Camus's *La Peste* (1947) was heralded on its publication as the first great post-war novel. It deals with how a group of people respond to a fictional plague which strikes the town of Oran, in Algeria, at some unspecified time during the 1940s. The plague has been read as an allegory of the German Occupation of France, and more generally as a symbol of evil in the world. The crucial issue in the novel is how, in the proximity to the senselessness and arbitrariness of death, human values may be maintained. The central characters discover a core of strength and selflessness within themselves which permits them to struggle against the plague even though their struggle often seems hopeless. This allows the narrator to conclude, after the withdrawal of the plague, that there are more things to admire in people (he says: in men) than there are to despise. The optimism of the novel lies in its attempt to ground a system of values in collective struggle against a common enemy.

However, even at its moments of greatest optimism, Camus's fiction throws doubt upon its own system of values. *La Peste* makes clear that the solidarity achieved by its central characters is both untypical of the people of Oran in general and entirely ineffective against the plague, which abates for reasons unrelated to human effort. Whilst some are combating the plague, others are trying to escape or profiteering from the black market. A bleaker picture shadows the more optimistic perspective foregrounded in the novel. The other side of the story, in which people appear as despicable rather than admirable, is highlighted in *La Chute* (1956). In the later novel the speaker, Jean-Baptiste Clamence, illustrates the duplicity of our moral impulses: even in our most selfless actions we are behaving selfishly, creating a favourable image that we as well as others will mistake for our true selves. Clamence's cultivated cynicism is in part a satire of Camus's self-satisfied intellectual contemporaries (in particular, it has been suggested, Sartre). But the contrast between the surface optimism of *La Peste* and the moral pessimism of *La Chute* is both illuminating and troublesome. Clamence draws the reader into a disorienting verbal labyrinth which is at the same time seductive and desolate.

Camus makes Clamence unappealing, but the conclusion to *La Peste* is glib and unpersuasive, even on its own terms. Neither the treacherous pessimism of *La Chute* nor the surface optimism of *La Peste* can be taken as representing Camus's own position. His work dramatizes an uncompleted dialogue with moments of hope and despondency but without resolution. So Camus's fiction oscillates between the search to establish values and the awareness of the futility of any such search, between the knowledge that nothing is better than anything else and the awareness that such knowledge is intolerable and unacceptable.

The key problems of many of the texts of this period crystallize around the issue of humanism: in the absence of objective or universal criteria, can man (to use the term which, despite de Beauvoir's ground-breaking feminist study *Le Deuxième Sexe*, 1949, goes largely unquestioned until the 1960s) forge for himself a scale of values which will save him from chaos? Texts of the post-war period oscillate between the poles of humanism and anti-humanism in the attempt to deal with the sense that established systems of belief were no longer valid. Roger Nimier gave voice to a cult of dis-enchanted youth in novels such as *Le Hussard bleu* (1950) and *Les Enfants tristes* (1951); and Boris Vian assumed a flippant but sinister tone in a series of comic, absurd, violent and despairing novels beginning with *L'Écume des jours* (1946). The political struggles of the period, and women's search for self-emancipation, are described in Simone de Beauvoir's *Les Mandarins* (1954), *La Force des choses* (1963), *Les Belles Images* (1966) and *La Femme rompue* (1967).

The war was followed by a period of political and moral debate in which authors often appeared at odds as much with themselves as with one another. Ambiguities within individual literary texts are compounded by shifts in the stance of authors throughout their careers. In *Les Mots* (1964), Sartre ironizes the power of committed literature which he had done so much to promote. The work of Marguerite Yourcenar, who in 1980 became the first woman to be admitted to the Académie française, also illustrates both hope and despair in the force of the values she attempts to maintain. In *Mémoires d'Hadrien* (1958) she goes back to the second century AD and to the Roman Emperor Hadrian to depict a brief time when, in the absence of the gods, man came into his own; but in her later novel *L'Oeuvre au noir* (1968) she depicts her humane hero hounded to his death by the prejudice and stupidity of those around him. The humanists are clinging on to a faith in humankind which their own texts often show to be unwarranted. Some, like Sartre, found a provisional answer in existentialism and Marxism; others, like the poet and novelist Louis Aragon, stuck with the Communist Party. All are engaged in a search for values. What gives Camus his particular status in this period is the manner in which his work attempts to negotiate the logical absurdity at the heart of writing during the immediate post-war period: the simultaneous preservation of faith in humankind as a centre of real value, and the bitter knowledge that so much accumulated evidence from the war years and later had undermined the foundations of such faith.

Experimentation: 1950–80

In 1953 Samuel Beckett's play *En attendant Godot* was first performed. On a nearly bare stage two clowns (later usually represented as tramps) pass the time. They are waiting for Godot, who never comes; for a while they are joined by a man named Pozzo and his slave Lucky. In the second act, they are still waiting; Pozzo, who is now blind, returns with Lucky. Godot does not come, the play ends. Audiences were understandably baffled. Compared with the moral seriousness of Sartre and Camus, the play seemed trivial or unintelligible. Yet the shock occasioned by the play was also in part a shock of recognition, as audiences felt that somehow their own lives were represented in this bleak drama of futility and disappointed expectations.

Beckett soon became associated with a number of other playwrights, such as Eugène Ionesco, Jean Genet and Arthur Adamov, who shared a willingness to explore new types of theatrical writing. In 1961 the critic Martin Esslin described their work as the Theatre of the Absurd, and the label has stuck. Amongst avant-garde playwrights, poets and novelists it became commonplace to argue that the best-known writers of the immediate post-war period were intererested only in the message they wished to convey; they had neglected aesthetic values and their works, for all their radical content, were reactionary from an artistic point of view. The 1950s and 1960s saw an experimental explosion in French literature, as authors explored the limits of their chosen genres and sought to extend their aesthetic and expressive capabilities. Committed literature was depicted as a straitjacket that restricted the potential of art to the most predictable forms and messages.

The desire to experiment with new forms produced an extraordinary diversity amongst the works actually produced. Although, for example, Beckett and Ionesco are often cited together as belonging to the Theatre of the Absurd, their plays have little in common beyond a shared rejection of plot, rational dialogue and coherent characterization. Whereas Beckett is sparing with words and actions, Ionesco can be linguistically exuberant, with words and objects (such as the chairs in *Les Chaises*, 1952) proliferating to create an increasingly senseless and oppressive clutter. Genet is different again; in *Les Bonnes* (1947), *Le Balcon* (1956), *Les Nègres* (1959) and *Les Paravents* (1965) he sets out to provoke and shock with his grotesquely exaggerated characterizations, his lampooning of bourgeois culture, and the constant disorientation of the audience through role-play and illusion. Such bold experiments were encouraged by innovative directors (Roger Blin, Jean-Louis Barrault, Roger Planchon, Ariane Mnouchkine) who pushed production techniques to their limits, using sparse, bare stages or alternatively grotesque, ritualistic exaggeration in order to wrest theatre from its realist conventions.

The same diversity, combined with rejection of the tenets of commitment, can be seen in the poetry of the period. Poetry had never been considered to be a particularly suitable medium for commitment. In 'Qu'est-ce que la littérature?' Sartre had argued that poetry could not be committed because it made language into something opaque and therefore did not engage with the practical, social and political world. Although Sartre subsequently revised this view, many poets were only too happy not to be committed in the Sartrean sense. Individual writers such as Francis Ponge (*Le Parti pris des choses*, 1942; *Proêmes*, 1948) and René Char (*Feuillets d'hypnos*,

1946; *La Parole en archipel*, 1962; *Commune présence*, 1964) had for some time been pursuing their own projects on the margins of mainstream literature, attempting (in Ponge's case) to refine a language capable of expressing the human encounter with the world of objects or (in Char's) to find in language resonances lost in ordinary usage. The move to give greater fluidity to poetic forms begun in the nineteenth century continued to the point that the word 'poetry' comes to cover a range of texts with little obvious in common, from the lyrical effusions of Saint-John Perse (*Exil*, 1941–4; *Vents*, 1946; *Amers*, 1957) and the sober prose essays of Ponge to the sparse fragments of Char, the obscure, near-mystical visions of Yves Bonnefoy (*Du mouvement et de l'immobilité de Douve*, 1953), the Rabbinic dialogues of Edmond Jabès (*Le Livre des questions*, 1963) and the drug-induced visions of Henri Michaux (*L'Infini turbulent*, 1957).

In the field of narrative fiction, the fifties saw the beginning of what became known as the *Nouveau Roman*. This term was adopted to draw together a group of writers (Nathalie Sarraute, Alain Robbe-Grillet, Claude Simon, Claude Ollier, Jean Ricardou, Michel Butor) with little in common other than that most of them were published by the Éditions de Minuit. Explicitly rejecting committed literature and what they regarded as the outdated, ossified forms of realist fiction, they set out to thwart their readers' expectations of coherence in plot and characterization. They tended to attribute (often wrongly) to the Realist novelists of the nineteenth century (see pages 129–33) a naive faith in the power of language to encapsulate reality. The traditional novel, it was argued, clarifies and simplifies the world by implying that it can be impartially viewed, understood and judged. New linguistic, psychological and epistemological theories required new narrative strategies: if language is opaque, ordering our experience of the world rather than reflecting it, if identity is fragmented, elusive, constantly in flux, and if the world is never knowable except partially and unreliably, then fiction should also be opaque, disordered and confusing.

The New Novelists are linked by a preoccupation with the nature, limits and function of narrative. As a consequence, their texts often take literature itself as their own principal subject. Sarraute's *Les*

Fruits d'or (1963), for example, contains snatches of dialogue revolving around a fictional novel, also called *Les Fruits d'or*; opinions differ, contrary judgements are expressed, so that in the end we have the impression that the novel itself is not a fixed object, that the only knowledge we may have of it is treacherous, or more generally that any book only exists in our different readings of it. Butor's *Degrés* (1960) revolves around the attempt to describe in words an hour's lesson on the discovery of America; as the book progresses, it becomes increasingly clear that the lived reality eludes language. In such texts, as Jean Ricardou put it, literature is no longer 'le récit d'une aventure', but rather 'l'aventure d'un récit'.* The texts turn in on themselves and their own narrative procedures; the act of writing becomes the ultimate subject of the novel.

The 1950s and 1960s were, then, an extraordinarily fertile time for experimentation and innovation in all literary and intellectual fields. In 1960 Raymond Queneau and François le Lionnais brought together a group of writers and mathematicians to found L'Ouvroir de littérature potentielle (Oulipo), a group dedicated to extending the bounds of literature. The journal *Tel Quel* (founded in 1960) brought together some of the most radical writers and intellectuals of the period: Philippe Sollers, Roland Barthes, Julia Kristeva, Jacques Derrida. This was a period of intellectual and aesthetic hedonism, where conventions appeared as constraints to be rejected rather than as enabling paradigms. Anything seemed worth trying at least once: in 1947 Raymond Queneau had recounted the same banal incident ninety-nine times in *Exercices de style*, each time in a different style; in 1960 he published ten sonnets with interchangeable lines, which in different combinations could generate, as the title suggested, *Cent mille milliards de poèmes*. Georges Perec wrote a novel (*La Disparition*, 1969) in which the most common letter in the French language, *e*, did not appear once, and then a novel, *Les Revenentes* (*sic*, 1972) in which no vowel except *e* appeared; Philippe Sollers wrote without punctuation, for example in *H* (1973); and some of Derrida's essays (see also pages 241–7) are fragmented, written as dialogues or laid out on the page in parallel columns, or with incomplete sentences. Generic boundaries of literature are put into question,

---

* 'the story of an adventure' . . . 'the adventure of a story'

and particularly in the 1960s the general term *écriture* tends to be used indiscriminately to describe all forms of writing, with terms such as 'novel', 'poetry' and 'essay' depicted as reactionary and redundant.

The moral earnestness of post-war writing seemed to have been surpassed in the spirit of experimentation which took hold of the 1950s and 1960s. And yet, authors tended to simplify both their predecessors' and their own practice in order to emphasize the novelty of what they were doing. It was rarely the case that their texts were merely self-regarding artefacts. One of the constants of French avant-garde thinking is the belief that changes in the modes of writing have far-reaching consequences; new literary forms open up areas of meaning that were previously inaccessible, making possible new ways of thinking and perceiving the world. Robbe-Grillet gave the title 'Nouveau Roman, homme nouveau' to one of the essays collected in *Pour un nouveau roman* (1963), thereby suggesting that the difficulties and obscurities of the *Nouveau Roman* should not be regarded simply as exercises in self-absorbed narcissism. Although committed literature is rejected, experimental writing does turn out to have its own form of commitment. It is engaged in a project of demystification, attacking the deep-rooted myths of bourgeois society, our faith in the stability of our own identity, in fixed moral values and the intelligibility of the world around us.

So, the very obscurity and and apparent meaninglessness of some experimental writing can be interpreted as contributing to the meaning of the works in question. Beckett's static dramas, in which nothing happens (again and again), can be taken as metaphysical representations of human reality pared down to essentials. His characters typically come in pairs: Estragon and Vladimir in *En attendant Godot* (1953), Hamm and Clov in *Fin de partie* (1957), Winnie and Willie in *Oh les beaux jours!* (1963). These pairs are almost interchangeable in their names and characteristics, mutually antagonistic, always on the point of leaving one another, but kept together by a desperate need for some remnant of human contact. The difficulties of Sarraute's novels can be explained by reference to her theory of tropisms: these are, she suggests, imperceptible movements, emotions or thoughts of which we are usually only dimly aware, but which are constantly present just below the level of consciousness. The endeavour to capture them in words is necessarily paradoxical, since it entails the attempt to fix what is by nature fleeting and non-verbal. The hybrid mixture of dialogue, internal monologue and stream of consciousness which she develops in her books responds to the need for a literary technique supple enough to follow the rapid movements of these tropisms.

Even the texts which seem most rebarbative to interpretation can be understood in ways which emphasize their place within the tradition as much as their rejection of it. Robbe-Grillet's *La Jalousie* (1957) can be read as a pure exercise in writing technique: we are only disoriented by the repetitions, inconsistencies and oddities of the narrative if we maintain the traditional expectation that the text will have a subject with a coherent plot and characters. On the other hand we can, and most readers do, assume that the novel does tell a story of sorts, but one that is filtered through the perspective of a disturbed, obsessive narrator, observing the signs of his wife's possible infidelity. The text thus appears as not quite a Gidean *récit*, but nevertheless as a sort of first-person narrative (even though the first-person pronoun is not used) which focuses on the pathological study of jealousy. The narrator inhabits a terrifying world of unreliable memory and perception, hopelessly trying to make sense out of ambiguous signs and inconclusive evidence. Such a reading is to some extent recuperative, restoring, in a way that not all would accept, the implication that the text is more than a space where *écriture* explores its own navel, and that there is indeed something behind the words akin to characters and a story. In this reading, the aim of representing human reality has not fundamentally been abandoned; however, the techniques by which representation should be achieved have changed in accordance with revised views of the nature of the world to be depicted. Enigmatic, self-questioning, elusive modes of writing correspond to a reality without fixed identities and reliable access to intelligible experiences. Most crucially, they attempt to contend with a view of language which becomes commonplace during the structuralist and poststructuralist periods (see pages 233–47), namely that language actually moulds our knowledge of the world, providing tools which constrain the ways in which we understand ourselves and our experience. In this context, changing the forms of writing becomes a way of changing reality itself, at least in as far as we have access to it.

It would be a mistake to suggest that radical forms of writing necessarily go together with radical politics. The novels of Robbe-Grillet, for example, are full of the most reactionary racial, cultural and sexual stereotypes, with misogynistic elements shamelessly foregrounded. However, it is equally mistaken to make a sharp distinction between committed and experimental writing, implying that the latter does not have its own political and moral programme. This is clearest in the case of some of the feminist writing which emerged in the wake of the events of May 1968. Unhappy with the attitudes of male militants, which often did not match the ideals of liberation and equality they defended in principle, some women writers and intellectuals began to explore the possibility of specifically female forms of thought and experience, developing what became known as *l'écriture féminine*.

In their theoretical writings, Julia Kristeva, Luce Irigaray and Hélène Cixous (see pages 247–50) suggested that Western thought has typically claimed universality for what are in fact male-dominated perspectives; in the process, the female has been repressed and muted. Women's experience may be different from that of men, who have no first-hand knowledge of, for example, menstruation, childbirth or breast-feeding. The problem for the woman writer is that the literary forms available to her, and the very language of literature, are inappropriate for the expression of female experience. Following the lines of this argument, traditional literary forms were not just, as the New Novelists insisted, based upon misapprehensions about language and reality, but also based upon specifically male, partriarchal misapprehensions. Even avant-garde authors, from the Surrealists to Robbe-Grillet, often reproduced the most stereotypical images of women despite their rejection of stereotypes in other areas. A new subject-matter was sought by women writers, in particular woman's relationship to her body, and they required a new language in which to express it.

Écriture féminine gives a specifically feminist edge to the search for new literary languages in which many of the most prominent authors were engaged from the 1950s to the 1970s. A series of ground-breaking texts explored the possibility of a language of the body, following the rhythms of female experience and sexuality, giving voice to a muted group: Annie Leclerc's *Parole de femme* (1974), Hélène Cixous's *Le Rire de la Méduse* (1975), Chantal Chawaf's *Retable* (1974), Jeanne Hyvrard's *Les Prunes de Cythère* (1975), Monique Wittig's *Les Guérillères* (1969) and *Le Corps lesbien* (1973). The theoretical, political and aesthetic differences between these authors gave their texts a diversity which saved them from being dismissed as a group or movement of only local interest. Indeed, the notion of a unified, overarching perspective was one aspect of patriarchal thought which the authors in question sought to dismantle, the value of dialogue and diversity being emphasized by a number of important collaborative texts: *La Jeune Née* (1975) by Cixous and Catherine Clément, *Les Parleuses* (1974) by Marguerite Duras and Xavière Gauthier, *Autrement dit* (1977) by Leclerc and Marie Cardinal.

Much more than any formal innovation, the single most important development in French literature since 1940 has been the enfranchisement of women. Given the vote on an equal footing with men in 1945, they have also gained greater access to the institutions which influence the publishing, reception and study of literature. Marie de France, Marguerite de Navarre, Madame de Lafayette, Madame de Staël, George Sand or Colette are in danger of seeming to be isolated figures when literary histories are drawn up, even when we are reminded that they are only the best-known figures in an alternative, still unknown canon. Although still seriously under-represented on most university syllabuses, the vitality and diversity of writing by women, its intellectual and aesthetic sophistication, the boldness with which it tackles taboo subjects in challenging forms, are beyond dispute.

After the Age of Suspicion: 1970 – the Present

In the title of a well-known essay first published in 1950, Nathalie Sarraute dubbed the modern age 'l'ère du soupçon' (the age of suspicion). Everything could be put into doubt, nothing was beyond question. However, by the late 1970s the experimental hedonism of the previous couple of decades had to some extent run its course: *Tel Quel* ceased to be published in 1982, Philippe Sollers had put punctuation back in his fiction, and the New Novelists had declined in influence. Experimental writing was felt to be inaccessible to a popular audience, too concerned with questions of form and unwilling to make concessions to the expectations and interests of its readers. In more recent years there has been a renewed sense that good writing can also be accessible to a broad audience, increasing its potential impact as it maximizes its actual readership. This does not entail an outright rejection of the experimentation of the preceding years, or an uncritical return to the practices of earlier generations. After the age of suspicion comes ... more suspicion, though some of its strategies and objects have changed along the way. Literature is now in a situation where it must compete with the mass media, often acknowledging a dependence on popular culture but still endeavouring to distinguish itself from it.

In the 1970s and 1980s two authors, Marguerite Duras and Michel Tournier, emerged as being able both to achieve relative popular success (partly, it must be said, by their talent for self-publicizing) and to arouse the interest of a large academic audience. Duras had, in fact, been publishing fiction since the 1940s, and in the 1950s and 1960s she was linked with the New Novelists. Some of the now vast body of her writing is as opaque as anything written in the period; but some of her texts have a deceptive simplicity and directness which lead the reader into a obsessional world of unstable identities and obscure motivations. In *Moderato cantabile* (1958) the central character, Anne Desbaresdes, and a casual acquaintance, Chauvin, form an intense relationship on the basis of a shared fascination for a recent incident in which a man killed his female lover. Together

Anne and Chauvin discuss and perhaps try to recreate this doomed, violent love; yet the event itself remains mysterious, unexplained despite or because of the amount of speculation it generates. Much of Duras's work takes place in proximity to (but never quite in direct contact with) violence, be it a murder in *Moderato cantabile* or *L'Amante anglaise* (1967), the bombing of Hiroshima in the film-script (filmed by Alain Resnais) *Hiroshima mon amour* (1960), or the Nazi concentration camps in *La Douleur* (1985). Duras makes little attempt to justify the fascination of such violence; and rather than a causal explanation for the behaviour of her characters, it serves as a metaphor for the core of pain and bewilderment which their actions betray and which is never fully elucidated.

L'Amant (1984), the text for which Duras finally won the prestigious Prix Goncourt, is on the surface a fairly simple narrative in which an older woman recounts her first affair with a Chinese man when she was a girl in Indo-China. But the text is also a subtle meditation on past and present, memory and imagination, autobiography and fiction, self and other, and the complexities of erotic desire and sexual power. Perhaps more than any other writer, Duras succeeds in finding narrative forms to accommodate both the effects of large-scale violence (Hiroshima, the Holocaust) on the individual and the views of contemporary philosophers and psychoanalysts on the dissolution or decentring of the subject. Her characters are idiosyncratic, yet barely individuated; the same material is constantly, obsessively reworked either within one text or across cycles of interrelated works. The novel *L'Amante anglaise*, for example, drew on material from an earlier play, *Les Viaducs de la Seine-et-Oise* (1960), and was then reworked into another, very different play also entitled *L'Amante anglaise* (1968). Yet despite this constant reworking of obsessive themes, motivations remain elusive, dilemmas are unresolved; with successive retellings the incidents seem less rather than more intelligible. The pain of one character merges seamlessly with that of another and continues unabated from one text to the next.

Whereas Duras was frequently associated with the New Novelists, Michel Tournier defines his literary aims in sharp opposition to them. Accusing them of having privileged form above content and of having abandoned all that was most valuable in French literature, he sets himself up as the defender of tradition, adopting familiar, reassuring forms and adapting well-known stories for the modern age. But for Tournier, using familiar stories and narrative structures is part of a strategy of subversion. His first novel, *Vendredi ou les limbes du Pacifique* (1967), is based on Defoe's *Robinson Crusoe*. Unlike Defoe's Crusoe, Tournier's protagonist loses faith in the society he left behind; he explores an increasingly bizarre sexuality (copulating with a cave, a tree and then directly with the earth), and discovers that Friday, rather than being an ignorant savage, has a great deal to teach him. Finally, given the chance to escape from his island, he rejects society and chooses to stay where he is. Tournier's second and still most stunning novel, *Le Roi des Aulnes* (1970), follows a similar path from reassurance to disturbance. It begins with a comic description of a self-deluding but harmless garage owner in the 1930s, then leads by gradual stages into an increasingly disturbing encounter with perversion, violence and the abuse of power in Nazi Germany. In *Les Météores* (1975), Tournier's third and intellectually most ambitious novel, the initially cosy family drama of Paul and Jean Surin turns into a meditation on homosexuality and incest before culminating in violent dismemberment.

Tournier adopts reassuring, traditional narrative forms in order to subvert his reader's expectations all the more effectively. His highly structured style of writing seems to promise revelations, solutions and resolutions, but these are never unambiguously delivered. From the beginning, his novels present a familiar fictional world with characters, action and plots, a beginning and a middle and an end. But things begin to go wrong. Tournier opposes the New Novelists and rejects the most immediately disorienting narrative techniques which they employed. However, by showing how the traditional paradigms which he adopts fail to account for the experiences of his characters, in some respects Tournier fulfils the subversive aims which the New Novelists laid out but barely realized. From the first lines of their works it is clear that the dark, ambiguous fictions of the New Novelists will not make sense within traditional frameworks; therefore, they tend to preach to the converted, subverting the expectations and entrenched attitudes only of those readers who expect to be subverted. Tournier, on the other hand, initially adopts a reassuring stance in order to draw the reader into texts which turn out to be no less dark and ambiguous than those of the New Novelists. His novels overturn accepted values, explore alternative types of sexuality, give voice to those on the margins of society, and denounce racism in modern France (*La Goutte d'or*, 1985) and the oppressive authority of white, bourgeois, heterosexual attitudes.

In recent years the desire to reinvent literature has been no less ardent than in the 1950s and 1960s, though there have been shifts in the themes and aims adopted, and a greater awareness that the interests and capabilities of readers need to be respected. Whereas Tournier rejects the New Novelists and their most disorienting techniques, whilst reproducing their subversive aims, other authors have found ways of accommodating the avant-garde questioning of literature to their own concerns. Some feminists have explored more conventionally realist, accessible alternatives to *écriture féminine* in the attempt to give literature a role in the study of social conditions and sexual politics, hence in the raising of consciousness and struggle for equality. Claire Etcherelli's *Élise ou la vraie vie* (1967) describes conditions on the factory floor and the exploitation of immigrant workers at the time of the Algerian War; and Marie Cardinal's *Les Mots pour le dire* (1975) recounts the stages of a course of psychoanalysis during which a woman comes to terms with her past, her mother and her self. In her early novels (*Les Armoires vides*, 1974; *Ce qu'ils disent ou rien*, 1977; *La Femme gelée*, 1981) Annie Ernaux reproduces the pressures which condition the sexual and social identity of women in modern society; and in *La Place* (1983) and *Une femme* (1988), which are studies of the narrator's father and mother respectively, she develops a form of writing which combines real, reconstructed and imaginary memories, fiction and autobiography, art and sociological study.

In such texts, the falsehood of the distinction between radical aesthetic concerns and moral commitment is readily apparent. This is illustrated with equal clarity in the works of writers with direct experience of the Nazi concentration camps during the Second World War, such as Jorge Semprun (*Le Grand Voyage*, 1963; *La Montagne blanche*, 1986) and, in particular, Elie Wiesel. The literary career of Wiesel, a survivor of Auschwitz and Buchenwald, has been torn between the sense that the experience of the Holocaust cannot be narrated, least of all in fiction, and that to narrate it is an urgent moral imperative. His earliest texts, the autobiographical *La Nuit* (1958) and the fictional *L'Aube* (1960) and *Le Jour* (1961), are from a formal point of view relatively simple *récits*, with first-person narrators looking back over key incidents in their lives. However, his texts narrate the collapse of all familiar centres of authority in the wake of the Holocaust, with the dissolution of fixed beliefs and the corrosion of the narrators' own sense of selfhood. In his later novels, such as *Le Cinquième Fils* (1983), *Le Crépuscule, au loin* (1987) or *L'Oublié* (1989), Wiesel adopts narrative forms which convey the loss of security which, thematically, his texts describe: multiple narrators, combinations of letters, interior monologue and third-person narrative, rapid oscillations between past and present, memory and imagination. The forms adopted thus mimic Wiesel's central themes, communicating through formal means the anxieties which beset the Holocaust survivor.

The early novels of Patrick Modiano (*La Place de l'étoile*, 1968; *Ronde de nuit*, 1969; *Les Boulevards de ceinture*, 1972) also return to the war years, adopting a fragmented, unstable narrative to convey the unreliability of memory, the confusion of moral certainties and the perceived incoherence of the world. In his later novels he explores time and memory in a manner often reminiscent of Proust, but without the sense of a grand redemptive project whereby the inconsequentiality of life will be redeemed by its transformation into art. Modiano's near-anonymous characters drift through their narratives, recalling past encounters and events, but unable to penetrate their significance. The inconsequential remains resolutely inconsequential; this is characteristic of Modiano's novels and, more generally, represents an important trend in recent French fiction. Jean Echenoz, for example, explores the indirect ways in which grand events impinge on the lives of his protagonists. *Lac* (1989) is a confusing tale of espionage, double agents, abduction and betrayal; yet at the end of the novel what seems most important is that the protagonist is to spend the night at home on his own after his lover's husband returns. *Nous trois* (1992) describes a series of dramatic events (an exploding car, an earthquake, the first French expedition into outer space) which hardly seem to strike the principal characters as out of the ordinary; but at the end a normally suave and self-confident womanizer is made paralysingly indecisive when the woman he loves telephones to arrange a meeting. Having remained sanguine as he circled around the earth in a spaceship, he cannot now even decide which shirt to wear.

The novels of Jean-Philippe Toussaint, *La Salle de bain* (1985), *Monsieur* (1986), *L'Appareil-photo* (1988) and *La Réticence* (1991), are perhaps the boldest of recent attempts to write about nothing very much. They are sustained by the quirky and fragile accommodation of Toussaint's characters to the lack of any sense of purpose or significance. In *La Salle de bain*, for example, a man spends time in Paris, then in Venice, and returns to Paris; as far as we can tell, the novel ends more or less as it had begun. Apparently hovering on the edge of crisis, Toussaint's characters defend themselves with habit and a preoccupation with the inconsequential. The disjointed incidents which punctuate the texts are not transformed by the revelation of their initially hidden significance; instead they are preserved in all their anecdotal senselessness.

In the texts of Modiano, Echenoz and Toussaint there are incidents which befall the characters but no event which might transform their lives; things happen in disjointed series rather than meaningful sequence. In their different ways the authors are exploring new relationships between the tale and the manner of its telling. This involves the adoption of a style which respects conventions of syntax, aesthetic balance and intelligibility, but which preserves the disconnectedness of experience, eschewing the transformation of accident into necessity. In these texts, then, it is possible to observe the emergence of a literary practice which maintains the readability of the text whilst gently sabotaging its, or its reader's, desire for significant patterns. This corresponds to an uncertainty concerning the status or purpose of literature. Unable to redeem the self or recover the past, some of the best modern French writing has been characterized by the modesty of its aims and the banality of its subject-matter. The disenchantment which inhabits texts by Modiano, Toussaint and Echenoz is also a disenchantment with art. This is not to deny the seriousness of their writing; but on thematic and formal levels their fiction registers a loss of mission and purpose. As a disenchanted art of the inconsequential, without goals or overarching self-justification, literature participates in the contemporary epistemological and ethical impasse.

This chapter has followed a loose chronological progression, though the distinction between committed and experimental literature is neither essentially periodic nor ultimately reliable. On the one hand, French literature of the period has advanced through a series of reactions and counter-reactions (the New Novelists rejecting commitment in the name of aesthetic licence, more recent writers rejecting experimental fiction in the name of content and communication); on the other hand, the rejected term often did not have the negative characteristics polemically ascribed to it. Committed literature was ambiguous, with openness of meaning the inevitable consequence of its insight into the difficulty of choice and the complexities of freedom; the experimental writers of the 1950s and 1960s dreamed of transforming reality every bit as fundamentally (though by different means) as their committed precursors; and the return to more traditional forms and themes in recent writing does not curtail the radical self-questioning and self-renewal of the forms and functions of literature. Despite rumours to the contrary, French literature is alive and well; and the dead end which it seems to have reached has so far proved to be a source of tremendous creative energy.

Further Reading

Elizabeth Fallaize, *French Women's Writing: Recent Fiction* (London: Macmillan, 1993).

Emmanuel Jacquart, *Le Théâtre de la dérision: Beckett, Ionesco, Adamov* (Paris: Gallimard, 1974).

Ann Jefferson, *The Nouveau Roman and the Poetics of Fiction* (Cambridge: Cambridge University Press, 1980).

Christopher Robinson, *French Literature in the Twentieth Century* (Newton Abbot: David and Charles, 1980).

Michael Tilby (ed.), *Beyond the Nouveau Roman: Essays on the Contemporary French Novel* (New York: Berg, 1990).

CHAPTER 9

Francophone Literatures

BELINDA JACK

Francophone Literatures, Nationalisms and Nomenclature

The recognition of the existence of francophone (and for that matter anglophone, lusophone and hispanophone) literatures is a recent phenomenon. It implies the existence of literature in French (and other European languages) which can no longer be appropriated by, or unproblematically annexed to, the mainstream European 'parent', and often colonizer's, literature. That the writing of France's European neighbours Belgium and Switzerland displayed particular 'local colour' or certain local concerns was recognized early on; the same is true of French Canadian writing. The European countries were by the nineteenth century independent nation states (as was Haiti, the first black republic) and Canada became a dominion in 1867 with considerable autonomy. Institutions in these countries, and small literary groups in Martinique, Guadeloupe, Guyana and Madagascar, for example, were themselves concerned to propose national (loosely defined) literary traditions when questions of nationalism dominated political, cultural and intellectual life. But despite these attempts to assert difference and differing degrees of literary independence, texts deemed worthy of recognition by the French were, on the whole, assimilated into French literature; other texts were regarded as constituting 'regional literatures', tributaries or annexes of French literature. By and large, of course, the major literary influences in the areas mentioned were French, and many writers were participating in more or less orthodox ways in the major French or European movements (Romanticism, Parnassianism, Symbolism, and later and more problematically Surrealism, for example). Writing by Africans, particularly Sub-Saharan Africans, on the other hand, which emerged later than in other areas, was annexed by the colonial sciences, those disciplines serving the colonial venture. Thus the prefaces which accompanied the first texts in French by Africans were written by ethnologists and colonial administrators rather than literary historians or critics. They were concerned above all with 'colonial literature's' role in the adventure of empire. One such critic, Roland Lebel,* claimed in 1925 that works of 'colonial literature':

> *revêtiront un intérêt ethnographique et traduiront la psychologie des races; dans le domaine colonial, cette curiosité naturelle prend une signification plus précise: c'est l'expression du besoin de la connaissance intime du pays et de ses habitants, utile à notre domination.*†

It is now recognized that a plurality of literatures written in the French language (or languages) exists, even if the status of these literatures falls short of the autonomy of certain literatures written in English or Spanish. American and Australian literatures were the first to assert, and be widely recognized as having, literary traditions of their own. More recently American (and indeed Australian) critics have initiated and largely fired a lively debate concerning the 'postcolonial'. Drawing frequently on writers associated with 'French' theory (Michel Foucault, Jacques Derrida, Jean Baudrillard, Jean-François Lyotard, Louis Althusser, Michel Pêcheux, most persistently), they have explored the relationships between the 'postmodern', 'poststructuralist' and 'postcolonial'.

---

* Details of works quoted and marked by an asterisk appear on page 225.
† 'will provide ethnographic interest and will translate the psychology of the races; in the colonial domain, this natural curiosity takes on a more precise significance: it is the expression of the need for intimate knowledge of the country and its inhabitants, useful for our domination.'

Although French centres for the study of francophone literatures have been established (the Centre d'études francophones at the Université de Paris XIII, most importantly), France's relationship with the francophone world, in large part its former colonies, remains a highly complex one. In the literary field, the lack of consensus concerning nomenclature is symptomatic of the dissolution of the debate, and militates against the genesis of a more homogeneous discipline. Thus the literatures briefly discussed here are known by their national appellations (Belgian, Mauritian, etc.), but also under a wide range of different kinds of rubric and grouping: 'Negro', 'Neo-African', 'Negro-African', 'Sub-Saharan African', 'French-Canadian' or 'Québécois' (the difference is a significant one), 'Negritude', 'West Indian', 'Black', 'Third World', 'Southern' and so on. Within the francophone debate new nomenclature becomes ever more diverse; within the anglophone debate, American 'postcolonial' studies are rapidly gaining hegemony.

The Dispersion of French

The history of French exploration, missionary and trading activity, and colonization, and of the dispersion and adoption of the French language across the globe, is complex. Briefly, in North America, French arrived with the explorers, trappers and missionaries in the seventeenth century. Estimates vary but it is generally agreed that there were some 60,000 French-speakers in North America, who were then cut off from France by the Treaty of Paris in 1763, which ceded New France (with the exception of New Orleans) to Britain. Today more than a quarter of Canadians are French-speaking.

The size of the French-speaking community in the United States (in Louisiana, for example) was considerably enlarged by the arrival of Acadians deported by the British in 1755 and by refugees from Saint-Domingue (Santo Dominico until 1844, when it became the Dominican Republic) during the revolution in Haiti. There are also between two and three million French-speakers in the north-eastern States, immigrants from Quebec and Acadia.

In the Creole islands, French arrived with the French colonial forces in the seventeeth century. Although Creoles (each island has its own particular Creole) are the languages of everyday communication both publicly and privately, French remains the administrative, business and educational language. In the French Overseas Departments (Martinique, Guadeloupe, French Guyana, La Réunion), French is spoken by almost everyone. In Haiti, French is spoken only by a small minority. On Mauritius, in the Indian Ocean, French is spoken by half the population. Mauritius is one of the most linguistically rich Creole islands: English, French, a number of Indian languages and Chinese are all spoken by significant groups.

As in the Creole islands, French became a more significant presence in Africa with the arrival of the French colonial forces in the mid-nineteenth century. Since independence, attempts, mostly unsuccessful, have been made to institute African languages to replace French as the language of administration, politics, business and education. Again estimates vary considerably, but it is likely that only 15 per cent of the relevant populations in Sub-Saharan Africa (in the former French colonies and territories) are French-speaking.

In North Africa, Arabic has offered a practical alternative to French in the former colonies and protectorates, and Arabic replaced French in the schools after independence, though some had been bilingual all along. French is, however, seen as a means of maintaining intellectual and political communication with the non-Arab world.

Although French arrived with the missionaries in the Lebanon in the mid-nineteenth century, it was not until later, with the adoption of the French Mandate in the 1920s, that it became important. A large percentage of the present population (roughly half) is bilingual, although Arabic is the official language. In addition to the areas considered above, French remains important in most of the areas penetrated by French colonial activity (and was for a period in Indo-China). It is only in the areas already mentioned, however, that substantial literatures developed: in Belgium, Switzerland and French Canada, in the Caribbean region and the Indian Ocean, in Sub-Saharan Africa and Madagascar, and in North Africa and the Middle East.

Literatures in the or a French Language and the Figuring of *la Francophonie*

In spite of the growing importance of various centres of publishing outside France, and universities which support teaching and research in the area of francophone literatures (most importantly in Africa and North America, especially Quebec), Paris remains the powerful point of focus. Nor should one underestimate the fact that the French ideology of *francophonie* is bound up with French interests in the francophone world, particularly in Africa. French cultural centres in Africa, and the state-sponsored journal *Notre Librairie*, also support and promote, and of course influence, the production and consumption of African literature.

Yet a seemingly obvious but much-ignored *donné* of the francophone linguistic and cultural space is that it is at least a bilingual, and more often a multilingual, space. The consequences of this are far-reaching and historically determined in ways which Tzvetan Todorov (1985)* has explored:

> *Dans un passé pas très éloigné, tout ce qui pouvait se rapprocher de ce que nous appelons aujourd'hui dialogisme, était perçu comme une tare. Inutile de rappeler ici les invectives de Gobineau contre les races mixtes, ou celles de Barrès contre les déracinés . . . Qui de nos jours ne préférerait se réclamer du dialogue, de la pluralité des cultures, de la tolérance pour la voix des autres?*†

---

† 'In a not very distant past, everything which might come close to what today we call dialogism was seen as a defect. It is pointless to call to mind Gobineau's invectives against mixed races or those of Barrès against expatriates . . . Who, nowadays, would not prefer to give their allegiance to dialogue, to the plurality of cultures, to tolerance of the voices of others?'

The 'great patriotic moment' to which Todorov refers is also the moment at which 'national' literatures emerged. It is, too, the high point of colonialism. The great movements of people, one of the far-reaching consequences of colonialism and postcolonialism, have brought about an extraordinary mixing of peoples. The multiculturalism which results is a challenge. As Julia Kristeva (1988)* argues:

> A l'heure où la France devient le melting pot de la Méditerranée, une question se pose, qui est la pierre de touche de la morale pour le XXIe siècle: comment vivre avec les autres, sans les rejeter et sans les absorber ... ?†

The complexities of the linguistic and cultural spaces in which francophone texts are written, published, criticized and read are thus necessarily bound up in, and in part constitutive of, the complexities and ferment of contemporary literary, cultural and social theory, described, for example, in terms of the threat to cultural coherence in Jean-François Lyotard's stimulating and controversial book *La Condition postmoderne: rapport sur le savoir* (1979). Todorov's call for acceptance of difference and otherness becomes something closer to philosophical necessity in the polemic of critics who challenge the certainties imposed by 'Western' critics on the 'non-Western' world. It is members of the postcolonial third-world intelligentsia who have done much to shape the political conscience of literary theory (most recently of deconstruction) and to contribute a new urgency and complexity to the feminist debate. The contributions of writers like Frantz Fanon, Aimé Césaire, René Depestre, Albert Memmi, Abdelkebir Khatibi, Tahar Ben Jelloun, Édouard Glissant, Mbwill a Mpaang Ngal, Assia Djebar, Maryse Condé and Catherine N'Diaye are informed by (and inform) disciplines and ideologies as different as psychoanalysis, Marxism, Surrealism, Negritude, postcolonialism, postmodernism, poststructuralism, the new historicism, deconstruction and diverse forms of feminism.

---

† 'At the moment when France is becoming the melting-pot of the Mediterranean, a question arises which is the moral touchstone for the twenty-first century: how do we live with others without keeping them at a distance and without absorbing them ... ?'

The term *francophone* was first coined by the geographer Onésime Reclus at the end of the nineteenth century and used to designate both a socio-linguistic and a geopolitical phenomenon: to describe French-speaking populations and to describe a French-speaking bloc. It was not until the 1960s that it was used again in a special issue of the journal *Esprit* entitled 'Français dans le monde' (November 1962). For many the term describes an ideology, a neo-colonial French desire to retain links with the former French colonies and to deny or weaken national autonomy. For others, most obviously French Canadians, it is an ideology which protects and promotes French in a climate in which there is considerable fear that the number of French-speakers will rapidly decline. In other more urgent contexts – the North African, for example – French is seen as a crucial means of international communication in a society in which different forms of censorship interfere with the free expression of ideas.

The term 'francophone' effaces important linguistic differences between francophone areas. Four groups are crudely but generally designated. Most obvious is that of those countries where French is the mother-tongue of a large community which has been defined by its use of the language for centuries. This is the case in Europe and francophone Canada. In creolophone countries French is either the official language or remains commonly used, particularly within the public sphere, among a population largely familiar with it. Within this second group are the French Antilles (Martinique, Guadeloupe and French Guyana), Haiti, and Mauritius, Réunion and the Seychelles, in the Indian Ocean. Within the third group are the former French colonies where, for a variety of reasons, French remains an important language known to a significant number of people. This is the case in black francophone Africa, the Maghreb and the Lebanon. Finally, there are those regions where a tradition of French language learning or use established itself and where limited groups of people continue to speak French. This is the case among certain communities in the Near East, Eastern Europe and the Indo-Chinese peninsula in particular.

Francophone Literatures

Belgium

The relatively recent date of the country's birth (1830), the complexities and artificiality of its being, and the multiplicities of multilingualism (French, German, Flemish, Dutch, *brusselaire*) no doubt account in part for a certain lack of cultural confidence and an attitude of intellectual and political scepticism. One of the most striking manifestations of these in literary terms is the lack of consensus as to Belgium's 'major' literary works. There is very little sense of a canon of Belgian literature – in any or several of the country's languages. This is further complicated by many Belgian writers' reluctance to be described as Belgian at all. But to deny the Belgian dimension of many such writers – Michaux, Norge, Beck, Rolin – is to deny the so-called *extra-territorialité* which is a feature of so much francophone writing. Other major Belgian writers are often regarded as belonging in some sense within the canon of French literature – Maurice Maeterlinck, essayist, poet and dramatist, and Fernand Crommelynck, leading figure of the Symbolist movement (see also page 154), are the pre-eminent examples. Much of the writing associated with the Belgian Surrealist movement is often regarded as a regional version of French Surrealism, rather than marking an important moment in Belgian literary history.

Switzerland

Ramuz, one of Switzerland's best-known authors (see also page 160), succinctly expresses the difficulty experienced by so many of the country's writers: 'C'est bien le sort en gros de mon pays d'être à la fois trop semblable et trop différent, trop proche et pas assez.'* It is in part the absence of obvious difference that explains the absorption of so many Swiss writers into the French tradition: Rousseau, Madame de Staël, Constant, Cendrars, Jaccottet. In terms of writers' own allegiance, identity is often expressed in terms of belonging to a region, rather than the nation.

---

* 'It is indeed largely the fate of my country to be at once too similar and too different, too close and not close enough.'

The origins of Swiss writing go back to the thirteenth-century Jurrasien *trouvère* poets Simonin de Boncourt and Girard de Pleujose. Many of the broad phases of the country's literary production are marked by religious affiliation. The Reformation, for example, profoundly marked Neuchâtel, Lausanne and, above all, Geneva (see also pages 42 and 50).

Swiss literary history is generally told in relation to individual *cantons*. It is the Valais region that matters in much of Maurice Chappaz's writing, for example. Fribourg, a region in which Catholicism and conservatism have dominated, has produced a distinctive if marginal writing. The Vaud region, on the other hand, has produced the majority of Switzerland's francophone writers. Geneva has also been a major point of focus. As writing associated with cities – worldwide – has become a new generic means of classi-fication, Geneva has emerged as a major locus, not only in novels, most obviously, but also in films where the meaning and significance of the city, its energy, order and efficiency are explored in terms of what this has to do with people and their peculiar identity as *genevois*.

French Canada

The confrontation between English and French in French Canada is one of many oppositions and antitheses which characterize much French-Canadian writing: between different linguistic groups inside and outside Quebec, between French Canada and France, between secular and Catholic French Canada, between provincialism and cosmopolitanism, between 'folk art' and 'high art', between art and direct political action, etc.

Language, in the sense of both *langue* ('tongue') and *langage* ('linguistic system'), has been a central preoccupation, and a shift of focus from preoccupation with *langue* to *langage* marks the shift from a desire to find an appropriate language ('tongue') in which to write a national literature to a desire to find a language consonant with *québécité*. Very broadly speaking this is also reflected in a shift from a more obviously political text, or at least one with obvious political corollaries, to a more intimate and psychological text.

Whether or not the writings of travellers and other expatriate French should be seen as the origins of French-Canadian writing is uncertain. Descriptions of Jacques Cartier's expeditions, published in the mid-sixteenth century, are often cited as the founding texts. Annals, sermons and letters are the other early genres.

By the nineteenth century, poetry dominated literary production, often described as folkloric, patriotic, Romantic or associated with the École littéraire de Montréal, a Canadian Parnassus. The major literary figure of the nineteenth century was Abbé Casgrain, who favoured art which offered clear moral lessons. The Crémazie brothers were also influential (their bookshop was the hub of the Romantic revival). Émile Nelligan, who spent more than forty years in hospitals and asylums, was the major figure of the École littéraire de Montréal; this group rejected the reactionary patriotism of their predecessors (also exemplified by the *roman du terroir** of the period) and advocated 'art for art's sake'. Nelligan was much influenced by the Belgian Symbolists.

Many of the debates initiated in the nineteenth century continued into the twentieth, most particularly that between regionalists, who sought to preserve traditions and root literature in a sense of place, and exoticists, who argued for the primacy of aesthetic and formal considerations. Little known in his time, Hector de Saint-Denys Garneau's poetry (*Regards et jeux dans l'espace*, 1937) is written outside these debates and now regarded as the most important of the period. Its preoccupations with inner unease and its anxious mood were later read as representative of national feeling. The important shift in the novel is towards the subversion of the *roman du terroir*. Novels like Félix-Antoine Savard's *Menaud, maître draveur* (1937) and *Trente arpents de neige* (1938) by Philippe Panneton (better known under his pseudonym Ringuet) are pessimistic debunkings of earlier rural idealizations. After the Second World War the novel becomes increasingly preoccupied with political and social questions, with urbanization and industrialization, and there is a growing awareness of French Canada's independence from France, from which it was cut off for a six-year period.

---

* 'novel of the land'

The major event of the 1940s, however, was the publication of the manifesto *Refus global* (1948), a collective manifesto (Émile Borduas was the most important of the group). Variously described as Surrealist, anarchist, nationalist, Marxist and Freudian, its publication is often cited as the moment of modernity's arrival in French Canada. Four strands can be isolated: a brief and selective history of French Canada; an appeal for change, citing Lautréamont, de Sade and Breton as beacons; an attack on Catholicism and capitalism; and an assertion of the liberating power of individual and collective creativity.

During the 1950s industrial conflict became widespread, and novels of the period often describe these events. Gérard Bessette's *La Bagarre* (1958) is one of the most important, drawing on the condition of sweepers in the Metropolitan Transport Company. The aspect of the novel which now seems more influential, however, is its preoccupation with novel writing. Theatre also becomes a significant genre; Gélinas's *Tit-Coq* (1950) is a seminal play. Drawing on folklore (the 'little rooster' of the title searches hopelessly for love), the play was written in the popular spoken French-Canadian of the day.

The most significant development of the 1950s, in relation to literary production is, however, the founding of numerous publishing houses offering French-Canadian authors independence from France. Accelerating during the 1960s, at the time of the so-called 'Révolution tranquille', French Canada's move towards a more open society was made possible by the relative liberalism of the Lesage government. In 1961 the Rassemblement pour l'indépendance nationale was founded, the first of a number of groups committed to independence. The ideo-literary slants on these debates were discussed in *Parti Pris*, a journal (with a publishing house of the same name) founded in 1963. Although a heterogeneous group, its members were agreed about their political aim: an independent (described as 'postcolonial'), socialist Quebec.

Just as the novel of the 1960s challenged narrow definitions of the genre or novel types ('psychological', socialist realist, etc.), so poetry was no longer contained on the page. Poetry readings became political and cultural events, blurring the distinctions between art and action. Theatre, similarly, flourished in the climate of the time.

Less politically and narrowly bound up with socio-political questions, writing in the 1970s, and even more obviously the 1980s, becomes more self-conscious, more preoccupied with theory, more playful, more undecided. Women's writing exemplifies these tendencies while at the same time often being implicitly concerned with feminist ideology. Nicole Brossard's commitment to lesbianism is bound up, in her later texts, with a preoccupation with the relationship between writing and sexual desire (see, for example, *Le Désert mauve*, 1987).

The postmodern scene is one which questions writing, texts, boundaries, fields of meaning and meaninglessness. Simultaneously and somewhat paradoxically, there is an increased urgency about questions of the canon. Literary critics and members of the pedagogical community have set about investigating and systematically categorizing Quebec's literary culture. Bibliographies, literary encyclopaedias, syllabuses and essays – on language, the phenomenology of criticism, socio-criticism, mytho-criticism, 'textologie', etc. – have been published in large number.

If it is the writer's responsibility to renew language, writers in French Canada also feel a responsibility to their language in the French sense of *langue*. This dual concern has excited numerous textual strategies and a powerful sense of self-consciousness about the business of writing, fundamental to (post)modernity. Their writing contributes in vital ways to that wider question about the relationship between writing in (the) French language(s) and its relationship with the writing (and readership) of France.

Caribbean

Writing in French from the Caribbean has a long and interesting history. The present-day *départements d'outre-mer*, Martinique, Guadeloupe and Guyana, are best considered separately from Haiti, which has been independent since the nineteenth century.

Early writing (mid-seventeenth century to mid-eighteenth) is essentially travel writing. The accounts collected in Labat's *Nouveaux*

Voyages aux îles d'Amérique (1722–) are seminal. After the abolition of slavery (1794, reintroduced 1802) a significant genre of writing by anti-abolitionists emerged. Poirié de Saint-Aurèle's *Les Veillées françaises* (1826) is typical of the reactionary poetry of the time. A further group of texts can be discerned, treating the plight of the mulatto (born of a white and a black parent). The major text is the essay 'De la situation des hommes de couleur libres aux Antilles françaises' (1823), which argues for the acquisition of full French citizenship for *gens de couleur* (granted ten years later).

More properly literary production, whether by whites or by the growing number of mulattos, is imitative of dominant French genres (Parnassianism in particular). A shift can be seen in a growing recognition and, a little later, awareness of the complexities of racial difference among the area's populations. The writers whose texts most obviously testify to this are the Martinican René Maran (see pages 217–18), the Guadeloupean Oruno Lara (*Questions de couleur*, 1923) and the Martinican Suzanne Lacascade (*Claire Solange âme africain*, 1924).

Questions of race become the focus of Léon-Gontran Damas's *Pigments* (1937), as the title suggests, a founding text of Negritude (see below, pages 215–16). The manifesto *Légitime Défense* (1932), *L'Étudiant noir* (1935) and above all Aimé Césaire's *Cahier d'un retour au pays natal*,* a long epic of racial and cultural exploration and assertion, represent the major tendencies of the pre-war years. Under Vichy these tendencies were further encouraged. Césaire's journal *Tropiques* continued to explore the West Indian identity in so far as this was possible under the repressive governance of Vichy. Specialized articles on Martinique's botanical riches, for example, which were apparently apolitical, can be read as part of a systematic attempt to establish a new sense of real identity, no longer one based on outsiders' knowledge.

As in other francophone areas, the volume and diversity of publication increased after the war and more so from the 1960s onwards. The novel gradually asserts itself as the dominant genre, women's voices become more numerous, and the forms and language(s) of the novel become more daring. Francophone poetry, many would argue, is increasingly eclipsed by Creole poetry from the 1960s on. Notable plays written in French, however, include those by Daniel Boukman, Aimé Césaire, Ina Césaire, Maryse Condé and Vincent Placoly. Social satire, a naturalistic theatre preoccupied with contemporary social problems, and plays which explore West Indian history are the major traits. History is also crucial to the novels of Édouard Glissant, arguably the most important franco-phone Caribbean writer, preoccupied above all with the nature of Caribbean identity: his essays, particularly *Le Discours antillais* (1981), have been extremely influential. Among the younger generation Patrick Chamoiseau is a major voice, articulating the wit, humour and satire of local folktales: his novel *Texaco* won the Prix Goncourt in 1992. The Guadeloupean Simone Schwarz-Bart's novels are also historically preoccupied (although they look ahead too), as are Raphaël Confiant's: *Le Nègre et l'admiral* (1991) is an immensely detailed recreation of Martinique under Vichy. Other major novelists of the 1970s and 1980s, who are numerous and diverse in their concerns and techniques, include Vincent Placoly, Daniel Miximin and a growing group of women: Michèle Lacrosil and Myriam Warner-Vieyra (in addition to those already mentioned) are among the most important.

Haiti

Francophone Haitian writing proper, rather than French travel writing, begins with independence. The political instability which characterizes Haitian history explains the political preoccupation of literary production. Journals have been immensely influential, and one route through Haitian literary history can be charted using them as a guide. Solime Milscent's *L'Abeille haïtienne* (1817) and Hérard Dumesle's *L'Observateur* (1819) are important early examples. Preoccupied with identity at a personal level and with nationalism, their concerns were stimulated by Haiti's unique history and by French Romanticism. *Le Républicain* (1837) advocated *indigénisme*. The poet Oswald Durant was its leading exponent in verses which sing the uniqueness of the Haitian landscape and identity. As in the other Caribbean territories, essays on racial difference also constituted an important genre of writing: most significant was Anténor Firmin's 'De l'égalité des races humaines' (1885), answering Gobineau's title 'Essai sur l'inégalité de la race humaine' (1853–5).

La Ronde was an important forum for poetry at the turn of the century. The influence of French Symbolism is notable. La Nouvelle Ronde (1925), La Trouée (1927) and La Revue indigène (1927–8), on the other hand, influenced by the growing anti-intellectualism in France and looking to the Harlem Renaissance and Latin America for new ideas, published poetry by Émile Roumer, Jacques Roumain (also a major novelist), Carl Brouard and Philippe Thoby-Marcelin.

Jean Price-Mars's anti-assimilationist work Ainsi parla l'oncle (1928) emphasized Haiti's African origins, and the journal Les Griots (1938–40) encouraged allegiance to a broader, transnational pan-Africanism. These ideas remained marginal to political life, however. La Ruche, founded in 1946, reflected an increased post-war militancy. Marxism and Surrealism were the major influences, René Depestre and Jacques-Stephen Alexis the major spokesmen. Unpopular with Duvalier, Depestre has lived much of his life in exile; Alexis was killed by the Duvalier militia in 1961.

The repressive and anti-intellectual climate which has dominated life in Haiti for several decades has made Haitian literature a literature written in exile (by writers such as Depestre, Gérard Étienne, Anthony Phelps and Jean-Claude Charles).

Indian Ocean

The publication in 1951 of Jean Albany's collection of poems Zamal marked a crucial shift of perspective. The remarkable and often accomplished literary texts produced on the island since the late eighteenth century were written either by outsiders or essentially from the viewpoint of the outsider. Albany's text describes a familiar and particular place in a particular language (and one which incorporates the island's Creole). Boris Gamaleya's militant writing and Anne Cheynet's work, particularly her novel Les Muselés (1977), which is concerned with the island's poor, also testify to the vitality of La Réunion's literary production. Departmental status, as in the Caribbean territories, explains the liveliness of the (post)colonial debate. Language is often the focus of this debate: see, for example, *Du Créole opprimé au créole libéré* (1977) by Axel Gauvin.

Sub-Saharan Africa

The first texts written by Africans in French were monitored by the institutions which had taught and encouraged Africans: colonial schools and missions. French interest in African writing was essentially of two kinds: on the one hand, texts written in French testified to the success of linguistic, cultural and often religious assimilation, particularly where the African wrote in praise of the French; on the other, texts which drew on indigenous traditions and cultures provided useful information about Africans, necessary to successful colonial domination. Mapaté Diagne's *Les Trois Volontés de Malic* (1920), an edifying tale often likened to Bunyan's *Pilgrim's Progress* for use in schools, and Bakary Diallo's *Force Bonté* (1926), which praises France's civilizing mission, are well-known examples.

Between the wars, as interest in Africa grew in Europe, the colonial institutions gradually lost their monopoly on African written production, and a range of writings, transcriptions, translations and recreations of a number of genres (tales, myths, historical epics, proverbs) testified to the richness and diversity of African culture and traditions. Birago Diop's *Contes d'Amadou Koumba* (1947) were particularly influential. Novels which described rural life also appeared. Félix Couchoro's early novel *L'Esclave* (1929) was highly influential.

After the Second World War the number of texts published by Africans increased rapidly. A number of genres - crudely defined - emerged: regionalist (Camara Laye's *L'Enfant noir* (1953) and David Ananou's *Le Fils du fétiche* (1955) are the archetypes), urban socialist realist (the archetype is Ousman Socé's *Karim* (1935), which belongs to the pre-war period; Ousmane Sembène's are the most important) and satirical (novels by Mongo Beti and Ferdinand Oyono are the outstanding examples).

The move away from implicit commitment to Africa, rather than the colonial power, and towards explicit condemnation of colonialism and its vicissitudes is also reflected in the work of poets who become increasingly militant. David Diop, whose poetry belongs very obviously within the protest tradition, has been one of the most influential. Africa is sung, and African ways of looking at the world are explored, in the poetry of Negritude, Léopold Sédar Senghor's most famously. It was at the time when African poetry in French was first written that French literary manuals, anthologies and pedagogical texts began to distinguish between 'French literature' and writing *in* French from the various French-speaking areas worldwide. Léon-Gontran Damas, a West Indian but publishing in Paris, produced his anthology *Poètes d'expression française* in 1947, and Léopold Sédar Senghor published his influential *Anthologie de la nouvelle poésie nègre et malgache de langue française* in 1948, accompanied by Jean-Paul Sartre's seminal essay 'Orphée noir'.

A typically complex and often elliptically argued essay, Sartre's text offers a wide range of definitions and descriptions of Negritude. The relationship between Negritude and (Negro-)African literature is also proposed in a number of configurations. Rather than in any sense fixing Negritude, these paradoxes in Sartre's polemic stimulated secondary discourses surrounding (Negro-)African literature, and indeed diverse francophone literatures. Quotations from the essay were incorporated into a wide range of discussions to become the touchstones for distinct approaches to literary texts. For example, the paradoxes of an anti-French literature written in French have been seen by some critics of (Negro-)African literature as paramount. A further instance of the essay's legacy can be seen in discussions of the relative significance of race and class in considering the black writer's allegiances. Negritude's historicism, which Sartre also emphasized, was seen by later critics as a crucial point of departure. The versatility of Negritude, not as a literary doxy belonging to a particular historical moment but as an adaptable literary-critical trope, was guaranteed, to a large extent, by the multiplicity of meanings with which Sartre invested it in his seminal essay. In addition, in emphasizing Negritude in one configuration as a socio-political force or ideology, Sartre assured its place within political as well as cultural and literary debate.

The word 'Negritude' first appeared in the West Indian poet Aimé Césaire's long poem, *Cahier d'un retour au pays natal* (1939 in the Parisian journal *Volontés*, 1947 in book form and 1971 in English translation), in the section which begins 'Ma négritude n'est pas une pierre'.* The meaning of 'Negritude' within the complex poetics of the *Cahier* cannot be simply defined. But what is proposed is a state of being, a particular consciousness.

Thus while Negritude often emerges from a poetic text as an essence, a fixed black ontology, the history of the term bears witness to the fact that there is no stable, original and base doctrine to be unproblematically discovered, and in relation to which all other definitions can be seen as simple derivations, extensions or perversions. Commentaries on Negritude are often drawn to investigate its 'origins', that is to say the moments of its initial articulations in the texts of Césaire and Senghor in particular. The quest for synoptic sense, based on their texts, and the abundance of widely differing commentaries subsequently produced on those canonical texts, themselves testify to a history of the continuous adaptation and transformation of those origins. Thus Negritude cannot now be understood independently from the numerous commentaries, explanations or extensions to which it has given rise, and in which it is now diversely embodied. The most significant, both because of its seminal status and because of its complexities, remains Sartre's 'Orphée noir'.

After Independence, African poetry diversifies. A number of major voices emerged: Malick Fall, Tchicaya U Tam'si, Jean-Baptiste Tati-Loutard, Kine Kirama Fall. These poets have produced *oeuvres* which cannot be briefly characterized. The types of novel visible pre-Independence continue, but the focus shifts. Satire, for example, is directed not at the colonial official but at the corrupt African politician (Ousmane Sembène's *Xala*, 1973, for example). Urban social realism criticizes (Aminata Sow Fall and Ibrahima Sall) but also offers a vision for the future (Nokan's *Le Soleil noir*, 1962).

Independence notwithstanding, Paris remained of course the

---

* 'my Negritude is not a stone …'

centre of the francophone world and increasingly became the powerful *locus* of French language publishing, despite the emergence of
important publishing houses in many francophone areas. A number
of publishers in Quebec, for example, have long been and are
becoming steadily more influential, not only publishing French-
Canadian writers but attracting authors from all over the French-
speaking world. An early and in many ways revolutionary text,
Ahmadou Kourouma's *Les Soleils des indépendances*, was first
published in Montreal in 1968. Rather than 'respecting' the norms of
the colonial language, the French of the text is often a literal
translation from the Malinke, as in the title of the novel, which means
'the era of Independence'. The expectation that francophone writers
'respect' the colonial language had been made very clear in a review
of René Maran's controversial novel *Batouala: véritable roman nègre*
(1921), which won the Prix Goncourt two years after its award to
Proust for part of *A la recherche du temps perdu* (see also page 160).
Maran, a Martinican, had been posted to Africa as a colonial official,
and *Batouala* was written in part in response to this experience. A
contemporary reviewer (de Lacharrière, 1922)* wrote:

> *M. Maran a pris soin de truffer son style d'une abondante*
> *terminologie petit nègre, voire même tout à fait nègre. Cette*
> *précaution n'ajoute rien de pittoresque, – tant il est vrai que*
> *l'exotisme ne réside pas dans le vocabulaire, mais dans la peinture*
> *vivante . . . Le vocabulaire nègre de M. Maran est dangereux, il*
> *souligne l'incertitude et la pauvreté de son vocabulaire français.*†

The assumptions underwriting the reviewer's perspective are
clear: that the author will be seeking to participate in the established
conventions of the 'picturesque' or 'exotic', and that he should wish
to exhibit the degree to which he has been successfully assimilated
by writing a 'correct' French. The reviewer's contention that there is
something 'dangerous' about Maran's project is consistent with the
text's banning in Africa by 1928. What is revealed here is the degree

---

† 'M. Maran has taken care to scatter an abundant Negro-French, even wholly
Negro vocabulary throughout his language. This precaution adds nothing
picturesque – for exoticism does not reside in vocabulary but in vivid depiction [. . .]
The Negro vocabulary of M. Maran is dangerous, it underlines the uncertainty and
poverty of his French vocabulary.'

to which the subversion of 'la langue' (tongue) is read as subversive of a *national* language, related to, if not synonymous with, the subversion of the nation and its interests. That the subversions of Kourouma's text, published several decades later, should have attracted the attention of a Canadian (and indeed Québécois) publisher, rather than a French publisher, is revealing.

African novels of the 1960s and 1970s are often explicit indictments of oppressive African regimes: Camara Laye, *Dramouss* (1966), Fantouré, *Cercle des tropiques* (1972) and Williams Sassine, *Le Zéhéros n'est pas n'importe qui* (1985) are all indictments of Guinea pre- and post-Touré, while Mongo Beti, *Remember Ruben, Perpétue ou l'habitude du malheur* (both 1974) and *Main basse sur le Cameroun* (1972) expose Ahidjo's rule in Cameroon. Novels of the 1980s become increasingly formally innovatory while their subjects often remain the indictment of contemporary society and its institutions.

African women writers emerged in the 1960s. Aminata Sow Fall and Werewere Liking are perhaps the most important. The former's dry irony is directed against both reactionary forces (the blind adherence to tradition, for example) and spurious modernity (the thoughtless imitation of Western ways). Liking's writing subverts genre, violently combining fragments in militantly feminist texts. She also directs and writes theatre. Calixthe Beyala and Ananda Devi have contributed to the urban socialist realist novel. Mariama Bâ's writing, on the other hand, is more concerned with individual women's experience.

North Africa
Algeria
Unlike other French colonies in North Africa, Algeria had a substantial settler community, principally immigrants from France. It is writing in French by members of this group which is generally cited as the origins of francophone Algerian writing. Some stories, those of Musette (pseudonym for Auguste Robinet) are settler tales written in a French which includes *pataouète*, a local patois made up of the various languages spoken.

From the 1920s onwards the major trends in Algerian literary production are associated with groups and journals. The Association des écrivains algériens, founded in 1921, was concerned to define and promote *algérianisme*, a notion of (white) Algerian identity distinct from that of the French. Robert Randau first coined the term; Jean Pomier and Louis Lecoq were major exponents. The École d'Alger, founded in the 1930s by Gabriel Audisio, was less politically and racially concerned than the earlier movement. This was at a time when Algerian Muslim nationalism was first making itself felt. But the racial groups were not exclusive. Abdelkader Hadj Hamou, one of the first writers of non-European origin to write in French, was associated with the *algérianistes*, as was Jean Amrouche. Among the best-known writers associated with the École d'Alger are Albert Camus (see pages 180–2 and 231–2), Emmanuel Roblès and Jules Roy.

After the war the novel emerges as the major genre of francophone Algerian writing. The seminal works are Mouloud Feraoun's *Le Fils pauvre* (1950), a largely autobiographical account of the author's peasant childhood, and Kateb Yacine's more formally innovatory and complex *Nedjma* (1956). More or less committed, most novels are concerned to depict the complexities of contemporary Algeria. Many are largely autobiographical accounts of the difficulties of biculturalism (Mohammed Dib, Mouloud Mammeri).

Debates about the responsibilities of *engagement* become more urgent with the outbreak of the Algerian War (1954). Important and militant poetry was produced by Henry Kréa and Anna Greki, in particular. Nationalist concerns also dominate the narratives of novels written in the early 1960s (by Dib, Djebar and Mammeri).

After Independence, the Front de libération nationale's commitment to Arabization led many commentators to predict the demise of francophone Algerian writing. This has not occurred, although many Algerian writers live outside the country and the concerns of their novels are not necessarily exclusively bound up with their homeland. The formal range displayed by Algerian novels testifies to authors' participation in an international (post-) modernism. Major writers include: Mohammed Dib, who has been publishing novels and poems since the 1950s; Nabile Farès, whose work describes Kabylian culture and the experience of exile from it; Mourad Bourboune and Rachid Boudjedra, two of Algeria's most subversive writers; Assia Djebar, a novelist and film maker increasingly concerned with the relationship between women's (oral) history and colonial (written) history; and Aïcha Lemsine, equally concerned with Algerian women's experience.

In the 1990s, increasing Islamic fundamentalism has made intellectuals the victims of assassination. Fewer and fewer writers live in Algeria. As the amount of writing produced in Algeria decreases so Beur literature has flourished. This is writing by authors whose parents migrated to France from Algeria. The relationship between Beur literature and francophone Algerian literature (which is no less difficult to define accurately) is a complex one.

Morocco

Morocco's relationship with France (like Tunisia's) was quite different from that of Algeria, and accounts for the later and less prolific flowering of francophone Moroccan writing. Until the 1950s the 'ethnographic novel' dominated literary production. It described local life and customs and was written for a French readership. Ahmed Sefrioui's novels are characteristic of the genre (*Le Chapelet d'ambre*, 1949; *La Boîte à merveilles*, 1954). Published a little earlier (from the late 1940s on), Mohammed Aziz Lahbabi's translations of Arabic poems were also influential.

Driss Chraïbi's *Le Passé simple* (1954), in which family relationships are symbolic of relationships with the homeland, represents a shift in focus. While in many ways resembling the ethnographic novel, Chraïbi's text also exploits the tension between various antitheses, ones which become increasingly important in the Moroccan novel, most importantly the conflict between loyalty to tradition and the Arab world, and the appeal of the new and European.

From the 1960s, Moroccan writing diversifies. Abdellatif Laâbi's journal *Souffles* , founded in 1966 with the poet Mostafa Nissaboury, is an important forum for discussion. Other major novelists include Mohammed Khaïr-Eddine, Abdelkebir Khatibi and Tahar Ben Jelloun, winner of the Prix Goncourt in 1987 for *La Nuit sacrée*. His training in psychiatry informs his texts' preoccupation with sexuality, and *La Nuit* describes the effects of bringing up a girl as a boy. The next generation of writers includes Abdelhak Serhane and Omar Berrada.

Significant poetry has been written by many of Morocco's novelists, and also by Mostafa Nissaboury, Mohamed Loakira and Abdalleh Bounfour, most importantly.

Tunisia

Francophone Tunisian writing is dominated by Albert Memmi. His early writing, much influenced by Sartrean existentialism (see pages 176–80 and 228–33), was concerned with the effects of colonialism and cultural alienation (manifest in bilingualism and mixed marriages, for example). His essays of the 1960s are particularly concerned with the ways in which power affects relationships – between men and women, between colonizer and colonized, etc.

Other major writers include Mustapha Tlili, whose work can be compared to that of Memmi (although the relationship between exile and creativity, important in Tlili's work, is not a major concern of Memmi's). Abdelwahab's writing is experimental and formally daring in its postmodernist range. Tahar Bekri, who started publishing poetry in the 1950s, has now produced a substantial *oeuvre* in which questions of identity and self-knowledge dominate. The poetry of Salah Garmadi and Moncef Ghachem is militant and violent in its denunciation of contemporary social and political problems. Amina Saïd is Tunisia's best-known woman writer: her concerns are wide-ranging, often bound up in questions of eroticism and identity and the relationship between them.

Middle East

Missionary activity which made contact with Christian Copts in Egypt included the founding of schools, thus gradually creating a francophone community. Literary production reached a peak in the 1920s and 1930s. Notable writers include Albert Adès and Albert Cossery, whose concerns are principally social, and Albert Josipovici, whose writing is fantastical. Georges Henein's work, influenced by French Surrealism, is also important.

In the Lebanon, francophone literary production gathered pace under the French Mandate (after 1920). Chekri Ghanem, whose heroic play *Antar* had been a great success in Paris in 1910, and later Georges Schéhadé and Andrée Chedid are major figures. During the civil war which began in the mid-1970s and lasted almost two decades, many Lebanese writers have been exiled. Amin Maalouf, winner of the Prix Goncourt for *Le Rocher de Tanios* in 1993, a story which mixes mid-nineteenth-century Lebanese history and fiction, is now the best known.

Writing and Reading the Francophone

To write in the French (or a French) language is to participate in *la francophonie*, if the term is taken to mean use of the French (or a recognizably French) language by a writer who is not French, or by a writer who believes his or her identity is not French (even if he or she has become a French national). To describe a literary text as 'francophone' is to distinguish it from a 'French' text and therefore emphasize a certain difference. Some of the interest of reading francophone texts, as a student of French literature, is to identify the francophone (or non-French, anti-French or 'supra-French') aspects of the francophone literary text.

The etymology of the term 'francophone' refers, of course, to spoken language: when the term was first coined relatively little had been written. The *literary* designation needs, though, to be stressed, however linguistically impure it may be to propose 'francophone literatures'. Another way of looking at this is to see the francophone *literary* project as inherently subversive. Until recently many of the texts examined in this chapter were read almost exclusively 'abroad'. The context from which the text emerged was 'exotic' or at least 'foreign'. One of the many consequences of this was that, crudely speaking, texts were read as mimetic representations. Readings thus privileged sociological, anthropological, racial or geographical *difference* as opposed to *linguistic* (new practices, the direct translation of foreign idioms, for example) or intertextual difference (such as the subversion or adaptation of French literary typologies, exoticism or Surrealism, respectively). Thus a further interest is to investigate the *language* of the francophone text, in the French sense of both *langue* and *langage*, and to consider the relationship between these two; in particular to ask whether the francophone text, in many instances, stages a dramatic confrontation between *langue* and *langage*. Within the francophone debate, one of the most powerful statements on language which privileges the first sense, and one of the most frequently quoted, is that of Frantz Fanon (1952),* the West Indian spokesman of decolonization:

> *Parler, c'est être à même d'employer une certaine syntaxe, posséder la morphologie de telle ou telle langue, mais c'est surtout assumer une culture, supporter le poids d'une civilisation.*†

It is, on the other hand, the potential for the transformation of French to allow for the articulation of difference that the North African writer Nabile Farès* stresses in an article in a special issue of *La Quinzaine littéraire*, associated with the 1985 Salon du livre, entitled 'Écrire les langues françaises'. Farès lists a large number of 'auteurs, écrivains qui pourraient paraître "étrangers" à figurer ici',‡ starting with: 'Beckett, Ionesco, Jabès, Todorov, Kristeva'. He continues:

> *On le voit, la liste est longue, écrivains, traducteurs, ou essayistes qui par leur pratique de la communication active ont installé la francophonie dans un autre lieu que celui où elle fut à l'origine, pauvre doctrine de la ségrégation coloniale. Désormais la francophonie ... est cet espace des oeuvres et analyses où entrent en*

---

† 'To speak means to be in a position to use a certain syntax, to grasp the morphology of this or that language, but it means above all to assume a culture, to support the weight of a civilization.'

‡ 'authors, writers whom it could seem "strange"/ "foreign" to include here'

communication les différents domaines de la pluralité culturelle et humaine.†

Further denying the fixity of the French language (despite institutional attempts to fix language, Farès defines language in terms of *practice*), he writes:

C'est à un espace de l'étrangeté dans la langue et de la langue que la francophonie doit son développement: la littérature dite francophone dépasse en son mouvement les multiples étroitesses réductrices. ‡

Linguistic complexity, *diglossie, polyglossie*: these phenomena are inherent in the francophone. Whatever theoretical problems accompany these, French-speakers have access (although the degree to which this is the case is an important subject of debate) to these texts which are still, unfortunately, outside the most widely recognized canons or syllabuses. These texts are assumed by many to be 'marginal'. Gayatri Spivak (1990)* has pointed out that 'marginalia' are the essential notes about the text made in the margin. The 'marginal' may generate the important debate. Francophone texts were deemed unimportant (to use an etymologically less complex term), and still are by many, because their literary merit, their linguistic complexity and formal innovation, their political and philosophical urgency, their often complex intertextual relationships with canonical texts of the French tradition which they may parody, subvert or deconstruct, have frequently been overlooked.

---

† 'One sees that the list is long, writers, translators or essayists who through their practice of active communication have moved *la francophonie* into a different place from where it was originally – a miserable doctrine of colonial segregation. Henceforth *la francophonie* is that space – of works and analyses – where the different domains of cultural and human pluralism enter into communication.'
‡ 'It is to a strange space in and out of the language that *la francophonie* owes its development: so-called francophone literature surpasses in its movement multiple reductive narrownesses.'

References

Aimé Césaire, *Cahier d'un retour au pays natal*, in *Volontés*, 1939; *Return to My Native Land*, translated by Émile Snyder (Paris: Présence Africaine, 1971), p. 116.

Frantz Fanon (1952), *Peau noire, masques blancs* (Paris: Présence Africaine); *Black Skins, White Masks*, translated by C.L. Markmann (London and Sydney: Paladin, 1967), p. 17.

Nabile Farès (1985), 'En d'autres lieux', *La Quinzaine littéraire*, **436** (March), p. 24.

Julia Kristeva (1988), *Étrangers à nous-mêmes* (Paris: Fayard), back cover.

J. Ladreit de Lacharrière (1922), *'Batouala'*, *L'Afrique française* (January–June), pp. 103–6.

A.-Roland Lebel (1925), *L'Afrique occidentale dans la littérature française (depuis 1870)* (Paris: É. Larose), pp. 225–9.

Gayatri Chakravorty Spivak (1990), *The Post-colonial Critic: Interviews, Strategies, Dialogues* (London and New York: Routledge), p. 156.

Tzvetan Todorov (1985), 'Bilinguisme, dialogisme et schizophrénie', in Abdel Kebir Khatibi (ed.), *Du bilinguisme* (Paris: Denoël), pp. 11–26.

Further Reading

G. Clavreuil and A. Rouch (eds), *Littératures nationales d'écriture française* (Paris: Bordas, 1986).

J.L. Flood (ed.), *Modern Swiss Literatures: Unity and Diversity* (London: University of London Press,1985).

B. Galland, *La Littérature de la Suisse Romande expliquée en un quart d'heure* (Geneva: Zöe, 1986).

B. Jack, *Francophone Literatures: An Introductory Survey* (Oxford: Oxford University Press, 1996).

B. Jack, *Negritude and Criticism: The History and Theory of 'Negro-African' Literature in French* (Westport, CT: Greenwood Press, 1996).

J.-L. Joubert *et al.*, *Les Littératures francophones depuis 1945* (Paris: Bordas, 1986).

L. Kesteloot, *Black Writers in French: A Literary History of Negritude* (Washington, DC: Howard University Press, 1991; first published in French, 1963).

L. Mailhot, *La Littérature québécoise*, 2nd edn (Paris: P.U.F., 1975).

Yale French Studies, Nos 82 and 83, 'Post/Colonial Conditions: Exiles, Migrations and Nomadisms' (1993).

CHAPTER 10

French Thought since 1940

CHRISTINA HOWELLS

French thought of the last fifty years has moved with considerable rapidity through a series of dramatic reversals, tracing a pattern of radical rejection of the positions of the previous intellectual generation. Rather than any notion of philosophical 'tradition', the overwhelming impulse has been parricidal, revealing an 'anxiety of influence' far stronger than the common desire for academic originality. The Second World War, its impact, its partial occlusion and the subsequent rediscovery of the horrors of the Holocaust seem to have been a major factor in the formation of the philosophical preoccupations of the last half-century. The recent revival of interest in the 'end of history' may perhaps be attributed also to the imminent end of the current millennium.

In this chapter, I shall explore the development of philosophy in France through the particular focus of conceptions of the human subject, and questions of agency and authority. The chapter will have four main sections, arranged as far as possible chronologically: existentialism and phenomenology; structuralism; deconstruction; and feminist theory.

Existentialism and Phenomenology: The Subject of History

Phenomenology and existentialism were at the height of their popularity in the 1940s. Sartre's ecstatic discovery that phenomenology permitted him to make philosophy out of all kinds of phenomena, even a glass of beer, is well known and apparently well accredited. Phenomenology examines things 'as they are', as they appear to us, in their materiality and contingency. Things do not have some hidden essence; in this sense they are precisely what they seem. And existentialism makes similar claims about people: they do not have a secret inner essence either, they are their existence, they are what they make themselves, any fixed essence comes only with death. Together, phenomenology and existentialism could be seen as a refusal of a philosophy of 'depths'; they argue that the world as we know it is the only world we can know, an apparently tautological statement whose truth is none the less difficult to accept intuitively.

Existentialism and phenomenology may be traced back to Kant in the eighteenth century, and to Hegel and the Danish theologian Kierkegaard in the nineteenth, but they originate more immediately in the philosophy of two German thinkers, Heidegger (1889–1976) and Husserl (1859–1938). In France existential phenomenology was developed by Sartre, Merleau-Ponty and, to some extent, Camus. The main focus of this section will be Sartre, with occasional reference to Camus. (See also the discussion of Sartre's and Camus's works on pages 174–82.)

The war years (1939–45) were a period of considerable change in the existentialists' attitudes towards humanism. (Humanism is understood here in the modern sense of belief in the value, autonomy and agency of the human subject.*) At the onset of war, Sartre and Camus were professing theories of human alienation and *angoisse*† in the face of the meaninglessness of life. In *L'Étranger* (1942) Camus shows his protagonist Meursault apparently indifferent to the death of his mother, committing a pointless and racist murder of an Arab 'à cause du soleil',‡ and welcoming the cries of hatred from the crowd which greet him at his execution. Meursault reckons, retrospectively,

---

* For the alternative meaning of humanism for the Renaissance, see pages 44–5.
† anguish   ‡ 'because of the sun'

that his life was a happy one, but given its self-confessed monotony and futility it would seem to have been very much the happiness Camus attributes to Sisyphus in *Le Mythe de Sisyphe* (1942). Sisyphus is a hero of the absurd, who repeatedly pushes a rock to the top of a mountain only to see it roll down again. This paradigmatically routine task is his source of happiness, for in an absurd world, where the human desire for meaning is always frustrated, a form of defiance of the absurd by lucidly accepting a life without future seems to be the supreme value.

Roquentin, hero of Sartre's *La Nausée* (1938), has little more point to his life. An academic historian engaged in writing a history of the Marquis de Rollebon, Roquentin's nauseous discovery of the absurdity, contingency and general meaninglessness of life leads him to abandon his biography, to attempt an abortive reunion with an old girlfriend, Annie, and eventually to contemplate, somewhat vaguely, the possibility of turning to art as an alternative source of pattern and purpose in life. The brilliance of Sartre's evocation of a disintegrating consciousness interacting with an unpredictable and even hostile world does nothing to mitigate the pessimism of his novel.

Sartre's major philosophical work of this period is scarcely more positive, though it is intellectually invigorating. *L'Être et le néant* (1943) paints a bleak picture of the human condition, in particular with respect to human relations, which are described in terms of conflict. Men (and women) are inevitably hostile to each other, congenital enemies, doomed to attempt to maintain their own position as subjects by envisaging the other as an object. No form of relationship seems able to break out of this vicious circle of power and domination, not even love, and certainly not desire, though Sartre does insist that he is describing an alienated state of affairs which does not necessarily exclude the possibility of 'une morale de la délivrance et du salut'.* And, indeed, the extent of human freedom in Sartre's account would suggest that we are, theoretically at least, able to construct a more satisfactory mode of interaction. Human beings are, for Sartre, in an ontological if not a practical sense, radically free. Human consciousness is *pour soi*,† it has no essence, it exists only in relation to something other than itself, it is not self-

---

* 'an ethics of deliverance and salvation'   † for-itself

identical but self-divided, and this is both its curse and the condition of its freedom. Consciousness is a being which 'est ce qu'il n'est pas et … n'est pas ce qu'il est'.* And the key to the freedom of consciousness lies in the imagination. Imagination, for Sartre, is not merely the formation of images; it is constitutive of the human ability to stand back from the immediate situation and totalize it – in other words, to make a world out of the brute givens of nature and the *en soi*† (or undifferentiated being). It is imagination too that constructs a 'self' out of the flux of each person's consciousness, experiences and choices. For the self is not given, it is made, and it is this ability and necessity to make oneself that constitutes the hub of human freedom. Our choices and decisions, our successes and failures, our relationships, lifestyles and even our emotions are not causally determined by our character. On the contrary, it is these which gradually produce our 'character', and indeed our 'self'.

Sartre analyses our self-constitution from a theoretical point of view in *La Transcendance de l'ego* (1936), where he argues that our ego or 'self' is not, as Husserl would have it, transcendental – that is, an imminent core and source of our being – it is rather transcendent – that is to say a construct, out in the world, along with all the other human creations. My brief account of its construction should have suggested some more practical implications. Despite Sartre's emphasis on the radical nature of human freedom, its enactment in the real world is clearly bound to be circumscribed. All my previous choices and actions have set up patterns of behaviour, not to mention expectations from others, which cannot be lightly or whimsically overthrown. I am free at any moment to change, since only I determine who I am, but this does not mean that change is easy. On the contrary, major change involves what Sartre refers to as a 'radical conversion', and for this the difficult exercise of purifying reflection seems to be necessary. Even small-scale change has major implications, because, as I am a totality, not a random collection of elements, all my activities are intricately bound up with one another. Discussing the deceptively simple case of a hiker who declares himself too tired, and gives up on a walk well before his friends, Sartre comments coolly, 'J'aurais pu faire autrement, soit, mais à quel

---

* 'is what it is not and is not what it is'
† in-itself

prix?'* The cost, of course, would have been a reassessment of his values and priorities, to enable him to choose perseverance, or simply pleasing his friends, above physical comfort – a harder task than it might at first appear.

And it is not simply the character I have constructed for myself that makes change difficult. I also have to contend with the brute 'givens' of my facticity: my age, sex, race and class of origin; not to mention the current conditions of my situation: my marital, social and professional status, my economic position, the geographical and historical features of the country in which I live, to cite just a few. If the characters in Sartre's plays seem to make dramatic decisions with startling rapidity, it should be remembered that they are not typical, they are in extreme situations: Oreste (*Les Mouches*, 1943) is a mythical character, 'sans famille, sans patrie',† arriving like a stranger in his home town, and he, in any case, longs for the inherent sense of belonging experienced by those from a more mundane background. Hugo (*Les Mains sales*, 1948) has been commanded by the Communist Party he has just joined to assassinate one of its leaders, and even this extraordinary task cannot enable him to hide from himself his bourgeois background, his alienation from the working-class members of the Party, and the poverty of his relationship with his wife. The cost of Hugo's determination to change is that he pays with his life.

Of course – unlike *La Nausée* – *Les Mouches* and *Les Mains sales* are marked very strongly by the war. Whereas humanism is explicitly mocked in the novel in the person of the Autodidacte, whose proclaimed love of mankind appears ultimately to be reduced to a pederastic fascination with small boys, Sartre's dramatic works reflect a more complex position. Oreste tests out a strong and decisive set of committed values, and turns even apparent failure to good use, when he proclaims that 'la vie humaine commence de l'autre côté du désespoir'.‡ Hugo and Hoederer argue about the right kind of humanism, showing an abstract idealism to be futile. And in the late 1940s Sartre also gave his famous lecture proclaiming existentialism to be a humanism, and produced an aesthetic theory

---

* 'I could have acted differently, of course, but at what cost?'
† 'without family, without fatherland'
‡ 'human life begins on the other side of despair'

clearly committed to humanist values. In this period too, Camus's *La Peste* (1947) appeared, with its passionate debates about aiming to be a man or a saint, far removed from the near nihilism of *L'Étranger*, and to be followed by *L'Homme révolté* (1951), an analysis of the relationship between political moderation and human wisdom. But even at the height of the existentialist espousal of humanism, the attitude to ethical values was a wary one, always opting for debate and ambiguity rather than assertion. Sartre's ethical meditations of this period were never completed and published only posthumously as *Cahiers pour une morale*; Simone de Beauvoir's work on ethics was appropriately entitled *Pour une morale de l'ambiguïté* (1947); and Camus hastened to throw off the mantle of moral mentor a few years later with the publication of the cruelly ambivalent *La Chute* (1956).

Sartre, moreover, was never really satisfied by the association of existentialism with humanism, and his desire for political commitment was soon to take a more radical path through his incorporation of Marxism. His *Critique de la raison dialectique* (1960) attempted both to revivify a Marxism he considered to have become sclerotic, by forcing it to take account of individual specificity, and to reinscribe existentialism as an 'ideology' within what he had come to view as potentially the most powerful and radical philosophy of his time. In the *Critique* Sartre makes existentialism come to terms with history: the individual factors of situation and facticity are now subsumed within the broader spectrum of socio-historical analysis. A dialectical relationship between man and history is expounded; taking over a phrase of Engels's, Sartre argues that men both make and are made by history: 'Les hommes font leur histoire eux-mêmes mais dans un milieu donné qui les conditionne.'* Conditioning is the operative concept rather than determinism or necessity, and consequently the *Critique* may be seen as fully compatible with the philosophy of freedom within the situation elaborated in *L'Être et le néant*, though the emphasis has shifted radically. One of Sartre's major concerns in the *Critique* is an analysis of human alienation: other people have constructed and are constructing a world which is not my product, and whose ends and purposes are not my own. I am 'predestined' from birth in the sense that I encounter a certain limited

---

* 'Men make their history themselves, but in a given milieu which conditions them.'

range of choices, but this does not diminish my freedom to choose within them. Sartre's critique is rigorously dialectical, but it is also paradoxical, and he analyses scarcity, groups and series, language, praxis and the practico-inert (that is to say human action and the dead results of that action once it has left man's control) with a brio and vigour that did little to endear him to the anti-intellectual Marxists he was aiming to inspire. His discussion of the revolutionary 'groupe en fusion'* was to prove more popular with the student activists of May 1968 than with the hard-nosed French Communist Party leaders, but perhaps we might not now consider this to be a failing. In any case, what is certain is that Sartre, whether in his pre-war non-political period, or in the heyday of immediate post-war commitment, or in his later phase of attempted reconciliation with Marxism, never espoused the naive, subjectivist, idealist humanism attributed to him by his structuralist detractors of the 1960s and 1970s.

Structuralism: The Subject as History

Although structuralism was probably at the peak of its popularity, in France at least, in the 1960s, it has its origins far earlier, most notably in the theories of the Swiss linguist Ferdinand de Saussure at the beginning of this century. Saussure envisaged language as a system of signs, comprising *signifiants* (signifiers – the aural or written form of the sign) and *signifiés* (signifieds – the meaning embodied in the sign). In Saussure's account, the relationship between signifier and signified is arbitrary, and both are enshrined in a network of differences. Meaning in language thus depends on a differential system, made up of a web of oppositions, rather than being a 'natural' translation of an order pre-existent in the world. Saussure's theories influenced not only linguistics but also anthropology, psychoanalysis, social studies and literary theory. In all these domains, the notion that structure determines the elements that compose it, rather than vice versa, is what marks structuralism out from empirical or humanist theories.

---

* 'group-in-fusion'

French structuralism envisaged itself as antithetical to existentialism. To this end it depicted existentialism as a body of beliefs which recognized only individual intention and agency, and ignored the structures within which individuals are necessarily inserted. Such a depiction misrepresents existentialism; it distorts the grounds for debate between existentialism and structuralism by inviting the former to defend positions that are not in fact its own; and it effectively masks any clear perception of the intriguingly large degree of consensus between the two philosophies. Structuralism was wilfully deaf to all but the simplest of existentialist statements. In the case of Sartre, which is probably the most interesting because the common ground is so extensive, structuralism focused almost exclusively on the most humanistic phase of his thinking, that is to say the immediate post-war writings, and contrived to ignore entirely early works such as *La Transcendance de l'ego*, which argues that consciousness is impersonal or at most pre-personal, and *La Nausée*, whose biting critique of naive humanism we have already referred to. More surprisingly, perhaps, it also ignored Sartre's later philosophy, such as the *Critique*, broadly contemporaneous with its own major works and certainly exploring many of the same issues.

Lévi-Strauss, Professor of Social Anthropology at the Collège de France, was the structuralist who engaged most directly with Sartre on his own terms, and even so, misunderstandings between the two, wilful or not, seem to have been manifold. Lévi-Strauss analyses the world in terms of its structures; that is to say, he examines phenomena, both natural and human, as manifestations of fundamental binary oppositions that make up a complex network within which human activity and understanding takes place. Oppositions such as male/female, earth/sky, raw/cooked, nature/culture, fire/water form the parameters of interpretation which determine our worldview in all its operations: language, myth, religion, marriage practices, social structures, institutions, literary and philosophical constructs. In *Les Structures élémentaires de la parenté* (1949), for example, he analyses the unwritten rules which implicitly underpin the choice of marriage partner in different social and tribal groups. In the volumes of *Mythologiques* (1964–1971) he similarly explores the basic elements which constitute the building blocks for even the most complex and elaborate of myths. What may look like a new creation, a free choice, an individual and specific operation is reduced to a variation within a closely determined theme.

This, of course, is the hub of the virulent antagonism between existentialism and structuralism: the issue of freedom. For Lévi-Strauss, human freedom is no more than an illusion, a misinterpretation of the effects of the complexity of the structures which traverse us. In his account, men do not create myths, myths are created through them, or, in a more radical version, myths think themselves through men. Similarly, men do not construct structures, they are themselves constructed by them. Lévi-Strauss accepts only one side of what Sartre sees as a dialectic: for Sartre, we are indeed formed and limited by social, institutional and other structures, but it is we – or, perhaps more accurately, our fathers and mothers – who produced these structures in the first place. This is precisely what Sartre means by praxis and the practico-inert (see page 233). He concurs with the structuralist attack on the individualism of bourgeois humanism, but believes thinkers such as Lévi-Strauss to have thrown the baby out with the bath water.

> *Il n'est pas douteux que la structure produit les conduites. Mais ce qui gêne dans le structuralisme radical . . . , c'est que l'envers dialectique est passé sous silence et qu'on ne montre jamais l'Histoire produisant les structures.**

Sartre and Lévi-Strauss do not even agree on the origin of the basic building blocks, the 'natural' oppositions such as fire and water, earth and sky. Sartre argues that these too are human constructs, whereas Lévi-Strauss insists that they are inherent in nature itself. At first sight, common sense might seem to be on the side of Lévi-Strauss, but this does not necessarily make him right. Sartre's argument is that the raw material for the oppositions is incontrovertibly part of nature, but that it is the human mind which perceives this in terms of oppositions rather than simply differences,

---

* 'There is no doubt that structure produces behaviour. But what is wrong with radical structuralism . . . is that the reverse side of the dialectic is passed over in silence, and History is never shown producing structures.'

for example. In so far as Lévi-Strauss recognizes the role of mind, it is not that of individual human subjects, but rather Mind, which, as part of Nature, plays out its determined destiny through its individual embodiments.

It is evident that many of the notions with which the two thinkers are operating have much in common, and that in different circumstances they might have worked cooperatively together, but the intransigence of both parties over the question of freedom made this impossible. What is more, Lévi-Strauss's analyses are resolutely synchronic – they describe structures as they are at a particular point in time, not how they evolve. Sartre's work is more preoccupied with historical development. Lévi-Strauss has been accused of being hostile to history, and even of misunderstanding or denying it, but such criticisms seem to me ill-founded. *Race et histoire* appeared in 1952, and in it Lévi-Strauss devotes himself to an extensive analysis of different types of history in different cultures. Twenty years later, in 1971, he contributed articles to commemorative collections for the ethnologist E. Evans-Pritchard and for the historian Raymond Aron, in which he extols both thinkers for their recognition of the necessity of combining historical and structural analyses. (These three examples of Lévi-Strauss's active acknowledgement of the import-ance of history are all collected in *Anthropologie structurale deux*, 1973.) It is clear that there is no theoretical reason why a historical account of the development of structures should not be possible, once the descriptive groundwork has been carried out. None the less, in the final chapter of *La Pensée sauvage* (1962), entitled 'Histoire et dialectique', Lévi-Strauss launches into a caustic and possibly misguided attack on some of the arguments in Sartre's *Critique*. In order to defend his own understanding of the 'primitive mentality' against what he sees as Sartre's erroneous account of it, he is led to accuse Sartre of confusion concerning the difference between analytic and dialectical reason, of having an essentialist conception of personal identity, and of promoting a mystical view of history. Sartre's brilliant turning of the tables against Lévi-Strauss in an interview with Pierre Verstraeten in 1965 seems to have marked the end of the exchange, in its published form at least.

The historian Michel Foucault would appear to be closer to Sartre than Lévi-Strauss both on the question of history and in the debate as to whether the origin of structural oppositions and of intelligibility lies in nature or the human subject. Like a character in one of Beckett's plays, Foucault would agree that 'There's no more nature.' So-called 'objective' knowledge always contains an element of power. Foucault's studies of the history of the major organizations and discourses, such as medicine, education, prisons, psychiatric institutions, religion and sexuality, reveal the way in which interpretation has been controlled under the guise of setting up 'scientific' objectivity above 'subjective' judgement. Foucault always denied being a structuralist: 'I have never been a Freudian, I have never been a Marxist and I have never been a structuralist.' But he certainly shares with structuralism the total opposition to what he calls 'narcissisme transcendantal', that is the idea of a founding subject, ground of knowledge and object of its own self-knowledge.

Foucault is fascinated by the Cartesian and Kantian projects; they represent the moment in the history of philosophy when the modern conception of 'Man' was at its height: man as rational subject, his consciousness transparent to itself, the 'empirico-transcendental doublet' of the 'analytic of finitude'. When Foucault makes his apocalyptic reference in *Les Mots et les choses* (1966) to the disappearance of man, it is to this specific, historically determined conception of man that he is referring. And what the 'transcendental subject' of humanist thought is blind to is precisely its own determinations, and in particular those of its thought processes. In *L'Archéologie du savoir* (1969) Foucault denies the charge we have already seen levelled at Lévi-Strauss: that structural analysis is incompatible with the study of history. On the contrary, he maintains, he always recognized what he calls 'la possibilité de changer le discourse';* what distinguishes his position is his refusal to acknowledge 'le droit exclusif et instantané à la souveraineté'† to originate such change, that is, to make history. We should note the term 'exclusive'. Foucault is not espousing some vulgar Marxist version of deterministic interpretations of social and intellectual change. His aim is rather to discover the concrete ways in which a

---

* 'the possibility of discourse change'
† 'the exclusive and instantaneous right of the sovereign subject'

particular discourse (be it on medicine, prisons or sexuality) is articulated with other social practices.

Les Mots et les choses is perhaps the best text to illustrate his method in that it draws on a multiplicity of different cultural codes, in particular natural history and biology, economics, grammar and philology. The text is subtitled *Une archéologie des sciences humaines*; by 'archaeology', Foucault means an exploration of forms of thought in so far as they are unconscious and anonymous. Foucault calls these forms 'epistemes'; they are conceptual strata which underlie the different areas of knowledge and delimit the kinds of perception, experience and theorizing that can be recognized as valid in a particular epoch. Foucault's epistemes are discontinuous; in *Les Mots et les choses* the epistemes are, broadly speaking, those of Renaissance thought, classical thought (that is, of the seventeenth and eighteenth centuries), modern thought (from the nineteenth century up to around 1950), and late twentieth-century thought. His discussions concern primarily the classical and modern epistemes. What is perhaps frustrating for the reader of Foucault is that his conception of 'enigmatic discontinuity' leads him, quite consciously, to describe epistemic mutations but not to explain them. They are in his view essentially arbitrary. What is more, since the epistemes are unconscious, they do not correspond to theorized epistemological beliefs as these would be analysed by, say, a historian of ideas.

Foucault's position with respect to the questions of subjectivity, agency and history is a complex one. When he claims in an interview in *Les Nouvelles littéraires* (28 June – 5 July 1984) that his earlier texts with their references to the death of man were all part of a history of the subject, he is maintaining that the polemical form of his views in the 1960s was necessary to his anti-humanist strategy. *La Volonté de savoir* (1976) explores the constitution of knowledge of the subject: 'un savoir du sujet; savoir, non pas tellement de sa forme, mais de ce qui le scinde; de ce qui le détermine peut-être, mais surtout le fait échapper à lui-même.'* In this description of the subject Foucault is intriguingly close to Sartre, and especially to *L'Être et le néant*.

The split subject also lies at the heart of the theories of the third structuralist thinker to be discussed here, the psychoanalyst, Jacques

---

* 'a knowledge of the subject; a knowledge not so much of its form, but of what splits it; of what determines it, perhaps, but especially of what makes it escape itself'

Lacan. Lacan is best known for his *Écrits* (1966), a collection of his writings, supplemented since 1975 by J.-A. Miller's reconstructions of his teaching at St Anne, published as a series of volumes of *Séminaires*. Lacan's proclaimed aim was a 'return to Freud', that is to say, a return to the letter of Freud's theories, uncontaminated by the interpretations and misconceptions that have accumulated around them. However, the density and difficulty of Lacan's writings make it almost impossible to judge the faithfulness of his 'return', and it is probably more fruitful to consider Lacan rather as a psychoanalytic theorist in his own right. Like the other structuralists, Lacan is fascinated by the ways in which the subject can be shown to differ from the autonomous agent of humanist thought. In what is probably his best-known paper, 'Le Stade du miroir comme formateur de la fonction du Je' (1949), he refers to Lévi-Strauss's essay on 'L'Efficacité symbolique'(1949). In this essay Lévi-Strauss puts forward a conception of the unconscious that has special appeal for Lacan: he argues that the unconscious is not a reservoir of personal experiences and recollections, which should more properly be called 'pre-conscious'; it is rather a collection of structural laws which carries out a specific symbolic function in all human beings:

> *L'inconscient cesse d'être l'ineffable refuge des particularités individuelles, le dépositaire d'une histoire unique, qui fait de chacun de nous un être irremplaçable. Il se réduit à un terme par lequel nous désignons une fonction: la fonction symbolique, spécifiquement humaine, sans doute, mais qui, chez tous les hommes, s'exerce selon les mêmes lois; qui se ramène, en fait, à l'ensemble de ces lois.**

In 'Le Stade du miroir', Lacan sets out his theory of the formation of the ego (or 'self') and 'l'armure d'une identité aliénante'† which it will offer to the subject. In terms of the three orders, Imaginary, Symbolic and Real, which Lacan elaborated in the 1950s, the ego belongs to the domain of the Imaginary. In Lacan's model of psychic

---

* 'The unconscious ceases to be the ultimate haven of individual peculiarities — the repository of a unique history which makes each of us an irreplaceable being. It is reducible to a term by which we designate a function – the symbolic function, which no doubt is specifically human, and which is carried out according to the same laws among all men, and actually corresponds to the aggregate of these laws.'

† 'the armour of an alienating identity'

development, the infant passes – somewhere between six and eighteen months, though the model is, strictly speaking, structural rather than chronological – through what he calls the 'mirror phase'. In the mirror phase the child loses its early impression of itself as one with its mother in an idyllic and imaginary unity, and comes to see itself (as, for example, in a mirror) as a separate and autonomous object. This is not, for Lacan, a truer picture than that of imaginary union. It involves a further alienation in that the independence the infant perceives is itself illusory. The specular image deceives the infant into a 'méconnaissance',* a misconceived view of itself as object, as other, and as a unified identity.

Like Sartre, Lacan conceives the 'self' or ego as a construction, unified only retrospectively through a form of socially necessary self-deception. Separation from the mother also inaugurates the symbolic order (the realm of language and desire), and creates the unconscious. The mother represents the infant's primary object of identification; it is only when the child experiences separation from its mother that it is in a position to desire her. Desire depends on absence and is expressed through language. Language is precisely the expression of loss: I only need to name or call for that which I do not possess. The symbolic order arises as a result of alienation from the object of desire. Desire can never be satisfied; language moves ever onwards, always seeking the original, imaginary union from which it has been banished. The unconscious is the universal repository of human loss, language and fragmentation. It is the site of the subject, the non-self-identical, the impermanent, as opposed to the fraudulently self-sufficient ego with its delusions of wholeness. When Lacan famously claims that the unconscious is structured like a language and that 'l'inconscient, c'est le discours de l'Autre'† he is not speaking metaphorically, and his formula, with its apparent simile, does not do justice to his meaning. Language, the subject and the unconscious are coeval; they are born simultaneously from the interruption of imaginary union, and from the irruption of desire.

Like Sartre, Lacan considers the human subject's lack of self-identity to be, paradoxically, its salvation: he writes in what sounds a very existential tone of 'la faute heureuse de la vie, òu l'homme, à

---

* 'misrecognition'
† 'the unconscious is the discourse of the Other'

se distinguer de son essence, découvre son existence'.* It is precisely lack that constitutes us as subjects: 'Sans cette béance qui l'aliène à sa propre image, cette symbiose avec le symbolique n'aurait pu se produire, òu il se constitue comme sujet à mort.'† However, after about 1956, language becomes increasingly dominant in Lacanian theory, to the extent that he seems to envisage language as the only real agent, and human autonomy is eroded to the point where existentialism and structuralism are again forced to part company. In Lacan's view, 'L'homme est, dès avant sa naissance et au-delà de sa mort, pris dans la chaîne symbolique … il est … un pion, dans le jeu du signifiant.'‡ For Sartre, clearly, this is only half the picture: 'L'homme ne peut "être parlé" que dans la mesure où il parle – et inversement.'§

Deconstruction: The De/Reconstruction of the Subject

Of course, Sartre was not the only philosopher to be dissatisfied with the limitations of the structuralist position. Poststructuralism attempted to retain some of the analytic tools of structuralism whilst jettisoning its more doctrinaire and ossified aspects. Deconstruction is probably the best-known and most intellectually exciting poststructuralist theory – to the extent, in fact, that the two terms are often used interchangeably – and the major exponent of deconstruction is the philosopher Jacques Derrida. In the 1960s, Derrida may have appeared fairly close to some aspects of structuralist thought, and indeed, in *L'Écriture et la différence* (1967), he discusses the contribution made by structuralism to the development of deconstruction, but with hindsight it is clear that Derrida's agenda

---

* 'the happy fault of life, where man, in being distinct from his essence, discovers his existence'
† 'Without that gaping lack that alienates man from his own image, the symbiosis with the symbolic, in which he is constituted as a mortal subject, could not have been produced.'
‡ 'Man is, from before birth and beyond his death, taken up in the symbolic chain … He is a pawn in the play of the signifier.'
§ 'Man can only "be spoken" to the extent that he speaks – and vice versa.'

has always been very different. It is true that the two movements were at one in their opposition to humanism, and indeed in their apparent determination to misrepresent Sartre's position in this respect. Foucault's scandalous proclamation of the 'disappearance of Man' and Derrida's paper on 'Les Fins de l'homme' (1968) both ignore Sartre's prior claim in the *Critique* that 'l'Homme n'existe pas',* and Derrida relegates Sartre's attack on humanism in *La Nausée* to a footnote. None the less, despite their common enemy, the methods of structuralism and deconstruction develop in antithetical directions. Structuralism must surely be the most striking example of an interpretative theory based primarily on binary oppositions; binary oppositions are the *bête noire* of deconstruction. They represent precisely the kind of hierarchicized, metaphysical way of conceptualizing the world that Derrida believes has dominated Western philosophy since Plato and needs to be dismantled.

Derrida is harder to categorize than the structuralist thinkers whose ideas I have been examining. This is due in part to his own attempts to undermine the rigid categorizations with which we operate most of the time, and in part to the nature of his work itself. Deconstruction is a form of textual analysis. The texts it analyses may come from any domain, not simply philosophy and literature, but also history, anthropology, psychoanalysis, linguistics, theology, etc. In fact, Derrida has devoted several essays to a deconstruction of texts by precisely the three structuralists we have just discussed: Lévi-Strauss in 'La Structure, le signe et le jeu dans le discours des sciences humaines' (1966), Foucault in 'Cogito et histoire de la folie'(1964) and Lacan in *La Carte postale* (1980). It is not easy to define deconstruction: to ask what it *is* is to pose a question from the very realm of essences which deconstruction is contesting. However, we may ask how it functions, and the formula closest to an answer may be Derrida's own expression, when he says we need a new 'logique paradoxale'. Now a 'paradoxical logic' is a deliberate contradiction in terms, since logic is defined as following correct reasoning and consistent argument, and not contravening the 'laws' of thought, whereas a paradox is quite the opposite: self-contradictory, against reason and, etymologically, beyond the *doxa*, or common-sense

---

* 'Man does not exist'

beliefs. This provocative aspect of Derrida's writing is what makes his work so unpalatable to many British philosophers, who tend to consider that his thought involves playing around with what the analytic tradition would consider, quite literally, to be nonsense. But Derrida's aim is to step outside what is generally believed and accepted, and he is not afraid of tackling his critics head-on, as was the case in his confrontation with John Searle in 1977.

Derrida first achieved public acclaim/notoriety in 1967 when he published three major texts: *La Voix et le phénomène* , *L'Écriture et la différence* and *De la grammatologie*. *La Voix et le phénomène* contains a critique of Husserl's phenomenological conception of the relationship between thought, speech and language. Husserl, Derrida argues, has a firm belief in the subject's unmediated presence to itself, in its self-transparency and self-understanding. What Derrida sets out to do is to show that, despite this belief, Husserl is unable to sustain his position, and that his own arguments undermine and indeed contradict the thesis he is attempting to put forward. This demonstration of self-contradiction is the essence of the 'classical' deconstructive strategy. It differs from the standard philosophical technique of finding flaws in the logic of an argument in order to show it to be false, in that the contradictions are neither simply logical slips nor necessarily explicit arguments; rather they reveal an underlying incompatibility between what the writer believes himself to be demonstrating and what his text itself actually says. Derrida focuses on Husserl's discussion of interior monologue, when the subject's simple presence-to-itself is arguably the most evident, and shows that, on the contrary, the notion of 's'entendre parler' contains within itself the seeds of the destruction of self-identity. 'S'entendre parler' has, of course, in French, a double meaning: both to hear oneself and to understand oneself speaking. For Derrida, the phrase itself illustrates precisely the internal division of the subject: only a self-divided subject could speak to itself. The very notion of self-presence is indicative of division rather than unity.

This, ironically, is why Derrida is wrong in his analysis of Sartre's conception of the subject: the subject of *L'Être et le néant* is not, as

Derrida claims, a self-identical plenitude, it is, as we have seen, 'diasporique', always elsewhere. Sartre, like Derrida, but twenty years earlier, defines 'présence à soi' as 'une façon de *ne pas être sa propre coïncidence*, d'échapper à l'identité'* And what is more, Sartre cites Husserl as evidence that even the most determined philosopher of presence cannot overcome entirely the reflexivity implicit in all consciousness. However, leaving aside the misrepresentation of Sartre, Derrida's deconstruction of a cornerstone of the phenomenological enterprise is a brilliant introduction to the kind of close textual analysis which shows him at his most convincing.

De la grammatologie is also a classic of its kind. Here Derrida is considering not a single text or author but rather some of the assumptions about the nature of speech and language that underlie the Western philosophical tradition. In this sense it is a much more ambitious and indeed controversial work. Derrida's argument is that the conception of language that posits the priority of thought over speech and speech over writing may be deep-rooted and apparently 'natural', but it is fundamentally flawed. He refers to this conception of language by the term 'logocentrism'. In his view the notion of 'priority' is not merely temporal, it also implies an evaluative element. Speech is considered superior to writing because closer to the thought of the speaker, unmediated by the processes of inscription. In speech, the speaker's 'self-presence' is more apparent. His identification with what he is saying is more complete. Derrida's contention, as in the case of Husserl, is that there is no fuller presence in speech than in writing: the illusion of presence produced by the physical proximity of the speaker belies his own absence and self-division. There is no unmediated thought, to be mediated through speech and further mediated through writing. Speech, Derrida maintains, is already a form of *écriture*† in so far as it is a network of traces that necessarily fail to represent fully what the speaker intends. We have already seen him argue that thought itself (in the form of interior monologue) is riven by self-division rather than self-identical.

In his eagerness to show speech as already derivative, Derrida goes so far as to claim that 'writing' is actually prior to speech. It is this sort of claim that has led Derrida to be ridiculed by those of an

---

* 'self-presence'; 'a way of *not coinciding with oneself*, of escaping identity'
† writing

empirical turn of mind; however, it seems to me much more interesting to try to understand what Derrida means than to attack him for what he clearly is not really saying. Derrida does not mean that, historically, people wrote before they spoke. He means rather that there is no pure, pre-linguistic thought which is translated into first speech and later writing. Thought itself, and speech, share many of the features of writing: conventionality, iterability, etc. Derrida's formulations are part of what he later called the 'reversal phase' of deconstruction. He is inverting the most common oppositions – here speech/writing, elsewhere real/imaginary, male/female, presence/ absence, mind/body, original/derivative, etc. – in order both to show the hidden hierarchy underlying an apparently neutral opposition, and also, more importantly, to undermine the stability of the opposition itself by exposing the degree to which the two poles of it are interdependent and inseparable.

In the last section of *De la grammatologie*, where Derrida discusses Rousseau's ideas on language, he demonstrates this method clearly in his analysis of the paradoxes and self-contradictions inherent in the notion of the 'supplément'. According to *Littré's* definition, the supplement is a slippery term: 'Suppléer: ajouter ce qui manque, fournir ce qu'il faut de surplus.'* *Littré* respects 'comme un somnambule l'étrange logique de ce mot',† Derrida dryly remarks. The supplement is described as adding to what is already complete and as compensating for a deficiency; it is both superfluous and essential. In Rousseau's case the notion of supplement recurs in several different contexts, always disrupting the coherence of what he is attempting to argue. Writing is a supplement to speech, culture is a supplement to nature, art is a supplement to reality, and masturbation is a supplement to heterosexual intercourse. Speech, nature, reality and heterosexual love are the ideal, distorted by the 'dangerous' supplements of writing, culture, imagination and narcissistic sexuality. However, the boundaries between the domains are far from clear: culture, for example, is sometimes seen as a late arrival on the human scene, sometimes as coinciding with the advent of speech, which means it is present from the outset, since Rousseau sees speech as what distinguishes humans from animals. All the

---

* 'to supplement: to add what is lacking, to provide the necessary surplus'
† 'like a sleepwalker the strange logic of this word'

apparently dangerous supplements turn out on closer analysis to be essential: they constitute us rather than pervert us. Culture, writing and even masturbation are the suppressed halves of a hierarchical opposition which Derrida will reverse. Derrida sees clearly what Rousseau is refusing to see: the implications of his own arguments. Culture is constitutive of humanity; writing is endemic in all communication; and what Derrida calls 'auto-affection' as well as an element of imagination is inherent in all sexuality.

To use Derrida's own argument in our account of deconstruction, we might say that deconstruction itself is not a dangerous alien method that threatens the integrity of philosophy and literary theory. Deconstruction is perhaps constitutive of all good theory: it is essential not supplementary, and if it is not, in a pure sense, original, this is only because Derrida has taught us to be wary of any notions of origins or ends. Derrida himself is the first to recognize the impossibility of a clean break where philosophy is concerned: he, like Heidegger in his critique of metaphysics, or Nietzsche in his, is unable to escape the metaphysical discourse he is attempting to deconstruct. Deconstruction certainly forces us to question our assumptions about meaning, presence, subject-hood, intention and agency, but it is not destructive of our ability to philosophize. Indeed, in the Oxford Amnesty Lectures of 1992, Derrida accepted the suggestion that deconstruction could perhaps alternatively be called reconstruction.

Of course, on other occasions, Derrida would certainly refuse to recognize such a positive depiction of deconstruction: the political context is perhaps determining. But in recent years Derrida has become increasingly sensitive to the ethical consequences of his own positions. Like Foucault, who latterly claimed to have been engaged all along on a history of conceptions of the subject, so Derrida shifted position from the 1960s to the 1980s, from an analysis of 'Les Fins de l'homme' (1968) to one of the rights of man. Already in an interview in 1972 he denied ever having maintained that there was no 'subject of writing', or indeed, no subject; and in the Cerisy colloquy in 1980 he insisted that the question of 'man' needed reopening, and rescuing from its association with naive, reactionary humanism.

More recent texts such as *Psyché II* (1987), *De l'esprit* (1987) and *Spectres de Marx* (1993) deal with precisely these issues.

Feminism: The Subject of Gender

French feminist theorists might also agree that the question of 'man' needed reopening, but it is less certain that they would mean by this the same thing as Derrida understands by it, though a deconstruction of the male/female opposition is clearly on some feminist philosophical and political agendas. When Simone de Beauvoir published *Le Deuxième sexe* in 1949 she was writing primarily a work of sociology and politics rather than a philosophical text. The nub of her argument was that femininity is socially constructed, not biologically determined. Women are conceived of by men as 'other', that is to say, not merely different from men but somehow aberrant: man is the norm from which woman diverges. And women tend to internalize this male conception of themselves and to consider themselves in certain ways as inferior. At the end of *Le Deuxième Sexe* (see also page 182), Beauvoir denies being a feminist: she considered herself primarily a socialist, and maintained that the oppression of women would only end with socialist revolution. By 1972 she had changed her mind; she joined the MLF (le Mouvement de libération des femmes) and explained that she now believed that it was necessary to fight for an improvement in women's situation before true socialism could be achieved. Even in socialist countries, she argued, women's equality had not been won.

Le Deuxième Sexe was the first major feminist work in French and was very influential. However, its significance has been played down by contemporary French feminists in a move that parallels the relegation of Sartre's works by his successors, and which may well be related to it. Beauvoir's daughters are less matricidal than Sartre's heirs appear parricidal, but they are experts in damning with faint praise.

One of the more substantial points of difference between Beauvoir and later feminists (see also pages 189–90) may well be over the question of psychoanalysis. Beauvoir's attack on the Freudian concepts of penis envy, female narcissism and female masochism were appreciated more by feminists in the USA (such as Kate Millett) than in France. French feminists were unwilling to reject Freudian theory out of hand. In an interview in 1986, for example, Hélène Cixous associates the feminist prohibition of Freud with the early 1970s, and argues that an understanding of the unconscious (and, indeed, of deconstruction) is vital for any serious contemporary theory. This does not simply represent a willingness to acknowledge important modern thinkers; Freud's ideas are being actively harnessed by certain French feminists to further their own arguments. The concept of the unconscious, in particular, implies a powerful critique of the idea that rational mental processes necessarily govern our thoughts and actions. A major strand of feminism would approve this attack on the power of reason. This was not, of course, Beauvoir's position: her intention was to show women as, potentially at least, free, rational subjects. But few of the major contemporary French feminists are philosophers, and reason itself has come to be considered by some a tool of patriarchal power and oppression. What is more, since the mid-1960s, Lacan's so-called 'return to Freud' has opened up a new way of reading Freudian theory that has considerable potential for the feminist cause.

It is interesting that, as was the case with structuralism, few of the major 'feminist' theorists are prepared to accept the feminist label. Julia Kristeva is a philosopher and psychoanalyst, Luce Irigaray is also a psychoanalyst, and Hélène Cixous is a creative writer. What this may perhaps indicate is that feminism is not so much a theory as an ideological position, which draws on, and has implications for, politics, philosophy, psychoanalysis and indeed literature. Contemporary French feminists certainly have as much in common as the structuralists of the 1960s and 1970s, but they also disagree on a wide range of issues.

One of the most fundamental, and at first sight perhaps surprising, points of difference, is the nature of male–female relations, and in particular the question of (in)equality. For Irigaray, biology makes an ineradicable difference – women are qualitatively different from men, and their writing and thinking should reflect this difference, not ape the logical binary patterns of male discourse. Women's writing should express their gender; this is summed up in the notion of *écriture féminine*, and some of the literary exponents of *écriture féminine* were discussed in Chapter 8 (see page 190). Cixous also promotes *écriture féminine*, but unlike Irigaray she believes that it can also be practised by men, Genet and Joyce for example, whose writing is freed from the rigidity of analytic discourse. For Cixous, femininity is a subject position, not just a biological given, and its expression should be further developed and opened up to men. Kristeva would agree with Cixous that male writers may produce this kind of fluid and iconoclastic writing. One of the most fruitful ways of understanding this conception of feminine writing is to use Kristeva's notion of the semiotic level of signification, the pre-linguistic level which is repressed when we enter (Lacan's) symbolic order. In Kristeva's view, women find entry into the symbolic order particularly problematic; it is associated with patriarchy, and the loss of the mother (the female figure). Consequently women tend to retain a closer relationship to the semiotic, and this subversive force may help them produce the kind of anarchic and disruptive writing termed by others '*écriture féminine*'.

However, Kristeva has been influenced not only by Lacan but also by Derrida, and she proposes, ultimately, a deconstruction of the binary opposition of male/female. For Kristeva, it is neither a matter, as Beauvoir proposes, of demonstrating female equality with men and showing how women's social conditioning prevents them achieving their potential, nor a matter of espousing a kind of Irigarayan separatism, which promotes biology and gender differences and labels certain qualities as both female and superior. For Kristeva, male/female is one of the false and distorting essentialist antitheses that a post-logocentric (deconstructive) philosophy could help overturn. As she boldly expressed it in an interview in 1974: 'Se croire "être une femme" c'est presque aussi absurde et obscurantiste que de se croire "être un homme" ... Plus profondément, une femme, cela ne peut pas être.'* We have associated Kristeva with Lacan and

---

* 'The belief that "one is a woman" is almost as absurd and obscurantist as the belief that "one is a man" ... On a deeper level ... a woman cannot "be"; it is something which does not even belong to the order of being.'

Derrida. Here she is also close to Sartre's notion of subjectivity: Sartre of course also believed that men and women had no essence, and he enjoyed exploring the paradoxes his own anti-essentialism created. Kristeva uses Lacan and Derrida to set up a new conception of subjectivity and gender, which goes beyond the narrow confines of political feminism and enters the psychoanalytic and philosophical arenas at a high level of theoretical sophistication.

This chapter began by looking briefly at the series of reversals that French thought of the second half of the twentieth century has undergone. Perhaps it would be appropriate to end with a paradoxical constant: the last fifty years have been witness to a constant rejection of authority and the 'self-evident' in favour of the most recent philosophical/theoretical vogue. This is not merely the schoolchild's rejection of 'thought control'; it is rather the philosopher's rejection of the answers (and sometimes the questions) of the previous generation. French thought has been iconoclastic since at least the classical period: Descartes himself started afresh from the *cogito* (see page 72). French subversiveness has been theorized in the twentieth century. Existentialism, structuralism, deconstruction and feminism are all modes of rejection of established 'common-sense' beliefs and value systems. The 'obvious', modern French philosophers claim, belongs to the realm of ideology rather than truth. The gap between truth and common sense has been known to philosophers for millennia and to scientists for centuries. It has now become so wide that the critic and journalist have also been forced to recognize it. Contemporary French theory may be rebarbative in its anti-intuitive nature, but this is precisely its strength. Mistrust of the obvious is initially the feature of theory which is most difficult to accept and comprehend, but it is the feature which turns out to be the most exhilarating and invigorating.

Further Reading

Primary sources

S. de Beauvoir, *Le Deuxième Sexe* (Paris: Gallimard, 1949).

S. de Beauvoir, *La Force de l'âge* (Paris: Gallimard, 1960).

H. Cixous, *La Jeune Née* (Paris: UGE, 10/18, 1975).

J. Derrida, *Marges de la philosophie* (Paris: Minuit, 1972).

J. Derrida, *De l'esprit* (Paris: Galilée, 1987).

J. Derrida, *Spectres de Marx* (Paris: Galilée, 1993).

M. Foucault, *Histoire de la folie à l'âge classique* (Paris: Gallimard, 1964).

M. Foucault, *La Volonté de savoir* (Paris: Gallimard, 1976).

M. Foucault, *Le Souci de soi* (Paris, Gallimard, 1984).

L. Irigaray, *Speculum; De l'autre femme* (Paris: Minuit, 1974).

J. Kristeva, *La Révolution du langage poétique* (Paris: Seuil, 1974).

J. Kristeva, *Soleil noir* (Paris: Gallimard, 1987).

J. Lacan, *Écrits* (Paris: Seuil, 1966).

J. Lacan, *Encore; Le séminaire, livre XX* (Paris: Seuil, 1975).

C. Lévi-Strauss, *Tristes Tropiques* (Paris: Plon, 1955).

C. Lévi-Strauss, *Mythologiques*, 4 vols (Paris: Plon, 1964–71).

J.-P. Sartre, *L'Être et le néant* (Paris: Gallimard, 1943).

J.-P. Sartre, *Critique de la raison dialectique* (Paris: Gallimard, 1960).

J.-P. Sartre, *Les Mots* (Paris: Gallimard, 1963).

Secondary Sources

M. Bowie, *Lacan* (London: Fontana, 1991).

P. Caws, *Structuralism: The Art of the Intelligible* (Atlantic Highlands, NJ: Humanities Press, 1988).

V. Descombes, *Le Même et l'autre* (Paris: Minuit, 1979).

C. Howells, *Sartre: The Necessity of Freedom* (Cambridge: Cambridge University Press, 1988).

E. Leach, *Lévi-Strauss* (London: Fontana, 1970).

J.G. Merquior, *Foucault* (London: Fontana, 1985).

T. Moi, *Sexual/Textual Politics: Feminist Literary Theory* (London and New York: Methuen, 1985).

C. Norris, *Derrida* (London: Fontana, 1987).

Chronology

Note We have been able to include only some of the most obvious 'landmarks' in literary history in this summary table. For earlier periods, especially pre-1600, the date of composition/publication of a work is often unknown, and only approximate indications are given.

1 REIGNING MONARCH OR REGIME IN FRANCE	2 HISTORICAL EVENTS	3 LITERARY WORKS AND EVENTS
751–987 Carolingian Dynasty		
	800 Coronation of Charlemagne as Holy Roman Emperor	
	842 Strasbourg Oaths	
		9th century 'Carolingian renaissance'
		c.880 *Cantilène de Sainte Eulalie*
987–1328 Capetian Dynasty		
987–96 Hugues Capet		
996–1031 Robert II		9th–11th centuries Early saints' lives
1031–60 Henri I		c.1050 *Vie de Sainte Alexis*
1060–1108 Philippe I	1066 Norman Conquest of England	
	1096–9 First Crusade	c.1098 *Chanson de Roland*
1108–37 Louis VI		
1137–80 Louis VII	1147–89 Second Crusade	
		12th century Early epics, romances, lyric poetry, histories
		c.1138 Geoffrey of Monmouth, *Historia regum Britanniae*
		Mid-12th century *Adam*
	1152 Eleanor of Aquitaine married to future Henry II of England (1154–89)	
		c.1150–70 *Romans antiques*
		c.1155 Wace, *Roman de Brut*
		1170–80 Marie de France, *Lais*
		1170s Romances of Gautier d'Arras
		1175 onwards *Roman de Renart*
		c.1176 Thomas, *Tristan*
1180–1223 Philippe II (Philippe-Auguste)		1180s Romances of Chrétien de Troyes Beroul, *Tristran*
	Late 12th century Beginning of University of Paris	*Folies*
		c.1200 Robert de Boron, *Joseph*
		c.1200 Jean Bodel, *Jeu de Saint Nicolas*
		Perlesvaus

1 REIGNING MONARCH OR REGIME IN FRANCE	2 HISTORICAL EVENTS	3 LITERARY WORKS AND EVENTS
		*c.*1200 Romances of Jean Renart *fabliaux*
	1202–4 Fourth Crusade	
1223–6 Louis VIII		
		Early 13th century Villehardouin; Robert de Clari
		1215–35 *Vulgate Cycle*
		1225–40 Prose *Tristan*
1226–70 Louis IX (Saint Louis)		
		*c.*1230 and 1270 *Roman de la Rose* (parts 1 and 2)
	1244 Christians lose Jerusalem	
		*c.*1250 Robert de Blois Philippe de Novarre *Aucassin et Nicolette*
		1270s Plays of Adam de la Halle
1270–85 Philippe III (le Hardi)	1270 Eighth Crusade	
	1271–95 Travels of Marco Polo	
1285–1314 Philippe IV (le Bel)	1309–77 Papal schism (Avignon papacy)	
		1310–20 *Roman de Fauvel*
1314–16 Louis X		
1316–22 Philippe V		
1322–8 Charles IV		
		Early 14th century Joinville *Voeux de paon* Deguilleville, *Pèlerinage* *Perceforest*
1328–1498 Valois Dynasty		1300–77 Guillaume de Machaut
1328–50 Philippe VI	1337–1453 Hundred Years War	
	1346–50 Black Death	
	1346 Battle of Crécy	
1350–64 Jean II (le Bon)	1356 Battle of Poitiers	
1364–80 Charles V		
1380–1422 Charles VI		
		*c.*1389 Philippe de Mézières
		1346–1407 Eustache Deschamps
		Mid-14th century Froissart
		1393 *Ménagier de Paris*
		Late 14th century *Querelle de la Rose*
		*c.*1400 Christine de Pizan
	1415 Battle of Agincourt	
		*c.*1420 *Quinze Joies de mariage*
		*c.*1420 Alain Chartier
		1394–1465 Charles d'Orléans
1422–61 Charles VII	1431 Joan of Arc burnt by English	
	1450–3 France recovers Normandy and Gascony	
		*c.*1456 Antoine de la Sale, *Petit Jean de Saintré*
		1456 and 1461 François Villon, *Lais* and *Testament*
1461–83 Louis XI		
		1460s *Cent Nouvelles nouvelles*

1 REIGNING MONARCH OR REGIME IN FRANCE	2 HISTORICAL EVENTS	3 LITERARY WORKS AND EVENTS
		c.1465 Farce de Pierre Pathelin
	1470 First printing press in Paris	
	1482 Burgundian lands divided between France and the Empire	
1483–98 Charles VIII		1489–98 Philippe de Commynes, Mémoires
		Late 15th century Grands Rhétoriqueurs
1498–1589 Valois-Orléans Dynasty		
1498–1515 Louis XII	1499 Louis XII invades northern Italy	
		1503 Champier, Nef des dames
		1511–13 Lemaire de Belges, Les Illustrations de Gaule
	1513 French expelled from Italy	
1515–47 François I	1515 Leonardo da Vinci invited to Amboise	
		1516 Budé, L'Institution du prince
	1517 Luther's 95 theses published in Germany	
	1520 François I and Henry VIII meet at the Field of the Cloth of Gold	
	1525 François I defeated at Battle of Pavia	
	1530 Collège des Lecteurs Royaux founded	
		1531 Marguerite de Navarre, Miroir de l'âme pécheresse
	1532 Treaty of Union between France and Brittany	
		1532 Rabelais, Pantagruel Clément Marot, Adolescence clémentine
	1534 Affaire des Placards Jacques Cartier reaches Canada	1534 Rabelais, Gargantua
	1535 Reformation adopted at Geneva	
		1538 Hélisenne de Crenne, Les Angoisses douloureuses
		1539 Edict of Villers-Cotterêts
		1540–6 French translation of Amadis de Gaule
	1541–64 Calvin in Geneva	1541 Calvin, Institution de la religion chrétienne (first French edition)
		1544 Scève, Délie
	1545–63 Council of Trent	1545 Pernette du Guillet, Rimes
		1546 Rabelais, Le Tiers Livre
1547–59 Henri II		
		1549 Du Bellay, Défense et illustration
		1552 Jodelle, Cléopâtre captive Rabelais, Quart Livre
		1552–3 Ronsard, Les Amours
		1555 Ronsard, La Continuation des amours; Hymnes Labé, Oeuvres

1 REIGNING MONARCH OR REGIME IN FRANCE	2 HISTORICAL EVENTS	3 LITERARY WORKS AND EVENTS
		1558 Marguerite de Navarre, *Heptaméron* Du Bellay, *Les Antiquités de Rome*; *Les Regrets*
	1559 Peace of Cateau-Cambrésis between France and Spain	1559 Boaistuau and Belleforest, *Histoires tragiques*
1559–60 François II		
1560–74 Charles IX	1560–3 Regency of Catherine de Médicis	
	1562 Outbreak of Wars of Religion	1562–3 Ronsard, *Discours des misères de ce temps*
	1572 Massacre of St Bartholomew	1572 Ronsard, *La Franciade* Jean de la Taille, *Saül le furieux*
		1573 Garnier, *Hippolyte*
1574–89 Henri III		
		1576 Bodin, *Six Livres de la république*
		1578 Ronsard, *Sonnets pour Hélène* Du Bartas, *La Première Semaine*
		1580 Montaigne, *Les Essais*
		1587 La Noue, *Discours politiques et militaires*
	1589 Assassination of Henri III	

1589–1792 Bourbon Dynasty

1589–1610 Henri IV	1594 Entry into Paris and coronation of Henri IV	1594 (anon.) *Satire Ménippée*
	1598 Edict of Nantes	
	1599–1611 Ministry of Sully	
		1599 Comédiens du Roi established at Hôtel de Bourgogne
		c.1606 Malherbe's Commentary on Desportes
		1607–27 D'Urfé, *Astrée*
	1608 Founding of Québec	
		1609 Saint François de Sales, *Introduction à la vie dévote* Lescarbot, *Les Muses de la Nouvelle-France*
	1610 Assassination of Henri IV	1610 Béroalde de Verville, *Le Moyen de parvenir*
1610–43 Louis XIII	1610–17 Regency of Marie de Médicis	
		1616 D'Aubigné, *Les Tragiques*
	1618–48 Thirty Years War	
		c.1620–50 Salon of Marquise de Rambouillet
		1621–6 Théophile de Viau, *Oeuvres*
	1624–42 Ministry of Richelieu	
	1627–8 Siege of La Rochelle	
		1629 Théâtre du Marais established
		1634 Mairet, *La Sophonisbe*
	1635 French arrive in Caribbean	1635 Foundation of Académie française by Richelieu
		1636 Pierre Corneille, *L'Illusion comique*
		1637 Descartes, *Discours de la méthode*

1 REIGNING MONARCH OR REGIME IN FRANCE	2 HISTORICAL EVENTS	3 LITERARY WORKS AND EVENTS
		1637 Corneille, *Le Cid*
	1638 St Louis (Senegal) founded	
	1639 Rising of Va-nu-pieds in Normandy	
	1642–61 Ministry of Mazarin	
1643–1715 Louis XIV	1643–51 Regency of Anne of Austria	
		1645 Rotrou, *Le Véritable Saint Genest*
		c.1646–96 Letters of Madame de Sévigné
		1647 Vaugelas, *Remarques sur la langue française*
	1648–53 Civil Wars of La Fronde	
		1649–53 Madeleine de Scudéry, *Le Grand Cyrus*
		1651–7 Scarron, *Le Roman comique*
	1653 Papal condemnation of Jansenism	
		1656 Thomas Corneille, *Timocrate*
		1656–7 Pascal, *Lettres provinciales*
	1661 Louis XIV assumes personal control of government; work starts on Versailles	1661 Molière's company moves to Palais Royal
	1661–83 Ministry of Colbert	
		1662 Molière, *L'École des femmes*
		1664 *Les Plaisirs de l'île enchantée* at Versailles, including Molière's *Tartuffe*
		1666 Furetière, *Le Roman bourgeois*
	1667–8 War of Devolution	
		1668 Racine, *Andromaque* La Fontaine, *Les Fables* (Books I–VI)
		1669 Académie royale de musique established by Lully
		1670 Pascal, *Pensées*
	1672–8 Second War against Holland	
		1673 Molière, *Le Malade imaginaire*
		1674 Boileau, *Art poétique*
		1677 Racine, *Phèdre*
		1678 Madame de Lafayette, *La Princesse de Clèves*
	1680 Dragonnades against Protestants	1680 Comédie-Française established
	1682 Court moves to Versailles	
	1683 Secret marriage of Louis XIV and Madame de Maintenon	
	1685 Revocation of Edict of Nantes	
		1686 Fontenelle, *Entretiens sur la pluralité des mondes*
		1687–8 Main episode of *Querelle des Anciens et des Modernes*
	1688–97 War of League of Augsburg	1688–96 La Bruyère, *Les Caractères*
		1691 Racine, *Athalie*
		1694 First *Dictionnaire de l'Académie française*
		1697–1706 Bayle, *Dictionnaire critique et historique*
		1699 Fénelon, *Télémaque*

1 REIGNING MONARCH OR REGIME IN FRANCE	2 HISTORICAL EVENTS	3 LITERARY WORKS AND EVENTS
	1702–5 Camisard risings in Cévennes	
	1702–13 War of Spanish Succession	
	1709 Expulsion of nuns from Port-Royal	1709 Lesage, *Turcaret*
	1715 Death of Louis XIV	1715 Lesage, *Gil Blas*
1715–74 Louis XV	1715–23 Regency of Philippe d'Orléans	
		1721 Montesquieu, *Lettres persanes*
	1726–43 Ministry of Fleury	
		1730 Marivaux, *Le Jeu de l'amour et du hasard*
		1731 Prévost, *Manon Lescaut; Cleveland*
	1734 Spread of Anglomania	1734 Voltaire, *Lettres philosophiques*
		1736 Crébillon *fils, Les Égarements du cœur et de l'esprit*
		Voltaire, *Le Mondain*
		1737 Marivaux, *Les Fausses confidences*
		1750 Rousseau, *Discours sur les sciences et les arts*
	1755 Lisbon earthquake	
	1756–63 Seven Years War	
		1757 Diderot, *Le Fils naturel*
		1759 Voltaire, *Candide*
		1760 Palissot, *Les Philosophes*
		Diderot, *La Religieuse*
		1761 Rousseau, *La Nouvelle Héloïse*
		1762 Diderot, *Le Neveu de Rameau*
		Rousseau, *Émile; Du contrat social*
	1763 France cedes most of Canada to Britain	
	1764 Expulsion of Jesuits from France	
	1766 Lorraine incorporated into France	
	1768 France acquires Corsica	
		1769 Diderot, *Le Rêve de d'Alembert*
	1770 Marriage of Dauphin and Marie-Antoinette	
		1773 Diderot, *Jacques le fataliste; Paradoxe sur le comédien*
1774–92 Louis XVI	1774–6 Ministry of Turgot	1775 Beaumarchais, *Le Barbier de Séville*
	1776–81 Ministry of Necker	
	1778 France enters War of American Independence	
		1782 Rousseau, *Rêveries du promeneur solitaire*
		Laclos, *Les Liaisons dangereuses*
		1782–8 Rousseau, *Les Confessions*
	1783–7 Ministry of Calonne	
		1784 Beaumarchais, *Le Mariage de Figaro*
		1788 Bernardin de Saint-Pierre, *Paul et Virginie*

1 REIGNING MONARCH OR REGIME IN FRANCE	2 HISTORICAL EVENTS	3 LITERARY WORKS AND EVENTS
	1789 (14 July) Storming of Bastille	
	1789 (4 August) Declaration of the Rights of Man	
	1791 Flight of Louis XVI to Varennes	1791 Sade, *Justine, ou Les Malheurs de la vertu*
1792–1804 First Republic		
	1793 Louis XVI and Marie-Antoinette executed	
	1793–4 The Terror	
	1794 Downfall of Robespierre	
	1795–9 The Directory	
	1798–9 Napoleon's Egyptian campaign	
	1799 (10 October) Napoleon seizes power	
		1801 Chateaubriand, *Atala*
		1802 Chateaubriand, *René; Le Génie du christianisme* Madame de Staël, *Delphine*
	1803–14 Napoleonic campaigns in Europe	
1804–1814 First Empire 1804–14 Napoleon I		
	1804 Napoleon crowned Emperor Independence of Haiti	1804 Senancour, *Obermann*
		1807 Madame de Staël, *Corinne*
	1814 Napoleon abdicates and retires to Elba	
1814–30 Bourbon Restoration 1814–24 Louis XVIII		
	1815 Return of Napoleon (The Hundred Days); Battle of Waterloo; Napoleon exiled to St Helena	
		1816 Constant, *Adolphe*
		1816–20 Milscent, *L'Abeille haïtienne*
		1820 Lamartine, *Les Méditations poétiques*
	1821 Death of Napoleon I	1821 Nodier, *Smarra*
1824–30 Charles X		
		1826 Hugo, *Odes et ballades* Vigny, *Cinq-Mars*
		1827 Hugo, *Cromwell*
		1829 Hugo, *Les Orientales* Mérimée, *La Chronique du règne de Charles IX*
	1830 July Revolution, abdication of Charles X	1830 Hugo, *Hernani*
1830–48 Orléans (July) Monarchy 1830–48 Louis-Philippe		
	1830 Colonization of Algeria begins Independence of Belgium	
		1831 Hugo, *Notre-Dame de Paris* Balzac, *La Peau de chagrin* Stendhal, *Le Rouge et le noir*
		1832 Dumas *père, La Tour de Nesle* Sand, *Indiana*
	1833 Guizot's charter for primary education in France	
		1834 Musset, *Lorenzaccio* Balzac, *Le Père Goriot*

1 REIGNING MONARCH OR REGIME IN FRANCE	2 HISTORICAL EVENTS	3 LITERARY WORKS AND EVENTS
	1835 Assassination attempt on Louis-Philippe	1835 Vigny, *Chatterton* Gautier, *Mademoiselle de Maupin* *Revue belge* founded
		1836 Musset, *Confession d'un enfant du siècle*
		1839 Stendhal, *La Chartreuse de Parme*
		1843 Hugo, *Les Burgraves* Balzac, *Illusions perdues*
	1844 Dominican Republic established	1844 Dumas *père*, *Les Trois Mousquetaires*
		1844–5 Sue, *Le Juif errant*
		1845–8 Garneau, *Histoire du Canada*
	1846 Economic crisis in France	1846 Balzac, *La Cousine Bette*
1848–52 Second Republic		
	1848 Abdication of Louis-Philippe; proclamation of Second Republic; Louis-Napoleon Bonaparte elected president	1848 Dumas *fils*, *La Dame aux camélias*
		1849–50 Chateaubriand, *Mémoires d'outre-tombe*
	1851 *Coup d'état* of Louis-Napoleon	
1852–70 Second Empire 1852–70 Napoleon III	1852 Louis-Napoleon proclaimed emperor	1852 Gautier, *Émaux et camées* Leconte de Lisle, *Poèmes antiques*
	1853 Haussmann begins reconstruction of Paris	1853 Hugo, *Les Châtiments*
	1854–6 Crimean War	1854 Nerval, *Sylvie*
	1855 Exposition universelle	1855 Nerval, *Le Rêve et la vie*
		1857 Flaubert, *Madame Bovary* Baudelaire, *Les Fleurs du mal*
	1859 War with Austria	
	1861–7 Mexican campaign of Napoleon III	
		1862 Flaubert, *Salammbô* Hugo, *Les Misérables*
		1863 Fromentin, *Dominique*
	1864 Cambodia becomes French protectorate	1864 Goncourt, *Germinie Lacerteux*
		1866 Verlaine, *Poèmes saturniens*
	1867 Canada becomes a dominion	1867 Zola, *Thérèse Raquin*
		1868 Lautréamont, *Les Chants de Maldoror*
	1869 Opening of Suez Canal	1869 Flaubert, *L'Éducation sentimentale* Baudelaire, *Petits Poèmes en prose* Verlaine, *Fêtes galantes*
	1870–1 Franco-Prussian War; fall of Napoleon III	

1 REGIME IN FRANCE	2 HISTORICAL EVENTS (METROPOLITAN FRANCE)	3 LITERATURE AND THOUGHT (METROPOLITAN FRANCE)

1870–1940 Third Republic

	1870–1 Start of Third Republic; Paris Commune	
	1873 Death of Napoleon III	1873 Rimbaud, *Une Saison en enfer*
	1875 Republican Constitution established	
		1877 Zola, *L'Assommoir* Flaubert, *Trois contes* Goncourt, *La Fille Elisa*
	1879 Senate and Chamber of Deputies return to Paris from Versailles	1879 Goncourt, *Les Frères Zemganno*
		1880 Zola, *Nana*; Zola and others, *Les Soirées de Médan*
	1881–2 *Lois* Ferry establish universal free primary education	
		1884 Huysmans, *À rebours*
		1885 Zola, *Germinal*
	1889 Paris International Exhibition	
		1892 Maeterlinck, *Pelléas et Mélisande*
		1897 Barrès, *Les Déracinés*
	1898 Dreyfus affair	
		1902 Gide, *L'Immoraliste*
	1905 Separation of Church and state	
		1909 Founding of *NRF*
		1913 Alain-Fournier, *Le Grand Meaulnes* Apollinaire, *Alcools*
	1914 Outbreak of First World War	1914 Gide, *Les Caves du Vatican*
	1916 Battle of Verdun	1916 Barbusse, *Le Feu*
		1917 Valéry, *La Jeune Parque*
	1919 Treaty of Versailles	1919 Proust, *A l'ombre des jeunes filles en fleurs*
	1920 Foundation of French Communist Party	
	1924 Bloc National defeated by Cartel des Gauches	1924 Breton, *Manifeste du surréalisme*
	1925 Locarno Agreements	1925 Gide, *Les Faux-monnayeurs*
	1926 Papal condemnation of Action Française	
		1927 Mauriac, *Thérèse Desqueyroux*
		1928 Giraudoux, *Siegfried*
	1929 Wall Street Crash	
		1932 Céline, *Voyage au bout de la nuit*
	1933 Hitler comes to power in Germany	1933 Malraux, *La Condiiton humaine*
		1935 Giraudoux, *La Guerre de Troie n'aura pas lieu*
	1936 Popular Front government	1936 Bernanos, *Journal d'un curé de campagne* Gide, *Retour de l'URSS*

4 HISTORICAL EVENTS (FRANCOPHONE COUNTRIES)	5 LITERARY WORKS AND EVENTS (FRANCOPHONE COUNTRIES)
1881 Tunisia becomes French protectorate	1881 *Jeune Belgique* founded
1885 Treaty of Berlin: Africa divided between colonial powers	1885 Firmin, *Egalité des races humaines*
	1896 Chékri Ghanem, *Ronces et fleurs*
	1905 Ramuz, *Aline* 1906 First Congrès international de la langue française in Liège Marius and Ary Leblond, *Anthologie coloniale*
1912 Morocco becomes French protectorate	
	1914 Hémon, *Maria Chapdelaine*
1920 Lebanon under French Mandate	1920 Randau's Algérianistes' manifesto
	1921 Maran, *Batouala*
	1923 Lara, *Questions de couleur*
	1924 Lacascade, *Claire Solange âme africain*
	1928 Price-Mars, *Ainsi parla l'oncle* 1929 Couchoro, *L'Esclave*
1931 Statute of Westminster: Canada gains political independence	
	1935 Ousmane Socé, *Karim*

1 REGIME IN FRANCE	2 HISTORICAL EVENTS (METROPOLITAN FRANCE)	3 LITERATURE AND THOUGHT (METROPOLITAN FRANCE)
		1936 Sartre, *La Transcendance de l'ego*
	1937 Spanish Civil War	1937 Malraux, *L'Espoir*
		1938 Sartre, *La Nausée*
	1939 Outbreak of Second World War	
	1940 German troops occupy Paris and much of France	
1940–44 Vichy Regime		
	1940–4 Vichy regime under Marshal Pétain	1940 Sartre, *L'Imaginaire*
		1942 Camus, *L'Étranger* Vercors, *Le Silence de la mer* Ponge, *Le Parti pris des choses*
		1943 Sartre, *Les Mouches; L'Être et le néant*
	1944 Liberation of Paris	
1944–6 Provisional Government of de Gaulle		
		1944 Anouilh, *Antigone* Sartre, *Huis clos*
	1945 End of Second World War; de Gaulle head of provisional government; referendum votes to end Third Republic	1945 De Beauvoir, *Le Sang des autres*
1946–58 Fourth Republic		
	1946 Resignation of de Gaulle; Constitution of Fourth Republic accepted by referendum	
	1947 Adoption of Marshall Plan (1948–52) to assist economic reconstruction of Europe	1947 Camus, *La Peste* Genet, *Les Bonnes* Queneau, *Exercices de style*
	1948 Signature of North Atlantic Treaty	1948 Sartre, *Les Mains sales*
		1949 De Beauvoir, *Le Deuxième Sexe*
		1952 Ionesco, *Les Chaises*
		1953 Beckett, *En attendant Godot*
		1954 De Beauvoir, *Les Mandarins*
		1955 Lévi-Strauss, *Tristes Tropiques*
		1956 Camus, *La Chute*
	1957 Treaty of Rome ratified, founding Common Market	1957 Robbe-Grillet, *La Jalousie*
1958– Fifth Republic		
	1958 De Gaulle returns to power; Fifth Republic founded	1958 Yourcenar, *Mémoires d'Hadrien* Duras, *Moderato cantabile*
		1960 De Beauvoir, *La Force de l'âge* Sartre, *Critique de la raison dialectique*

4 HISTORICAL EVENTS (FRANCOPHONE COUNTRIES)	5 LITERARY WORKS AND EVENTS (FRANCOPHONE COUNTRIES)
	1937 Saint-Denys Garneau, *Regards et jeux dans l'espace* 1939 Césaire, *Cahier d'un retour au pays natal*
	1947 Borduas, *Refus global* *Présence africaine* founded
	1948 Senghor, *Anthologie de la nouvelle poésie nègre et malgache*
	1950 Feraoun, *Le Fils pauvre* Gélinas, *Tit-Coq*
1951 Beginnings of struggle for independence in Tunisia and Morocco	1951 Albany, *Zamal*
	1952 Chedid, *Le Sommeil délivré*
1954 Beginning of Algerian War 1954–62 Decolonization in Africa	1954 Chraïbi, *Le Passé simple*
1956 Independence of Tunisia and Morocco recognized	1956 First Congrès des écrivains et artistes noirs Yacine, *Nedjma* Damas, *Black Label* Beti, *Le Pauvre Christ de Bomba* 1957 Memmi, *Portrait du colonisé*
	1958 Bessette, *La Bagarre*
	1959 Blais, *La Belle Bête* Dadié, *Un Nègre à Paris*

1 REGIME IN FRANCE	2 HISTORICAL EVENTS (METROPOLITAN FRANCE)	3 LITERATURE AND THOUGHT (METROPOLITAN FRANCE)
		1963 Sarraute, *Les Fruits d'or*
		1964 Sartre, *Les Mots*
		Foucault, *Histoire de la folie à l'âge classique*
		1964–71 Lévi-Strauss, *Mythologiques*
		1966 Lacan, *Écrits*
		1967 Derrida, *La Voix et le phénomène; De la grammatologie; L'Écriture et la différence*
1968 Student revolt and general strike		1968 Modiano, *La Place de l'étoile*
1969 De Gaulle resigns (dies 1970); Georges Pompidou elected president		1969 Perec, *La Disparition*
		Foucault, *L'Archéologie du savoir*
		1970 Tournier, *Le Roi des Aulnes*
		1971–2 Sartre, *L'Idiot de la famille*
		1972 Derrida, *Marges de la philosophie; La Dissémination*
1974 Pompidou dies; Valéry Giscard d'Estaing elected president: abortion laws liberalized		1974 Leclerc, *Parole de femme*
		Derrida, *Glas*
		Irigaray, *Speculum; De l'autre femme*
		Kristeva, *La Révolution du langage poétique*
		1975 Cixous, *Le Rire de la Méduse; La Jeune Née (with Catherine Clément)*
		Lacan, *Encore; Le Séminaire, Book XX*
		Cardinal, *Les Mots pour le dire*
		1976 Foucault, *La Volonté de savoir*
		1979 Lyotard, *La Condition postmoderne*
		1980 Derrida, *La Carte postale*
		Kristeva, *Pouvoirs de l'horreur*
1981 François Mitterrand elected president; Socialist victory in general election; abolition of death penalty		
		1983 Wiesel, *Le Cinquième Fils*
		1984 Duras, *L'Amant*
		Foucault, *Le Souci de soi*
		1985 Toussaint, *La Salle de bain*
		1987 Derrida, *De l'esprit; Psyché*
		Kristeva, *Soleil noir*
1988 Mitterrand re-elected president		1988 Ernaux, *Une Femme*
		1992 Echenoz, *Nous trois*
		1993 Derrida, *Spectres de Marx*
		1994 Derrida, *Politiques de l'amitié; Force de loi*
1995 Jacques Chirac elected president		1995 Derrida, *Mal d'archive*

4 HISTORICAL EVENTS (FRANCOPHONE COUNTRIES)	5 LITERARY WORKS AND EVENTS (FRANCOPHONE COUNTRIES)
	1961 Fanon, *Les Damnés de la terre*
1962 Independence of Algeria proclaimed	1962 Nokan, *Le Soleil noir*
	Dib, *Qui se souvient de la mer*
	1963 Founding of *Parti Pris*
	1966 Haut Comité de la langue française founded
	1968 ADELF (originally Association des écrivains coloniaux) founded
	Kourouma, *Les Soleils des indépendances*
	1969 Memmi, *Le Scorpion*
1970 Agence de coopération culturelle et technique founded	1970 Hébert, *Kamouraska*
	1973 Sembène, *Xala*
	1975 Glissant, *Malemort*
1976 Parti québécois attains office	
	1977 Cheynet, *Les Muselés*
	1979 Sow Fall, *La Grève des Bàttu*
1980 Defeat of independence referendum in Quebec	1980 Depestre, *Bonjour et adieu à la négritude*
	1981 Glissant, *Le Discours antillais*
	1983 Khatibi, *Maghreb pluriel*
	1985 Djebar, *L'Amour, la fantasia*
	1987 Brossard, *Le Désert mauve*
	Ben Jelloun, *La Nuit sacrée*
	1988 Memmi, *Le Pharaon*
	Depestre, *Hadriana dans tous mes rêves*
	1991 Khatibi, *Un Été à Stockholm*
	1992 Chamoiseau, *Texaco*
	1993 Maalouf, *Le Rocher de Tanios*

Index

Except for anonymous works, titles appear under the author's name.